WARNING

What is disclosed herein about the Whitechapel, Paddington, Darlinghurst, Carcoar, Oxley and Gatton murders in England and Australia has been compiled principally from the public records of Australia, New Zealand and the United Kingdom, and the Report of the Royal Commission on Police Inquiry (1899), available online at the Queensland Parliamentary Service, Brisbane, Australia. Other records have been sourced from historical newspapers in Australia, New Zealand and the United Kingdom, and from *The Ultimate Jack the Ripper Sourcebook: An Illustrated Encyclopedia*. All measurements and distances are from the *imperial system*. There also are images and references to Aboriginal people no longer living, and language that some might find disturbing or offensive. No offence or disrespect is intended towards any person living or dead.

First published in 2015 as *Oxley-Gatton Murders: Exposing the Conspiracy* by BookPal, Brisbane, Australia.

Revised, updated and re-published in 2018 as *Jack the Ripper: His Australian Murders*.

Copyright © 2018 Neil Raymond Bradford

This book is copyright. Except for private study, research, criticism or reviews, as permitted under the Copyright Act, no part of this book may be reproduced, stored in a retrieval system or transmitted in any form or by any means without prior written permission. Enquiries should be made to the Publisher.

A copy of this publication can be found in the National Library of Australia.

ISBN: 978-0-646-99410-9 (paperback)

Published by Neil Raymond Bradford, Brisbane, Australia.

Subjects: Bradford, Neil Raymond.
            Murder -- Conspiracy -- Mystery -- True Crime.
            Murder -- England -- London -- Whitechapel.
            Murder -- Australia -- New South Wales -- Paddington.
            Murder -- Australia -- New South Wales -- Darlinghurst.
            Murder -- Australia -- New South Wales -- Carcoar.
            Murder -- Australia -- Queensland -- Oxley.
            Murder -- Australia -- Queensland -- Gatton.
            Murder -- Investigation -- England -- London -- Whitechapel.
            Murder -- Investigation -- Australia -- New South Wales -- Paddington.
            Murder -- Investigation -- Australia -- New South Wales -- Darlinghurst.
            Murder -- Investigation -- Australia -- New South Wales -- Carcoar.
            Murder -- Investigation -- Australia -- Queensland -- Oxley.
            Murder -- Investigation -- Australia -- Queensland -- Gatton.
            Jack the Ripper -- Serial Killer -- England -- London -- Whitechapel.
            Whitechapel Murders, 1888-89.
            Paddington Murder, 1892.
            Darlinghurst Murder, 1893.
            Carcoar Murders, 1893.
            Gatton Murders, 1898.
            Oxley Murder, 1898.

Front Cover Image: Monument erected for Michael, Norah and Ellen Murphy at Gatton (Courtesy of the Queensland State Archives), with a rose superimposed thereon.

Back Cover Images: Michael, Norah and Ellen Murphy (Courtesy of the Queensland Police Museum), and F. J. Hill Saddler at Nundah (Courtesy of State Library of Queensland).

JACK THE RIPPER

His Australian Murders

NEIL RAYMOND BRADFORD

BOOKS BY NEIL RAYMOND BRADFORD

Voices from The Past: Law Enforcement on the Central Highlands
&
Oxley-Gatton Murders: Exposing the Conspiracy

FUTURE BOOKS

Hornet Bank to Cullin-la-ringo: Truth behind The Massacres
&
Surviving the Joke: Honesty Does Not Always Pay

Dedicated to the memory of my younger brother,
Dale Richard Bradford

Gone far too early, but not forgotten

ACKNOWLEDGEMENTS

It is with great pleasure that I thank Virginia Gordon and Duncan Leask of the Queensland Police Museum, Vicki van Til of the Queensland Parliamentary Service, Paul Johnson of The National Archives, United Kingdom, and Stewart Evans, co-author of *The Ultimate Jack the Ripper Sourcebook: An Illustrated Encyclopedia*, for their valuable contributions.

CONTENTS

WARNING i
ACKNOWLEDGEMENTS vi
CHARTS/MAPS/SKETCHES viii
BACKGROUND ix
INTRODUCTION 1
1   WHITECHAPEL MURDERS 25
2   JACK'S AUSTRALIAN MURDERS? 35
3   SINS OF ANOTHER 53
4   OLD JACK COMES "HOME" AGAIN 73
5   OXLEY MURDER 91
6   BURGESS' ALIBI 102
7   GATTON MURDERS 130
8   DON'T ARREST JACK! 167
9   THE COVER-UP 189
10 DAMNING EVIDENCE 216
11 THE CONSPIRATORS? 254
CONCLUSION 274
ABBREVIATIONS USED IN ENDNOTES 280
ENDNOTES 281
BIBLIOGRAPHY 308
INDEX 314

CHARTS

Glasson, Innes and Webb families	64
Day and Urquhart families	190
Persons of Interest	260
Campbell, Palmer and Stephen families	268
Carus-Wilson and Churchill families	271

MAPS

Moran's paddock at Gatton	1
Brown and Walsh's paddock at Oxley	94
St Helena Island to the Bunya Mountains	106
Greenmount to Gatton	129

SKETCHES

How to Euthanize a Horse	100

BACKGROUND

Throughout the book, reference will be made to two Magisterial Inquiries and a Royal Commission in Queensland, Australia, that has relevance to the investigations conducted by police into the unsolved 1898 Oxley and Gatton murders.

The first Magisterial Inquiry was conducted into *the deaths of Michael, Norah and Ellen Murphy at Gatton on December 26, 1898* at the Gatton Police Court.

The inquiry was opened on January 24, 1899, by Acting Police Magistrate Augustus Henry Warner-Shand of Ipswich and closed on March 24, 1899, Inspector Frederic Charles Urquhart, head of the Criminal Investigation Branch, Brisbane, assisting Warner-Shand during the proceedings.[1,2]

The second Magisterial Inquiry was conducted *into the circumstances attending the death of Alfred Stephen Hill at Oxley on December 10, 1898* at the South Brisbane Police Court.

The inquiry was opened on February 17, 1899, by magistrates, William Harris and Thomas Austin, and adjourned *sine die* on the same day, Detective Sergeant Denis Collins Shanahan of the Criminal Investigation Branch, Brisbane, assisting Harris and Austin during the proceedings.[3]

The Royal Commission was appointed on July 20, 1899, *to inquire into the Constitution, Administration, and Working of the Criminal Investigation Branch of the Police Force of Queensland, as well as into the Relations subsisting between such Branch and the Police Force generally, and also into the general Organisation, Distribution, Control, and Enrolment of such Police Force, including such Branch, and also the Discipline and Efficiency thereof, and the System under which Promotions, Transfers, and Appointments are made therein.*

The inquiry was opened on August 1, 1899, at the Office of the Commissioner of Police in the Treasury Building, George Street, Brisbane, by the Chairman, Arthur Baptist Noel, a judge in the District

Court of Queensland, and closed on November 29, 1899, the Commissioners assisting being Frederick William Dickson, a Crown Prosecutor of Queensland, Superintendent Thomas Garvin, Officer in Charge of the Northern Division of the New South Wales Police Force, ex-Superintendent John Sadleir, who served for 44 years in the Victorian Police Force, and Theodore Oscar Unmack, a successful and influential businessman, former member for Toowong in the Legislative Assembly and Postmaster-General for Queensland.

The Secretary was James William Blair, a promising barrister of Ipswich.[4]

A "Magisterial Inquiry" is now referred to as an "Inquest," the title of "Police Magistrate" was replaced by "Magistrate," and those referred to then as "magistrates" are known today as "Justices of the Peace."

INTRODUCTION

A theory outlined in *Oxley-Gatton Murders: Exposing the Conspiracy* to the effect that the Government and police force protected Thomas Day from arrest for the murders of Michael, Hnora (Norah) and Theresa Ellen (Ellen) Murphy in Moran's paddock at Gatton, Queensland, Australia, on December 26, 1898, was not fully accepted.[1] Further research after publishing the book, however, uncovered evidence in historical documents at the Queensland State Archives to confirm that it was, in fact, a *cover-up*.

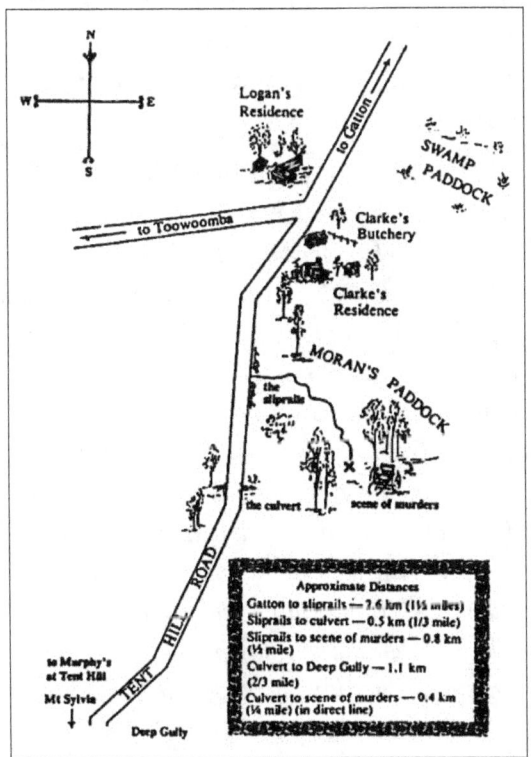

Moran's paddock at Gatton
(Courtesy of the Queensland Police Museum)

December 27, 1898 – the bodies of the Murphy siblings were found in Moran's paddock by their brother-in-law, William McNeil, a visitor from Westbrook, near Toowoomba.[2]

December 30, 1898 – Detective Acting Sergeant Michael Toomey from the Criminal Investigation Branch at Brisbane, Queensland, questioned Thomas Day and took possession of a jumper stained with blood.

Arthur George Clarke, who had recently employed Thomas Day at his butchery, confirmed that there were no *spots* of blood on the jumper when he saw Day wearing it on December 24, 1898.

Instead of having it expertly examined to determine if it was *animal* or *human* blood, the jumper was returned to Thomas Day, who scrubbed and washed it until all stains were removed.[3]

December 31, 1898 – five days after the murders, Toomey took a statement from John Carroll, which is the first of the documents alluded to in the opening paragraph, and which can be found at the end of this Introduction, as follows:

> *I was at the Mount Sylvia races on Monday, 26th instant, and came home in company with my mother and Mary Callinan, who lives near the Catholic church. When I passed the creek below the slip panels leading into Moran's paddock, it would be about twenty minutes past eight o'clock, and between the creek and the sliprails, I saw a man walking towards us. He was on my left-hand side. I looked at the man and noticed that he was wearing what I took to be a short blue coat or a shirt. He had dark trousers, and grey felt hat with a large leaf. It was pretty-well turned down over his face. The three Murphy's were about 50 yards in front of us. I noticed that he passed very close to their [buggy] as he passed them. He did not speak to any of them. The Murphy's came into Gatton before I did. I reached Gatton at 8.45 pm. I now believe that it was Clarke's butcher after he, being mentioned to me by Toomey, and at the time he passed me, I said to my mother, "I believe that is Clarke's butcher," and I am still of the same opinion.*[4]

Just prior to the murders, Carroll saw Thomas Day near the sliprails to Moran's paddock, referring to him in his statement as being *Clarke's butcher*. Day was wearing what appeared to be *a short blue coat or a shirt* which, apparently, was the *blue jumper* inspected by Toomey and shown to Clarke on December 30, 1898.[3,5]

Introduction

January 4, 1899 – in a telegram sent from Gatton to Chief Inspector John Stuart at Brisbane, Commissioner William Edward Parry-Okeden advised/instructed:

> *Telegraph Newspaper publishes information re missing whip. Although their representative here with all other pressmen agreed not to do so, try stopping it appearing in Week. Lewis cannot go strait. I spoke to Minister about this last night. Act quickly.*[6]

The *Minister* referred to by Parry-Okeden was the Home Secretary, Justin Fox Greenlaw Foxton, who, at the time of the Gatton murders, was responsible for the administration of the police force in Queensland, and *Lewis*, whom Parry-Okeden said *cannot go strait*, was Thomas Day.[7]

This telegram is the first piece of evidence, identifying that the Government and police in Queensland were protecting Thomas Day from arrest for the Gatton murders. It also identifies the importance placed on recovering the whip, used during the vicious rape, in my opinion, of Norah and Ellen Murphy.

Seeing as how Section 132 of the Criminal Code Act 1899 provides that *any person who conspires with another to obstruct, prevent, pervert, or defeat the course of justice is guilty of a crime*, does the telegram disclose a *conspiracy* between Foxton, Parry-Okeden and Stuart?[8]

Probably, but let us consider further documentary evidence before arriving at a conclusion!

January 5, 1898 – Parry-Okeden created a special district for the investigation into the Gatton murders, appointing Inspector Frederic Charles Urquhart as the Officer in Charge.[9]

With assistance from Toomey and other trusted police officers, Urquhart changed the course of the investigation to protect Thomas Day from arrest for the Gatton murders.

Afterwards, Urquhart wrote, "We have failed because from the very outset, we had no chance of success."[10]

Yes, there was no chance of success because the police force, identified clearly in Parry-Okeden's telegram, had been instructed by the Government that Thomas Day was not to be arrested.[6]

January 7, 1899 – in a telegram to Robert Hazlewood Lawson, the Chief Clerk in the police force located at the Police Depot, Brisbane, Parry-Okeden advised/instructed:

> *Yours today, exhibits are to be submitted to such minute examination, microscopical and otherwise, as may tend to eliciting of any indications of use in pursuit of offenders by best experts obtainable. Contact Doctor Wray and accept his advice as to selection of experts for this work. The greatest care must be taken to prevent any risk of Sergeant Arrell losing touch of the exhibits in such a way as to interfere with the value of his evidence in the future.*[11]

It is abundantly clear from this telegram that Parry-Okeden, obviously acting on instructions from Foxton, was protecting Thomas Day from arrest for the Gatton murders. Day's bloodstained jumper inspected by Toomey, consequently, was not seized by police along with clothing taken from other suspects and examined to establish if it was *animal* or *human* blood thereon.[3,5,12]

January 11, 1899 – ensuring that Thomas Day would not be arrested for the Gatton murders, the man seen near the sliprails identified by John Carrol as *Clarke's butcher* was not included in a second statement taken from Carroll, as follows:

> *I am the son of Margaret Carroll fruiterer of Gatton. I remember Monday the 26th December last. I left home on that morning about six o'clock for the Mount Sylvia Races in a spring cart in company with my mother and Mary Callinan. I left the racecourse about seven o'clock that evening in company with my mother and Mary Callinan. I was driving and sitting on the right-hand side of the cart as we were coming into Gatton. I know Moran's paddock where the murders were committed. I saw the three dead bodies of the Murphys there on Tuesday the 27th December last. About half-past eight o'clock on Monday the 26th December last I saw a man about 100 yards on the culvert side from the sliprails of Moran's paddock. He was walking towards me and passed close to the cart on my left-hand side. I saw him pass the three Murphys, who were about 15 yards ahead of us in a [buggy] and driving in the direction of Gatton. He passed close to*

Introduction

> the [buggy] the Murphys were driving in. I knew it was Michael, Norah and Ellen Murphy. They had passed me near the culvert, and I there recognised them. I was looking at the man from first I saw him in level with the Murphy's [buggy] until he passed me. The night was a bright moonlight night, and I saw the man distinctly, and I believe I would know him again.[13]

Carroll's second statement, which also can be found at the end of this Introduction, proves that the Government and police force protected Thomas Day from arrest for the Gatton murders.

That being so, the attention of police turned towards Day's good friend, Richard Burgess, who was arrested at the Bunya Mountains by Mounted Constable James Gillies of Dalby on suspicion of being concerned in the murders.

The charge, however, was withdrawn by Sub-Inspector Hubert Roland Pasley Durham and substituted with another for stealing a saddle so that Burgess could be escorted back to Toowoomba where a case could be built-up against him.

Suspecting that Burgess was about to be *framed* and *hung* for the Gatton murders, Austin McLaughlin of Pittsworth retained the services of Joseph Vincent Herbert, a leading solicitor of Toowoomba, to defend Burgess.

Through Herbert, Burgess provided an *alibi* that was checked out by police and found to be correct. Not only was he not at Toowoomba when the saddle was stolen but Burgess also was not at Gatton when the murders were committed.

When the *alibi* was proved, the charge of stealing the saddle was withdrawn and substituted with a charge of vagrancy. Being found *guilty* on that charge, Burgess was sentenced to two months' imprisonment at Boggo Road Gaol at Brisbane.[14]

March 22, 1899 – in a memorandum to various police stations, which was three days prior to the release of Richard Burgess from prison, Stuart advised/instructed:

> As Richard Burgess will be discharged from the Brisbane Gaol on 25th March instant, it is expedient that his movements be noted carefully

after he leaves the Gaol, and whatever road and direction he takes (when known), should be notified to the Criminal Investigation Branch, and the Police of the District to which he is apparently going. All police will keep as close an eye as possible on his movements, wiring ahead in likely directions, and informing the Officer in Charge of the C. I. Branch at Brisbane.[15]

April 4, 1899 – while *shadowing* Burgess to keep him and Thomas Day apart from each other, in a telegram to Durham at Toowoomba, Stuart advised/instructed:

Man answering description of Burgess passed Munbilla making direction of Killarney or Warwick at ten thirty (10.30) am on April 1st. Appears to be in habit of entering girls' bedrooms at night. Police to be well on alert to, if possible, catch this ruffian at his game. Think if you picked two smart constables and put them on him, they might succeed in getting a case against him as he is a menace to the general public.[16]

April 12, 1899 – complying with the instructions provided eight days earlier by Stuart, after *telling off* constables to observe and report the movements of Burgess, Durham advised:

I have the honour to report that on receipt of your telegram instructing me to tell off two constables to pick up the man Richard Burgess reported to have been seen at Munbilla on the 1st instant going in direction of Killarney, I told off Constables Haye and Kiely, who knows the man, to search the Condamine side of the district. This has been done with the result that I have received a wire from Senior Sergeant O'Loan stating that no reports of Burgess have been heard of. Sergeant McDonald of Stanthorpe has sent Constable Wilson to Lucky Valley in that district, making inquiries. The two constables Haye and Kiely have now been instructed to go towards Dugandan and see if he is on the eastern side of the range. The man James Ellis is at Killarney, and as soon as I hear that Burgess has been located, I will give every assistance.[17]

April 13, 1899 – in a telegram to Stuart, the day after he advised that Thomas Day, alias James Ellis, was at Killarney, "Re James Ellis,"

Introduction

queried Durham. "What instructions shall I give now Burgess has left colony."[18]

Parry-Okeden, in another telegram to Stuart, which has been decoded from the code used for his telegram to Stuart dated January 4, 1899, advised/instructed:

> Wire New South Wales police Burgess's movements and warn them of his particular bent. Explain what a ruffian he is. If our man unable get into work at Gatton College or elsewhere, put him on some other job. Have written you re Armitage. Awful weather. Continuous rain.[19]

Apart from requesting the police force in the neighbouring colony of New South Wales, Australia, to be involved in the *shadowing* of Burgess, Parry-Okeden instructed that if *our man*, who was Thomas Day, was unable to *get into work* at the Gatton College or elsewhere, Stuart was to *put him on some other job*.

"Well," you might ask, "how do you know that Thomas Day and Richard Burgess were known to each other?"

When he left Gatton after the murders, with the knowledge and consent of Urquhart, Toomey asked Day to go to Toowoomba to identify Burgess in the lockup *as the man he had seen between Brisbane and Gatton*.[20]

That being a fact was provided by Duncan Robert McGregor in a statement that he saw a man resembling Day with Burgess, whom he knew, in Brisbane during May 1898 and again close to each other at Oxley, Queensland, soon after Day arrived from New South Wales on December 6, 1898.[21]

The person referred to as *Armitage* by Parry-Okeden in his telegram to Stuart on April 13, 1899, was Acting Sergeant William Armitage of South Brisbane.[19]

Armitage took out a warrant on January 11, 1899, for the arrest of Claude William Carus-Wilson on a charge of committing *buggery* with his father, Edward Litton Carus-Wilson (referred to as Carus-Wilson from hereon) during the night of December 10, 1898, which was the day that Alfred Stephen Hill was shot and killed in Brown and Walsh's paddock at Oxley.[22]

When the warrant was taken out for Claude's arrest, another was in existence for the arrest of Carus-Wilson on a charge of committing an *unnatural offence* on a boy at Ipswich.[23]

May 16, 1899 – responding to public criticism after the arrest of Claude, Parry-Okeden corresponded with the Under Secretary, Justice Department, Brisbane, as follows:

> *When I was sending escort to Western Australia to bring back E. L. C. Wilson, I supposed the boy, Claude, would be a witness, and in order that I might have power to bring him back also, I directed, as a precautionary measure only, that a warrant for his arrest should be procured, to be used if necessary, not otherwise. When I found he had been arrested needlessly, I felt annoyed. Please supply report and copy of proceedings, if any.*[22]

Not only did Parry-Okeden protect Thomas Day from arrest for the Gatton murders, but he also was the instigator of action that impacted on the trial of Carus-Wilson for the wilful murder of Alfred Stephen Hill being aborted.

At the Royal Commission, Parry-Okeden conceded that Thomas Day was probably the *swagman* who, allegedly, received the revolver from Carus-Wilson that killed Alfred Stephen Hill in Brown and Walsh's paddock at Oxley and used later at Gatton to murder Michael Murphy.[24]

Eight years after the Oxley and Gatton murders, a revolver was found secreted in a hollow tree felled for firewood in the Swamp Paddock adjoining Clarke's butchery at Gatton. Same as the many other denials, the authorities told the public that it was not the revolver used in the murders.[25]

This *dark secret* of the *cover-up* orchestrated by the Government and carried out by police that protected Thomas Day from arrest for the Gatton murders has finally seen the light of day!

May 13, 1899 – when Thomas Day and another friend, William Charles Chaston, deserted from A Battery of the Permanent Artillery

Introduction

in Queensland, Parry-Okeden requested police in other colonies not to approach the deserters but to observe and report their whereabouts if located.[26]

October 11, 1899 – the South Australian Police Gazette instructed that *special and very cautious inquiries are requested with a view to locating offenders only, and the inquiry should be of such a nature as not to alarm them.*[27]

October 13, 1899 – the Tasmanian Police Gazette requested that *special efforts be made to locate these offenders, and that inquiries be of such a nature as not to alarm them.*[28]

October 25, 1899 – the New Zealand Police Gazette instructed that *special inquiry is requested for these men in New Zealand, but it is not desirable that they should be apprised of such inquiry.*[29]

Why were police in South Australia, Tasmania and New Zealand instructed to make discreet inquiries *of such a nature as not to alarm* Day and Chaston instead of arresting them for desertion?

The answer to that question was found in an article published in *The Darling Downs Gazette* to the effect that Richard Burgess made a statement at Greenmount, Queensland, which was after his release from prison on March 25, 1899, that it was *Jack the Ripper and someone else who committed* the Gatton murders.[30]

After considering that statement with evidence uncovered at the archives of Australia, New Zealand and the United Kingdom, the book *Oxley-Gatton Murders: Exposing the Conspiracy* was revised, updated and renamed *Jack the Ripper: His Australian Murders*.

Thomas Day's accomplice in Moran's paddock was apparently another friend, John Miller, who was from London, England, and who, two days after the Gatton murders, was seen in company of Burgess between Gatton and Toowoomba at Postman's Ridge.[31]

Miller, alias *Frisco, Yank* and *York,* together with Chaston, worked on the Howard Smith and Sons' and Dalgety's wharves at Newcastle, New South Wales, before going to Sydney, also in New South Wales, where they worked on the steamer *Peregrine*, subsequently terminating that employment at Brisbane in the early part of December 1898 to take part in the Gatton murders.[32]

During the 1888 and 1889 Whitechapel murders in England, it was revealed that *cattle boats* transporting live cargo into London, entered the Thames on a Thursday or Friday and left again for the continent on a Sunday or Monday.

Based on that revelation, investigating police formed the opinion that the alleged Whitechapel murderer known as *Jack the Ripper* was a *drover* or *butcher*, appearing and disappearing with the *cattle boat* on which he was employed.[33]

Day, Burgess, Miller and Chaston were seamen who worked, apparently, on boats between Australia and other countries, the handkerchiefs securing the hands of Norah and Ellen Murphy behind their backs at Gatton being tied with a *sailor's knot*.[34,35]

Was Thomas Day the notorious serial killer, *Jack the Ripper*?

One firmly believes that he was, and that he killed not only in Australia but also in England and possibly America. If you would like to know more, please read the *Background* before embarking upon the journey of discovery.

Introduction

Gatton,
31. 12. 98.

John Carroll states I was at the Mt. Sylvia races on Monday, 26th. inst. and came home in company with my mother and Mary Callinan who lives near the Catholic Church. When I passed the Creek below the slip panels leading into Moran's paddock it would be about twenty minutes past eight o'clock and between the Creek and the slip rails I saw a man walking towards us. He was on my left hand side. I looked at the man and noticed that he was wearing what I took to be a short blue coat or a shirt. He had dark trousers and gray felt hat with a large leaf. It was pretty well turned down over his face. The three Murphy's were about 50 yards in front of us. I noticed that he passed very close to their cart as he passed them. He did not speak to any of them. The MurphY's came into Gatton before I did. I reached Gatton at 8.45.P.M. I now believe that it was Clark's butcher after he being mentioned to me by Toomey and at the time he passed me I said to my mother,"I believe that is Clark's butcher", and I am still of the same opinion. Mrs. Carroll states I would not know the man that passed us as I did not look much at him.muck.

John Carroll's statement dated December 31, 1898
(Courtesy of the Queensland Government (Queensland Police Service))

Jack the Ripper

Parry-Okeden's telegram dated January 4, 1899
(Courtesy of the Queensland Government (Queensland Police Service))

Introduction

Received at Gatton on 24 April 99

Rule 6

Electric Telegraph, Queensland.

Wds. 81
Amt. 6/11 O/Hnd

From Gatton 1h 5 m.

Dated _____ 18 __

MESSAGE for R H Lawson
                Police Dept

BRISBANE.

Yours today exhibits are to be submitted to such minute examination microscopical & otherwise as may tend to eliciting of and indications of use in pursuit of offenders by best experts obtainable consult Doctor Wray & accept his advice as to selection of experts for this work the greatest care must be taken to prevent any risk of Sergeant Arrell

Parry-Okeden's telegram dated January 7, 1899, page 1
(Courtesy of the Queensland Government (Queensland Police Service))

Parry-Okeden's telegram dated January 7, 1899, page 2

(Courtesy of the Queensland Government (Queensland Police Service))

Introduction

John Carroll's statement dated January 11, 1899, page 1
(Courtesy of the Queensland Government (Queensland Police Service))

cart as we were coming into Gatton. I know Moran paddock where the murder was committed I saw the three dead bodys of the Murphys there on Tuesday the 27th December last. about half past eight o'clock on Monday the 26th December last I ~~was~~ saw a man about one hundred yards on the culvert side of from the slip rails of Morans paddock, he was walking towards me & passed, close to the cart on my left hand side

John Carroll's statement dated January 11, 1899, page 2
(Courtesy of the Queensland Government (Queensland Police Service))

Introduction

> I saw him pass the three Murphys who were about fifteen yards ahead of us in a dogcart & driving in the direction of Gatton, he passed close to the dogcart the Murphys were driving in, I knew it was Michael Nora & Ellen Murphy, they had passed me near the culvert & I then recognised them, I was looking at the man from ~~when~~ first I saw him in level with Murphys dogcart until he passed me, the night was a bright moonlight night & I saw the man distinctly

John Carroll's statement dated January 11, 1899, page 3
(Courtesy of the Queensland Government (Queensland Police Service))

> I believe I would know him again.

John Carroll

John Carroll's statement dated January 11, 1899, page 4
(Courtesy of the Queensland Government (Queensland Police Service))

Introduction

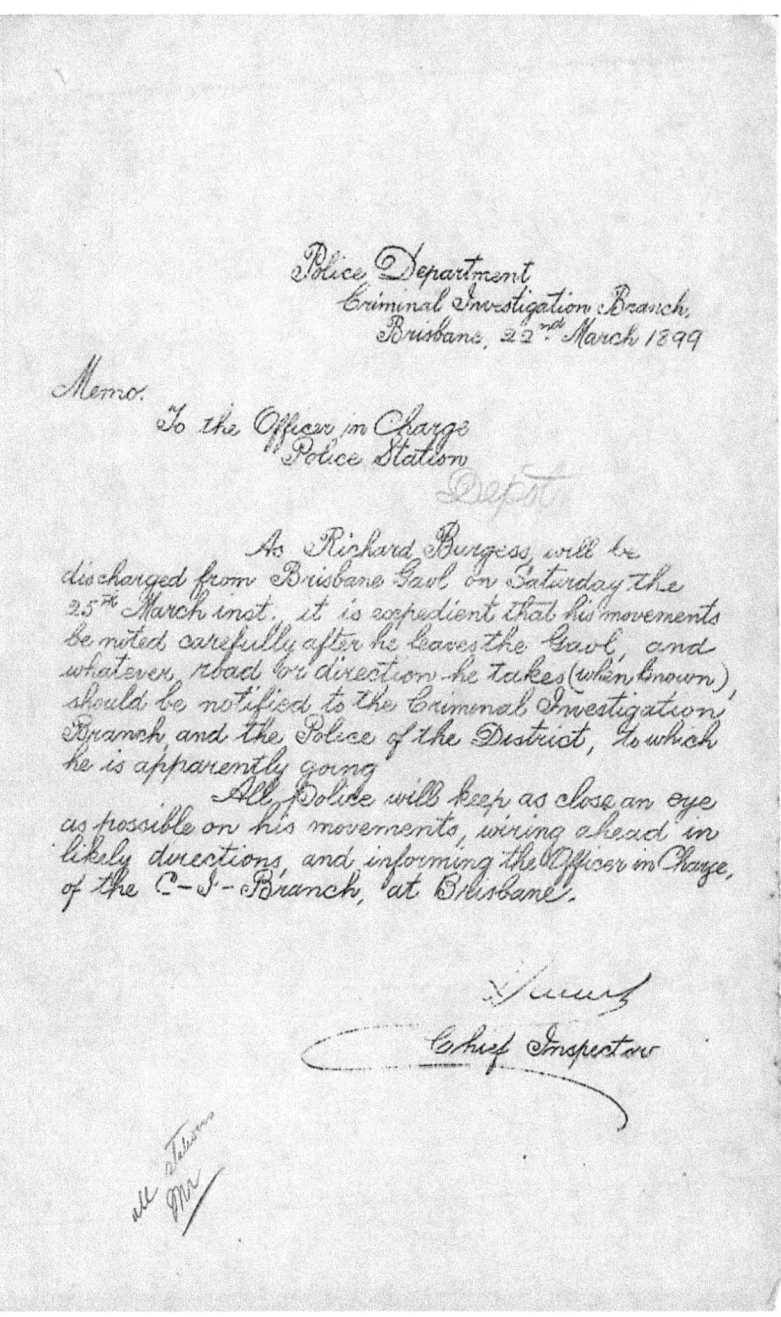

Stuart's memorandum dated March 22, 1899
(Courtesy of the Queensland Government (Queensland Police Service))

Copy.   J.B.: 253.

                                                 4.4.99.

Telegram to:—
            Sub Inspector Durham,
                Toowoomba.

Man answering description of Burgess passed Munbilla making direction of Killarney or Warwick at ten thirty (10:30) A.M. on April 1st: appears to be in habit of entering girls' bedrooms at night. Police to be well on the alert to, if possible, catch this ruffian at his game. Think if you picked two smart constables and put them on him they might succeed in getting a case against him as he is a menace to the general public.

                                    (sgd.) J Stuart.
                                        Chief Inspector.

Stuart's telegram dated April 4, 1899

(Courtesy of the Queensland Government (Queensland Police Service))

Introduction

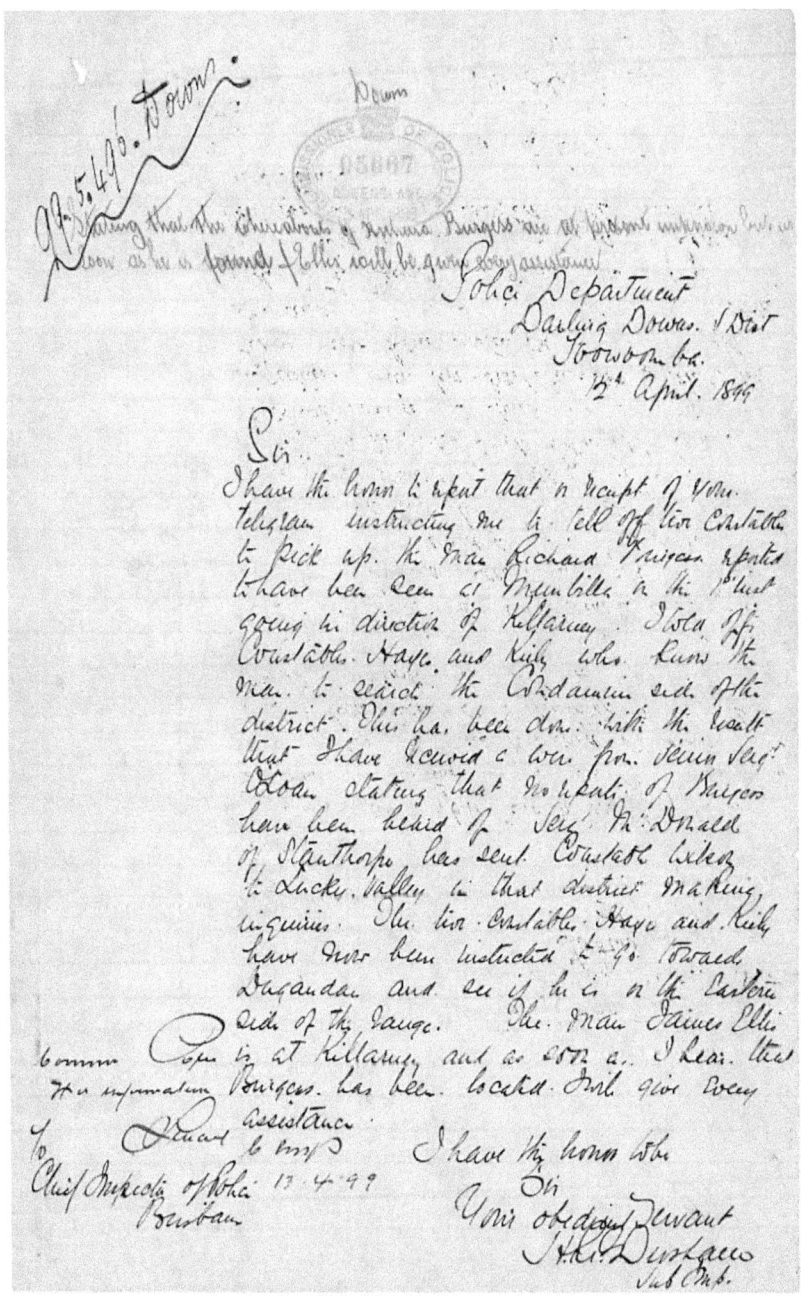

Durham's report dated April 12, 1899
(Courtesy of the Queensland Government (Queensland Police Service))

Jack the Ripper

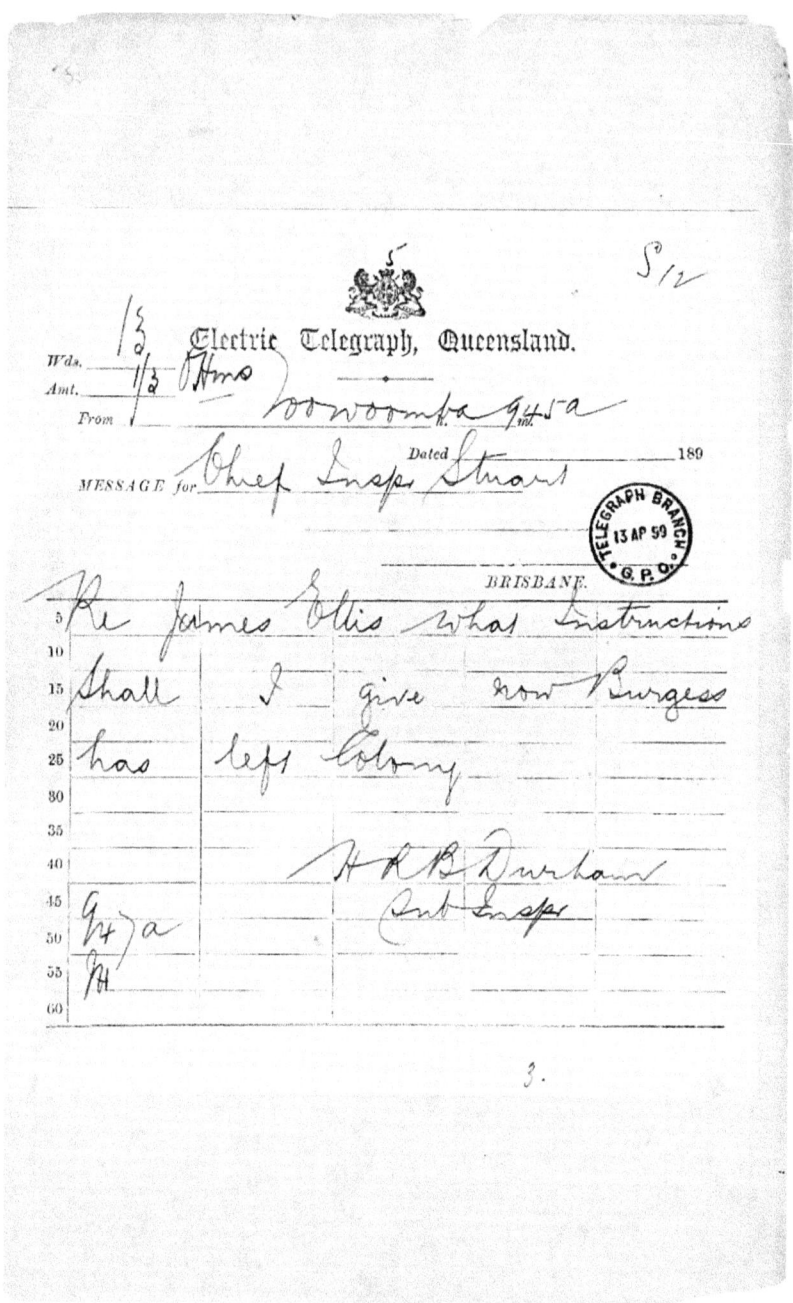

Durham's telegram dated April 13, 1899

(Courtesy of the Queensland Government (Queensland Police Service))

Introduction

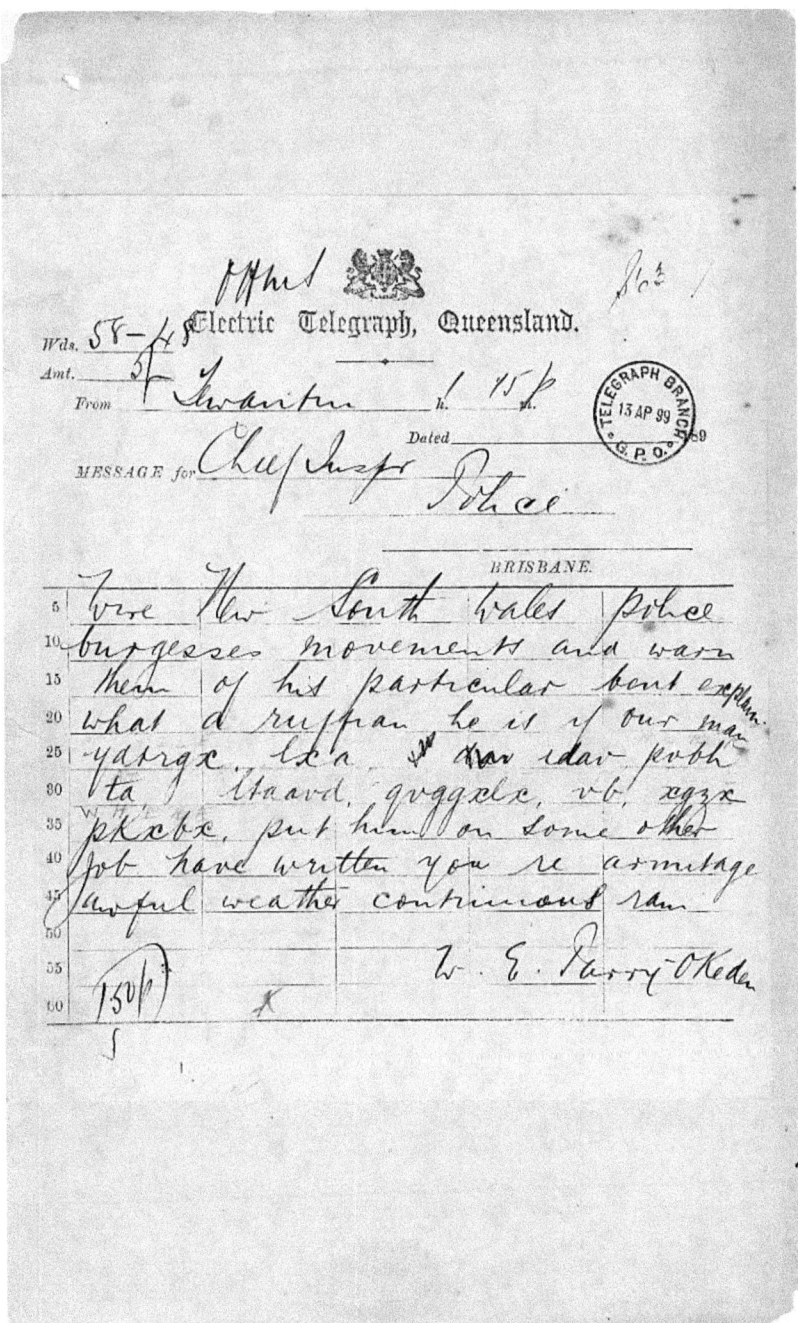

Parry-Okeden's telegram dated April 13, 1899

(Courtesy of the Queensland Government (Queensland Police Service))

1109 A.
8.2.99

William Chaston states I am a gunner in "A" Battery Queensland Permanent Artillery. About the month of September last I went to Newcastle from Sydney. I got a job on Howard Smith's and Dalgety's wharfes. While working there I made the acquaintance of a man called "Yank" who was also working on the wharf. I worked with him for about two months. About the 10th November myself and "Yank" left Newcastle and went to Sydney and joined the S.S. "Peregrine" and arrived in Brisbane. We parted company on arrival at Brisbane but I used to see him nearly every day. After I was about a week in Brisbane I joined the Artillery and he (Yank) got a job at Greens in Albert street. I visited him on two occasions. The first time I called I saw him but on the second I saw Mr Green who informed me that he (Yank) had left. One day about the first of January I was in Ann street near the Protestant Hall when I met the man "Yank" In course of conversation he said to me "I have been to the Hospital since I saw you last. I met with an accident; I scalded my head" I then noticed his head and saw that it (head) was painted yellow. I then parted with him and have not seen him since. While in Newcastle the man "Yank" used to board at Jal Hinda (a coloured man) near the Centennial Hotel "The Yank" is well known to a man named Harry who is foreman for Dalgety & Co., Newcastle. Harry used to call him by the name of "York" York or Yank is described as follows: About 30 years of age, 5 feet 6 or 7 inches high, slight build, fair complexion, small fair moustache turning grey (only) hair cut short and turning grey; scar or white patch of head on back left side; thin sharp features, blue eyes, pointed chin; smart active appearance; when last seen wore a light tweed suit, and black or brown soft felt hat; wears No 6 boot or lace up shoes; had a pair of blucher or cossack boots; a Cockney; told me he had been to Western Australia and 'Frisco. He also told me He was a vegetable cook in some restaurants in Sydney.

(Signed) W. Chaston. Q.P.A.

William Chaston's statement dated February 8, 1899
(Courtesy of the Queensland Government (Queensland Police Service))

1

WHITECHAPEL MURDERS

Jack the Ripper was the name given to the unidentified serial killer who, allegedly, was responsible for the deaths of at least nine females during 1888 and 1889 in the Whitechapel district of London, England.[1] Much could be written, but I am no expert on the murders, so I will confine my comments to salient points that have a bearing on the crimes also allegedly committed by *Jack the Ripper* in Australia. In that regard, one has relied heavily on documented facts provided in *The Ultimate Jack the Ripper Sourcebook: An Illustrated Encyclopedia* recommended to me by the Metropolitan Police Service, London.

Of the belief that there is an intertwining of events and circumstances relating to murders committed in England and Australia, as was done for the Introduction, what one has to say about the *Jack the Ripper* murders in England and Australia will be outlined chronologically.

January 23, 1880 – Annie Dickson, formerly Ann Ely, who was the wife of James Robert Dickson, the Premier of Queensland at the time of the Gatton murders, died from tetanus.[2]

Nine days earlier, Annie was searching for a burglar inside their residence named *Toorak* at Hamilton, Brisbane, when she accidentally shot herself in the hand, the wound becoming infected.[3,4]

January 5, 1882 – almost two years after the death of his first wife, Dickson married Mary MacKinlay, the Lady Principal of the Brisbane Girls' Grammar School.[5]

Despite being well-known at Brisbane, 11 years before the Carcoar murders in the Western districts of New South Wales, which will be outlined later, Dickson and Mary travelled to Carcoar where they were married by the Reverend Thomas Robert Curwen Campbell.[6,7]

That being so, there obviously was a personal connection between Campbell and either Dickson or Mary, who was from Scotland, but came to Australia from England.

September 19, 1882 – Edward Litton Carus-Wilson, whose trial 17 years later for the murder of Alfred Stephen Hill was aborted by the Government, married Margaret Jane Whitsitt at Palmerston North in New Zealand.[8]

Suffering from sciatica, Carus-Wilson walked with a halting gait and dragged his left leg after the right leg, turning the heel inwards as he did so.[9]

After the marriage, Carus-Wilson lived and worked briefly at Terrick Terrick, north-west from Melbourne in Victoria, Australia, before returning with Margaret to England.[10]

June 5, 1885 – a stowaway, Thomas Day, a name synonymous with the murders 13 years later of Michael, Norah and Ellen Murphy at Gatton, was on board the steamer *Bombay* when it arrived at Sydney from Plymouth, England.[11,12]

One assumes that the stowaway was sent back to England, being involved thereafter in the Whitechapel murders.

December 23, 1887 – suffering for several years with breast cancer, soon after giving birth to their son, Claude William Carus-Wilson, Margaret Carus-Wilson died at 97 Euston Road, St Pancras, Middlesex, England.[13,14,15]

Born with paralysis to both legs, Claude was pushed around in a perambulator or pulled along in a goat cart until he was able to walk with the aid of crutches.[9]

April 3, 1888 – Emma Elizabeth Smith, who appears to have been the first victim of the Whitechapel murders, was sexually assaulted and robbed by three men in Osborne Street, Whitechapel, one being a *youth of about nineteen*.[16,17]

The popular theory is that *Jack the Ripper* was not one person but part of a gang.

George Haslip, a surgeon at the London Hospital, gave evidence that the peritoneum was ruptured by a *blunt instrument* during the rape, resulting in Emma dying the following day from peritonitis, a report in *The Bendigo Advertiser* suggesting that a *walking stick* caused the injuries.[16,17,18]

Before the robbery, Emma was seen *talking to a man dressed in dark clothes with a white neckerchief around his neck*.[17]

Ten years later, Thomas Day was seen wearing a white handkerchief around his neck, which was during the morning after the Gatton murders.

August 7, 1888 – the second victim, Martha Tabram, also known as Turner, was murdered at the George Yard buildings in Commercial Street, Spitalfields.

Chief Inspector Donald Sutherland Swanson of the Criminal Investigation Department, Scotland Yard, outlined in his report dated October 19, 1888, that the victim suffered 39 stab wounds to the *body, neck and private part* from *a knife or dagger*.

At 11.45 pm, a prostitute, Mary Ann Connolly, alias Pearly Polly, saw Martha going into the yard with a soldier.

Around two hours later, a Grenadier Guard, described as being *22 to 26 years, height 5 feet 9 or 10 inches, complexion fair, hair dark, small dark-brown moustache turned up at ends, with one good conduct medal*, told Constable H. Barrett that *he was waiting for a chum, who had gone with a girl*.[19]

August 31, 1888 – the third victim, Mary Ann Nichols, was murdered in Buck's Row at Whitechapel.

Inspector J. Spratling outlined in his report dated August 31, 1888, that the victim was found *lying on her back with her clothes a little above her knees*, and that the victim's throat was cut *from ear to ear*, and *from left to right*.

Constable John Neil saw two men from the nearby slaughterhouse of Barber & Co, standing on the opposite side of the road.

A horse-slaughterer, Henry Tompkins, together with two other employees of Barber & Co, James Mumford and Charles Brittain, *satisfactorily accounted for their time, being corroborated in some portions by the police on night-duty near the premises*.

There was an *impression of a ring having been worn* by the victim, suggesting that it might have been stolen.[20]

September 8, 1888 – the fourth victim, Annie Chapman, was murdered in a yard at 29 Handbury Street, Spitalfields.

Bruising about the face, arms and hands suggested that Annie struggled with the perpetrator before being knocked unconscious to the ground where her throat was cut and abdomen mutilated.

Having relevance to the murder of Emma Harrison committed later in Australia, the victim was found with her *tongue* [protruding] *between the front teeth,* and with her head *turned on the right side.*[21]

Three *brass-rings* worn by Annie on the *third finger of the left hand,* which also has relevance to a *young man* then living at Aldgate in Central London, were stolen and never located.[21,22]

Doctor George Baxter Phillips gave evidence that the instrument used *must have been a very sharp knife with a thin, narrow blade,* and that *those used by a slaughterman, well ground down, might have caused* the injuries.

Phillips also expressed the opinion that the perpetrator had *anatomical knowledge,* but it appeared to him that the work was done hastily.[21]

September 30, 1888 – the fifth victim, Elizabeth Stride, alias Long Lizzie, was murdered at Dutfield's Yard in Berner Street, St George's-in-the-East.

Forced to the ground, the victim's throat was cut from *left to the right*.

Charles Preston identified that a *silk handkerchief* found around the neck belonged to the victim.

At 12.35 am, Constable H. Smith saw the deceased in the company of a man, about 28 years, 5 feet 7 inches, dark complexion, small dark moustache, dressed in a black diagonal coat, hard-felt hat, white collar and tie.

Ten minutes later, Israel Schwartz, who identified the body at the mortuary, saw the deceased with a man described by Schwartz as being about 30 years, 5 feet 5 inches, fair complexion, dark hair, small brown moustache, full face, broad shoulders, dressed in dark jacket and trousers, and a peaked black cap.

Upon entering Berner Street from Commercial Road, Schwartz saw the victim thrown onto the footpath.

When the victim screamed, Schwartz crossed to the opposite footpath where he was confronted by a second man, lighting a clay pipe, about 35 years of age, 5 feet 11 inches in height, fresh complexion, light brown hair and moustache, and dressed in a dark overcoat and black felt hat with a wide brim.

Chief Inspector Swanson outlined in his report dated October 19, 1888, that when the first alleged perpetrator called out to the other, referring to him as Lipski, *Schwartz walked away, but finding that he was followed by the second man, he ran as far as the railway arch*, which is where the pursuit ended.[23]

Often referred to as the *Double Event*, on the same day, after the murder of Elizabeth Stride, the sixth victim, Catherine Eddowes, was murdered in Mitre Square at Aldgate.

After cutting the throat and disembowelling the victim, the perpetrator laid the intestines over the body.

A *white handkerchief* draped across the victim's throat *below the cut* was, in my opinion, the *signature* of *Jack the Ripper*.

Swanson outlined in a further report dated November 6, 1888, that *the murder could have been committed by a person who had been a hunter, a butcher, a slaughterman, as well as a student in surgery or a properly qualified surgeon*.[24]

So, there you have it, *Jack the Ripper* was not necessarily a doctor or surgeon!

On it being suggested that the serial killer was a *butcher* or *slaughterman*, police made inquiries among the local butchers and slaughterhouses to see *if anyone recently employed in this capacity had lately become deranged*.[25]

During those inquiries, it was revealed that *cattle boats* transporting live cargo entered the Thames on a Thursday or Friday and left London again for the continent on a Sunday or Monday. That revelation resulted in investigating police forming the opinion that *Jack the Ripper* was a *drover* or *butcher*, periodically appearing and disappearing with the *cattle boat* on which he was employed.[26]

October 4, 1888 – an entry in Her Majesty's journal about the *dreadful murders of unfortunate women of a bad class in London* confirms that Queen Victoria was aware of the Whitechapel murders.[27]

October 19, 1888 – Albert Backert from the Whitechapel Vigilance Committee received information from a *respectable middle-aged woman* of Aldgate.

It transpired that a young man, who lived on the floor below the informant, paid the *respectable middle-aged woman* to clean his bedroom and adjoining lumber-room.

After saying *he had been to sea*, inferring that he was a *sailor* of some kind, the young man allegedly told the informant that he *was receiving £1 a week from his father and was also receiving an allowance from his brother, who was a doctor, and that he did not work himself*.

The young man *had plenty of clothes, including hunting breeches, revolvers, guns and many other articles which an ordinary working man would not have*.

Several times, it was brought to the young man's attention that *his towels were very bloodstained for which he accounted by saying that he was fond of painting and had wiped his brush on them*.

Seeing him one day with pieces of liver laid out on a newspaper, when asked how he came by the liver, the young man told the informant that it was given to him by a friend on a New Zealand boat, which has relevance to inquiries made after the Gatton murders to locate Day and Chaston in New Zealand.

Liver contained in a box was received through the post by the Whitechapel Vigilance Committee.

Five *brass wedding rings*, possibly including the rings stolen from Annie Chapman, were found in the young man's bedroom.[22]

October 27, 1888 – Inspector James McWilliams outlined in a report that George Lusk, chairman of the East End Vigilance Committee, also received a letter and portion of a kidney through the post from *Jack the Ripper*.

After examining the kidney, Doctor Frederick Gordon-Brown expressed the *opinion that it is human.*[24]

A letter received at the Commercial Street Police Station is of interest to what one says about *Jack the Ripper* in Australia as the address on the envelope was written in *black-lead pencil, and the contents, which were also written in pencil, were couched in ridiculous language, the police believing it to be the work of a lunatic.*[28]

November 9, 1888 – the seventh victim, Mary Jane Kelly, was murdered in a flat at 13 Miller's Court, Spitalfields.[29]

The notes made by Doctor Thomas Bond during the post-mortem examination included the following:

The body was lying naked in the middle of the bed, the shoulders flat, but the axis of the body inclined to the left side of the bed. The head was turned on the left cheek. The left arm was close to the body with the forearm flexed at a right angle and lying across the abdomen, the right arm was slightly abducted from the body and rested on the mattress, the elbow bent and the forearm supine with the fingers clenched. The legs were wide apart, the left thigh at right angles to the trunk and the right forming an obtuse angle with the pubes.[29]

Not only was the throat cut from *ear to ear*, down to the bone, and the face slashed beyond recognition, but also the abdomen was ripped opened and body parts were placed over and around the body as well as on a nearby table.[29]

George Hutchinson described a suspect as being 34 or 35 years of age, 5 feet 6 inches in height, pale complexion, dark hair and eyelashes, slight moustache turned up at the ends, very surly looking and of Jewish appearance.[30]

Anthony John Camp, author of *Royal Mistresses and Bastards: Fact and Fiction*, alleges that one of the mistresses of Prince Albert Edward was a Mary Jane Kelly.[31] The author, when asked, did not confirm or deny that the alleged mistress was identical with Mary Jane Kelly murdered at Spitalfields.[32]

More to the point, while with the army on manoeuvres in Ireland, Prince Albert Edward cohabitated for three nights, allegedly, with an actress, Nellie Clifden, who was hidden in the camp by his fellow officers.

The Prince of Wales was reprimanded for that misdemeanour by his father, Prince Albert, who died two weeks later.[33]

Blaming her son for the sudden and unexpected death of his father, Queen Victoria wrote in a letter to her eldest daughter, "I never can, or shall, look at him without a shudder."[34]

Based on the theory that where there's smoke, there's fire, one firmly believes that Prince Albert Edward and his son, Prince Albert Victor, possibly had liaisons with prostitutes, one being Mary Jane Kelly.

Following in his father's footsteps, Prince Albert Victor was implicated in the death of Lydia Miller, alias Manton, who allegedly drank *half a pint of carbolic acid*.

The apparent refusal of the coroner to give *access to depositions taken* combined with the jury being asked *to sign a blank paper instead of the usual record of the proceedings* suggests that there is some truth in the rumour then that the name and position of a young man *would authorise much effort to hush the matter up for the sake of society*.[35]

A verdict of *suicide whilst in a state of unsound mind* was returned by the jury.[36]

Even today, some believe that Prince Albert Victor was *Jack the Ripper*.

It might have been the case that he had some involvement in the murders, but he was not the serial killer as he was with Queen Victoria and other dignitaries at Balmoral in Scotland when Stride and Eddowes were murdered.[37]

Growing tired of her grandson's misdemeanours, Queen Victoria threatened to cancel his engagement to Princess Mary of Teck, resulting in the Duke of Clarence and Avondale severing his relationship with the socialite, Maud Richardson.

When Richardson threatened *to cause a scandal if* [Prince Albert Victor] *discontinued his visits*, it appears that Richardson was offered £5000 *to cease troubling the Duke*.

After declining the offer, Richardson partially carried out the threat by exposing the relationship to others.[38]

Once again, based upon the theory that where there's smoke, there's fire, it appears prostitutes in the Whitechapel district of London might have done the same and paid dearly with their lives!

November 13, 1888 – in a letter addressed to the Home Secretary, Queen Victoria's private secretary, Sir Henry Ponsonby, asked on behalf of Her Majesty, "Have the cattle boats and passenger boats been examined?"[27]

This involvement of Queen Victoria corroborates the theory that *Jack the Ripper* was employed as a *drover* or *butcher* on a *cattle boat* that entered the Thames on a Thursday or Friday and left again for the continent on a Sunday or Monday.[33]

December 20, 1888 – the body of the eighth victim, Rose Mylett, alias Lizzie Davis, was found in Clarke's Yard, Poplar, the victim allegedly *strangled with a four-lag cord (equal to packing-string of very moderate thickness)*.

According to some historians, the death of Mylett was not murder, nevertheless, the *signature* of *Jack the Ripper*, namely a *handkerchief*, was folded loosely around the victim's neck.

Before her death, Charles Ptolomey saw Rose with two seamen, one about 5 feet 11 inches, who *looked like a Yankee*, and the other 5 feet 7 inches, Ptolomey also noticing that *the shorter one was speaking to the deceased, and the tall one was walking up and down*.[39]

All seamen, Thomas Day's friend, Richard Burgess, often claimed that he was from America, and his other friend, John Miller from London, who appears to have been Day's accomplice in the Gatton murders, was known also as *Frisco*, *Yank* and *York*.

April 30, 1889 – then a widower with a young son, Edward Litton Carus-Wilson married Catherine Maud Hill in the Church of St Luke at Westbourne Park near London, England.[40]

Soon after, in company of Claude and his new bride, the Reverend Edward Carus-Wilson, allegedly with a Master of Arts degree from Oxford, England, arrived at Adelaide in South Australia.[10,15]

July 17, 1889 – the ninth and last victim of the murders, Alice McKenzie, had her throat cut and abdomen mutilated in Castle Alley, Whitechapel.[41]

The young man from Aldgate disappeared suddenly after McKenzie's death, leaving behind a pair of silent shoes, a bloodstained overcoat and several bags.[22]

Allegedly, the involvement of Her Royal Highness Queen Victoria and the Establishment in the investigations resulted in a rumour that Lord Salisbury *concealed Jack the Ripper at Hatfield House on the night of the last Whitechapel murder*, which appears to have been the death of Alice McKenzie.

Same as what happened after the Gatton murders, it was inferred that the Chief Commissioner of the Metropolitan Police, London, was instructed by the Home Secretary *to discontinue all further inquiries into the atrocities* on it being *discovered that Jack is a member of the House of Lords*.[27]

If that, in fact, did happen, one has a correlation between the murders committed in London and at Gatton, suggesting that the Government and police in England also protected Thomas Day from arrest for the Whitechapel murders.

Furthermore, if one's suspicion is correct, Thomas Day's father was a *Queen's Counsellor*, residing in 1887 at 25 Collingham Gardens, South Kensington, London, and his mother's father, together with the father of the Premier of Queensland at the time of the Gatton murders, was a former director of the Imperial Bank Limited, London.[42,43]

While Thomas Day was not *a member of the House of Lords*, his alleged father, however, was from the Peerage of the United Kingdom and elsewhere, providing credence to the rumour that Lord Salisbury *concealed Jack the Ripper at Hatfield House on the night of the last Whitechapel murder*.[27,43]

2

JACK'S AUSTRALIAN MURDERS?

During the 1890s, while *Jack the Ripper* was notably absent from England, two men proclaimed on the gallows in New South Wales that they did not commit the crimes for which they were about to be hanged.[1,2,3] Moreover, a third would have been hung in Queensland if he had not come up with an *alibi* that was checked out thoroughly and found to be correct.[4]

January 18, 1890 – it was rumoured that Prince Albert Edward's good friend, William Farmer of the prosperous Australian drapery business of Farmer & Co, with head offices in Sydney and London, would leave his estate of Coworth Park, Sunningdale, Berkshire, England, and return to Australia.[5]

Farmer, however, remained in England and was appointed Sheriff of London (1890-1891), Knight Bachelor (1891), High Sheriff of Berkshire (1895), and Master of the Worshipful Company of Gardeners (1898).[6]

March 27, 1890 – corresponding with the age of the youth involved in the murder of Emma Elizabeth Smith, and coinciding also with what was believed to be the last Whitechapel murder, a seaman by the name of T. W. Day from Kent, England, arrived at Sydney from London on the steamer *Coromandel*.[7,8]

One assumes that the seaman was Thomas Day, and that Day might have been banished from England, either by the authorities or his family.

His birthplace of Kent, England, also has significance with respect to associates of Day in Australia.

October 11, 1890 – after evading the police out of a concern that she might suffer a bodily injury from the young man suspected of being *Jack the Ripper*, the *respectable middle-aged woman* of Aldgate was finally located and interviewed. She described the suspect as being of *middle* *height, well-built, with a small, fair moustache, and light brown hair* that he made darker, now and again.⁹

As was the case with the suspects for the Whitechapel murders, the description of Day often differed from one witness to another, inferring that the prime suspect for the Gatton and possibly Whitechapel murders had some theatrical training.

That is more than a possibility as Day was reading *Rienzi*, converted into a theatrical play during the 1840s, when disturbed by police in his hut after the Gatton murders.

Not of *the appearance of a working man*, suggesting that he was living below the means of his upbringing, the young man's parents were *in a good position* but considered their son to be a *scapegrace*, in other words, a mischievous or wayward person, and would have nothing to do with him.

His brother, a doctor, who visited on two occasions, was much older than the young man, comparing with Doctor William Aloysius Day in the alleged paternal family of Thomas Day.

Speaking English with a *nasal twang*, he frequently used *Boss* in general conversation.⁹

The Australian accent is described by the *Australian Geographic* as having a *nasal twang* and the use of *Boss* is significant from colonial to present times in Australia.¹⁰

December 24, 1892 – at 10 am, Annie Morrison, aged 42 years, who appears to be the first victim of *Jack the Ripper* in Australia, in my opinion, left her place of abode with her brother-in-law, John Wilson, in Henry Street at Waverley, Sydney.

Annie had 15 or 20 shillings in her possession and was carrying a bag when she left Wilson's house.¹¹

At 5 pm, Annie visited her son, Freddie, then with her father, George Weller, who was boarding with Henry Brooks on the corner of Barcom and Oxford streets at Paddington.

"You must not think," said Annie to Brooks, "that I have been drinking."

Despite noticing the smell of liquor about her, "I know you have not, Annie," replied Brooks.

After a cup of tea with Brooks, Annie went with Freddie to a terminus in Oxford Street where she caught a tram.

Ten minutes after Freddie arrived back at the house, Annie returned and was seen by Brooks in possession of a flat parcel wrapped up in brown paper.

George Weller went a second time with Annie to the terminus where Annie said she would wait for a tram to Bondi.

When Weller last saw his daughter, Annie was wearing two rings and had a bag and the parcel in her possession.

Between 5 pm and 6 pm, George Davies, who was employed at the Commercial Hotel in Oxford Street, saw Annie by herself in the parlour bar. She appeared to be quite sober and was served with a glass of schnapps.

Soon after, Annie left in company of a young man.

Between 9.30 pm and 10 pm, George Everard Everill saw Annie in Oxford Street, still in possession of the bag, having an animated discussion with two men, one taller than the other.

One assumes that the two men were Thomas Day and Richard Burgess, so the alleged perpetrators will be referred to as Day and Burgess.

Day was wearing light-coloured pants, a dirty grey coat and a black slouch hat whereas Burgess was dressed in black or navy-blue clothing and a brown slouch hat.[17]

December 25, 1892 – around 4 am, Everill saw Day again in Oxford Street and afterwards near Woollahra where he was joined by Burgess described by Everill as a larrikin, carrying *a black pint bottle* in one of his hands.

With Annie between Day and Burgess, the trio were last seen by Everill, walking towards Ocean Street. All appeared to be under the influence, particularly Annie, who was carrying the bag in her left hand. There was no sign of *marks or bruises* on Annie, but her face *was very flushed*.

At 9 am, Thomas Oxley responded to someone groaning inside a partly-erected house in Liverpool Street at Paddington.

On entering, Oxley found Annie with a bruised face and black eye, lying on the ground floor. When asked *what brought her there*, Annie told Oxley that *she did not know but would like to go to the hospital as she was in pain.*

At 10 am, Constable John Alexander Hazlett of Woolahra said to Annie, "What is the matter with you?"

Annie did not respond at first, but when Hazlett repeated the question, Annie replied, "I am in pain."

"Where," queried Hazlett.

"Here," replied Annie, indicating the lower part of her body.

Upon seeing that Annie's left eye was discoloured, her head and face bruised, and lower lip cut, Hazlett said to Annie, "Have you been assaulted by someone?"

"No."

"Did someone give you that black eye?"

"No."

"What is your name?"

"Mary Morrison," replied Annie, who added, "I live at Paddington, but I have no home."

During further questioning, Annie told Hazlett that *she did not know how she got to the house or where she then was.*

A *broken beer bottle,* possibly the *black pint bottle* seen in possession of Burgess at 4 am, was found close to Annie.

When asked if she had any money, "None now," replied Annie.

Thomas Oxley found *a bag, bonnet and a piece of an old skirt in the kitchen part of a partly-erected building, about 20 yards* from where Annie was discovered, but the boots and stockings worn by Annie before the rape were never located.

On the way to the Sydney Hospital, Annie told Hazlett that her correct name was Annie Morrison.[12]

At 11 am, Annie was very weak and in a state of collapse when examined by Doctor Herbert Lethington Maitland, house surgeon at the Sydney Hospital.

Questioned as to how she came by the bruises all over her body, Annie at first told Maitland that she had been assaulted and afterwards denied the statement, possibly because she knew the identify of Thomas Day.[13]

A dressmaker by occupation, it is possible that Annie might have been employed at some time by Farmer & Co.

Annie Brook, nurse at the Sydney Hospital, assisted with the undressing of the victim when she was admitted. There was no ring on Annie's fingers, and no money was found in the pockets of her clothing.[14]

December 26, 1892 – when Henry Brooks asked Annie at the hospital if she went in the tram the second time, "No, I walked along Oxford Street to Paddington," replied Annie, who added, "Don't ask me any more questions. I am too weak."[12]

Annie did, however, tell her brother-in-law, John Wilson, that she was assaulted by two young men whom Annie, allegedly, could not describe. She remembered everything prior to suffering blows to the face in Oxford Street during the afternoon of Christmas Eve and after that she could not remember anything.[13]

December 28, 1892 – four days after the brutal assault and rape, Annie Morrison died from her injuries.

It was reported in *The Sydney Morning Herald* that at the inquest, Maitland gave evidence to the effect that the internal wounds *were caused by some blunt instrument used with violence.*

Doctor William Camac Wilkinson performed the post-mortem examination.

After Wilkinson outlined the injuries suffered by Annie, the City Coroner, John Chadwick Woore, said to Wilkinson, "How, in your opinion, were the internal injuries caused?"

"I should say by some iron instrument with a fairly small blunt point. A wooden instrument if of sufficient, resisting power would cause the injuries," replied Wilkinson, who added, "There were from three to four inches from the external to the internal injuries."

"The injuries could not have been caused by a knife?"

"No."

Responding to a question from the jury, "It would have been possible for the injuries to have been caused," replied Wilkinson, "with a walking stick with a small point or with an umbrella."

When asked by Woore as to how the deceased died, "Death had resulted from the internal wounds," replied Wilkinson. "The injuries on the face were just such as would be caused by blows from a man's fist."[11]

The jury found that the deceased was brutally ill-used and assaulted by some person or persons unknown.

"That is a verdict," clarified Woore, "of wilful murder?"

"Yes," replied the foreman.[12]

It will be remembered that rings were stolen in the Whitechapel murders, and that the *respectable middle-aged woman* at Aldgate found five *brass wedding rings* in the young man's bedroom.[9]

The rings worn by Annie Morrison before the incident were stolen, establishing a correlation between the murders committed in England and Australia.[12,14]

Same as the many descriptions provided for the suspects of the Whitechapel murders, the alleged perpetrators of the Paddington murder were two young men, one taller than the other, providing another correlation between the murders committed in England and Australia.

A third correlation was the *modus operandi* used during the murders in England and Australia, namely the luring of the victim to a secluded location where the victim could be assaulted, robbed and raped.

It also will be remembered that the first victim of the Whitechapel murders, Emma Elizabeth Smith, who was assaulted and robbed by two if not three young men, was raped with a *blunt instrument* described as a *walking stick*.[15,16]

Four years later in Australia, the instrument used to rape Annie Morrison was believed to have been either *a walking stick with a small point* or *an umbrella*, providing a fourth correlation between the murders committed in England and Australia.[11]

A suspect for the Paddington murder was placed under surveillance at Young, south-west from Sydney. It was expected that he would be arrested along with another observed in his company, but that apparently did not happen.[17,18]

One suspects that Edith Westby born in 1849 at Melbourne who lived off her own means in the 1880s at 50 Rutland Gate, Westminster, London, was Thomas Day's mother, Edith being about 20 years at the time of the birth.[19,20]

That being so, at the time of the Paddington murder, Day's uncles, Edmund Wright Westby and Alfred Ashley (Ashley) Westby; the former being born in England and the latter at Melbourne, lived on their property known as *Pullitop*, near Wagga Wagga, south-west from Sydney.[21,22,23,24]

One assumes that Day, together with Burgess, was making for the property of his uncles when spotted at Young, north-east from Wagga Wagga, where the two suspects for the Paddington murder were apparently last seen.[17,18]

At the Royal Commission, during questioning about Thomas Day's antecedents, Commissioner Frederick William Dickson, son of Premier Dickson, said to Urquhart, "… He said he came from Wagga?"

"Yes."

"And you do not appear to have wanted to know anything about Day's previous career?"

"I have not suggested anything of that kind," replied Urquhart, who was not asked any further question about Day's antecedents, leaving the public in the dark as to the identity of Thomas Day and his association with Wagga Wagga.[25]

Why did the Royal Commission stop short of revealing everything there was to know about Thomas Day? Did it have something to do with the close friendship between Ashley Westby and Sir Frederick

Matthew Darley, Lieutenant-Governor and Chief Justice of New South Wales?[26]

Understanding the significance of those relationships is the key to unlocking the mystery surrounding the 1888 and 1889 Whitechapel murders in England, and the 1892 to 1898 murders in Australia.

March 25, 1893 – Emma Harrison was found brutally raped and murdered inside a boarding house at 321 Bourke Street, Darlinghurst, Sydney.[27]

Same as the Whitechapel and Paddington murders, a watch and ring belonging to Emma were stolen.[28]

The day after the murder, a suspicion that *Jack the Ripper* committed the murder was published in *The Evening News*, as follows:

A married woman, who lives a few doors away from the ill-fated house, averred that it had been the work of Jack the Ripper, having seen a strange man in the vicinity that day whom she said had been vowing vengeance, sotto voce, to women in general. She seemed fully satisfied that the murderous Jack of London had turned up in our midst.[27]

In England, the murders were committed close to each other in the Whitechapel district of London.

The same pattern emerged in Australia as it was about 820 yards from where Annie Morrison was attacked and raped at Paddington to where Emma Harrison was raped and murdered at Darlinghurst.

Like Annie, Emma was a dressmaker employed by Sir William Farmer, the distance from where Emma lived to Farmer & Co in Pitt Street being about 1,640 yards.[27]

Another aspect that caught my attention was the way some of the bodies were positioned after death in England and Australia.

Doctor Bond outlined in his notes that the head of Mary Jane Kelly *was turned on the left cheek*, and that *the left arm was close to the body with the forearm flexed at a right angle and lying across the abdomen.*[29]

This was practically the same as how Emma was found by Doctor Frederick Milford, who noted that the victim's head was *turned towards the left side*, and that *the right hand rested on the abdomen*.[30]

Apart from different arms lying across the abdomen, there are similarities in the way the bodies were positioned on a bed in England and Australia, particularly the way their heads were turned to the left side.

March 27, 1893 – City Coroner Woore, who conducted the hearing into the demise of Annie Morrison, opened an inquest into the death of Emma Harrison.

One of the first witnesses to give evidence was a newsagent, William Henry Jeater, who had been engaged to Emma for three years, and who was taken into custody by police on suspicion of committing the murder.

At 8 pm on Saturday, the night of the murder, Jeater arrived at the boarding house to see his fiancée. Alone at the time, Emma ushered Jeater through the front door into the living room.

About an hour later, Emma went upstairs and returned to the living room with Sir Walter Scott's novel *Kenilworth*, which is about the secret marriage of Robert Dudley, 1st Earl of Leicester, and Amy, daughter of Sir Hugh Robsart.

Around 9.30 pm, while reading aloud from the novel, Jeater heard what appeared to be someone tapping on the window. "I wonder what that is," said Emma, who went outside to investigate.

Jeater did not see or hear Emma speak to anyone while she was away for about three minutes. Coming back into the house, Emma made some comment about it being a *runaway knock*, no doubt inferring that it might have been a prisoner escaping from the nearby Darlinghurst Gaol.

At about 10 pm, after talking for several minutes at the front door, Jeater left Emma on the best of terms, so he thought.[31]

Around noon the following day, a Sunday, Emma was found lifeless on the bed, fully-clothed, her underclothing and bedclothes saturated with blood.

Four red smears *resembling water mixed with blood* were found on the bedclothes near the feet, right knee, level with the chest, and left side of the mouth.[27,32]

When asked by the coroner if he could identify the body, "I don't know," said Jeater. "I can't identify it."

"You can't," said Woore to Jeater, "identify it?"

"No," replied Jeater, who by way of explanation added, "she has changed so much since I saw her last."[33]

Milford gave evidence during the inquest that Emma *had been perfectly chaste during life, and at or about the time of her death, had been outraged*, the internal examination revealing that *two organs bore abrasions, and a third had also recently been injured as a result of violence* accounting *for the blood found about the deceased and her clothing.*[30,32,34]

While it was never brought out in court, this was not a case of sexual intercourse between a male and female, albeit against the will of the female.

Sure, Emma was *virgo intacta*, and it would be expected that she bled from the vagina passage, but surely not to the extent of saturating the underclothing and bedclothes?

The rape, in my opinion, was with a *blunt instrument*, possibly a *walking stick*.

Seeing as how Milford appears not to have clarified the matter, one assumes that while wiping the *blunt instrument* clean on the bedclothes, blood mixed with urine caused the *red smears* described by Milford as *resembling water mixed with blood.*[32]

Apart from the face and head being darker than the rest of the body, *the tongue was clenched between the teeth, about a quarter of an inch from its tip, and was lacerated above and below the teeth.*[30]

It might have been coincidental, but Annie Chapman was found at Spitalfields, England, with her *tongue* [protruding] *between the front teeth*, and with her head *turned on the right side.*[35]

There also were bruises on both arms, left side of the forehead near the eye, and on the *left side of the neck, midway between the lower jaw and collar bone.*[30]

Milford determined that *the wounds about the throat had been caused by a person standing in front of the deceased, and grasping her throat with his right hand*, Emma died from *asphyxia, the result of strangulation.*[36]

A letter addressed to Jeater, calling off the engagement, was found on a dressing table near the body. Jeater confirmed that it was in Emma's handwriting, but the letter *was not signed and was written in lead pencil*.[31]

Of interest to Emma's unsigned letter *written in lead pencil*, the address on an envelope received at the Commercial Street Police Station, as alluded to before, *was written in black-lead pencil, and the contents, which were also written in pencil, were couched in ridiculous language, the police believing it to be the work of a lunatic*.[37]

Linking that statement with Emma's murder, one assumes someone of *unsound mind* forced Emma to write the letter that she apparently refused to sign.

After satisfying the coroner and police that he was not the perpetrator, Jeater was released from custody. The attention of police, surprisingly, then focused on a boarder, George Martin Walter Archer, who was a groom employed by the Sydney Tramway and Omnibus Company.

April 18, 1893 – Archer was committed for trial when the jury found him *guilty* of wilful murder.[38]

June 10, 1893 – the trial was conducted by Sir Joseph George Long (George) Innes, a very good friend of Emma's employer, Sir William Farmer.[39]

At 9.40 pm on the Saturday night, Isabella Halliday, who lived beside the boarding house with her husband, Charles, believed she saw Archer standing under poor street lighting in Burton Street.

When seen allegedly by Isabella, Archer was wearing a black soft-felt hat and appeared to be perfectly sober.[40]

Afterwards, from the top floor of her residence, Isabella saw someone, but could not say for certain that it was Archer, enter the boarding house, corroborated in part by another witness, Elizabeth Sheehy.[41,42]

Between 10 and 10.30 pm, William Freebairn, the licensee of the Caxton Hotel on the corner of Burton and Palmer streets, not far from the crime scene, provided Archer with some brandy.[43]

At 10.15 pm, corroborating in part the evidence of Isabella Halliday, while walking past the boarding house, Elizabeth Sheehy saw Emma standing on the footpath and a man at the front door she believed was Archer.

One assumes that it was Thomas Day seen by Isabella and Elizabeth at the boarding house, so he will be referred to as such.

When asked to go inside, "No," said Emma to Day, "do you think I am going in there?"[44]

It appears that Emma went back inside alone, locked the front door, and when she believed it was safe to do so, left the key in the usual hiding place for the other occupants, the key being found by Day who entered the boarding house.

At 10.40 pm, Charles Halliday heard a scream that came from the direction of the next-door boarding house. Opening the back door to see what was happening, Charles heard a scuffle going on inside, possibly on the top floor, and then he heard someone say loudly, "Take that and that!"

Coming downstairs to see what was happening, Isabella said to Charles, "Whatever is that?"

Hearing furniture moved around and upon seeing no light inside the boarding house, "It can't be the Archers," said Isabella to Charles, "because here is Mrs Archer coming now with her mother."[41]

At 10.45 pm, Archer's wife, formerly Emily Fanny Howe, arrived back at the boarding house in company of her mother, Esmeralda Howe.

When she went to open the front door, Emily found the key was missing from its usual hiding place and that the side door was closed but not locked.

Entering through the side door, which was witnessed by Charles and Isabella, Emily saw a stream of light shining down the stairs from Emma's room, indicating that the door was then open.

Soon after, Esmeralda went home through the side door, leaving it closed but unlocked for the return of the owner and other occupants, John Osborne and his wife.

At the same time, while making her way upstairs to the top floor, Emily saw the light in Emma's room had been extinguished but could not say for certain if the door was open or closed.

It can be assumed, consequently, that Emma was already dead, and that the perpetrator was still inside the house, putting out the lamp to make it appear to others as if nothing untoward was happening inside the bedroom.

After lighting a lamp and a candle in her room, Emily made her way back downstairs to go outside by candle-light, possibly to an outhouse, Emily's movements in the backyard being observed by Charles.

Walking past Emma's room on the way downstairs, Emily saw that the door was closed.[41]

At 10.50 pm, Hannah Henry took note of the time from the prison clock when she saw Archer at the corner of Burton and Bourke streets as she believed he was acting suspiciously.

Going back to have a better look at him, Archer allegedly said to Hannah, "What the – are you looking at?"

"At you," responded Hannah.[44,45]

At 11 pm, Emily was back in her bedroom when the Osbornes came home.[41]

Shortly afterwards, Emily went downstairs again, this time to the dining room, being there no more than two minutes before returning to her bedroom.[41]

Hannah Henry was adamant that she saw Archer standing on the corner of Bourke and Burton streets at 10.50 pm, and so too was Charles Halliday that it was 10.40 pm when he checked the clock upon hearing the scream inside the boarding house.

Considering those times with what Milford said about Emma being *raped at or about the time of her death*, it is obvious that the attack and rape would have been between 10.40 pm and 10.45 pm, the times when Charles Halliday heard the scream and Emily Archer entered the boarding house.

On either side of 10.50 pm, Emily made her way upstairs and back downstairs. That being so, Emily was adamant that if someone had gone downstairs while she was inside her bedroom, she would have heard as the stairs creaked.

So, between 10.50 pm and 11 pm, while Emily was outside the house and Archer was at the corner of Bourke and Burton streets, it appears Emma's killer used the window of opportunity available and exited the boarding house.

Archer and Thomas Day were about equal height and build, making it possible for Elizabeth to have mistaken Day for Archer at the front door. This also applies to Isabella, who believed she saw Archer enter the house around the same time.[46,47]

One assumes that after using the key to let himself into the boarding house, which would have been shortly after 10.15 pm, Day forced Emma to write the letter.

Obviously refusing to sign the letter, Emma was then brutally murdered and raped just before Emily returned home, a supposition based upon the evidence given by various witnesses and the window of opportunity available to the killer.

When questioned on the Sunday night, about how blood came to be on the singlet he was then wearing, "What is the meaning," said Detective John Roche to Archer, "of those bloodstains?"

"Oh, my nose had been bleeding on Saturday, and I must have got some of the blood on my hands," replied Archer, who added, "When I'm working, my trousers work down through not wearing braces, and I frequently push my shirt down with my hands."

"What caused your nose to bleed?"

"A horse kicked me."

"It didn't leave much of a mark."

"Well, it did not exactly kick me, but hit me with its head. It was a black colt, and while I was putting on the winkers, he swung his head around and hit me."

"What caused the small scar on your eyebrow?"

"That's what the horse did. At the same time, I must have been struck by the bit."[44]

Edwin (Ted) Delaney, Arthur Townsend, Edwin Vale, Charles Lawton, John Mitchell, Thomas Scollay and Robert Green gave supporting evidence for the Sunday. No one, however, supported Archer's claim that he suffered a nosebleed on the Saturday.[48]

Just prior to Roche taking Archer into custody at the stables on the Monday after the murder, "There's an old shirt of mine hanging up over there, Ted," said Archer to Delaney. "Throw an old coat or something over it."

Delaney saw the shirt hanging on a peg in the stables but did not do anything at first as suggested by Archer to conceal it. The next morning, however, he removed the shirt to a *manger* from where it was handed over to the police.[48,49]

Going against him at the trial, Archer's statement that he arrived home at about 1.30 am was not supported by Emily, who said it was more like 1 am.[41]

Immediately after instructing the jury that the evidence against Archer was mostly *circumstantial*, Justice Innes inferred that the *intent* of the accused was to rape Emma, and in the process, he murdered the victim.[50]

Ask yourself, what was Archer's *motive* for the criminal acts, lust or theft of the watch and ring?

Lust was possible but highly unlikely.

At the time of the murder, Archer was happily married and was living at the boarding house with his wife and daughter, May, who was born the previous year.

If it was theft, why not do it at a time when Emma was away from the house?

The *intent*, in my opinion, was to murder Emma, defile her body, and steal the watch and ring, same as what happened to Annie Morrison and some of the Whitechapel victims.

After telling the jury that *the public required their police officers to leave no stone unturned to find out the perpetrators of the outrage*, an outline of the extraordinary comments made by Justice Innes, about the actions of investigating police, was published in *The Sydney Morning Herald*, as follows:

> *There was no objection to their making inquiries of the prisoner, but it to him seemed objectionable that answers elicited by cross-questioning should afterwards be used against him, but the law allowed that. At the same time, he thought that no one who had attended to the case would say that Roche or Sawtell had perverted the truth. No doubt at times, police officers allowed their zeal to outrun their discretion, and under certain circumstances, this induced them, perhaps unconsciously, to vary the conversations that they may have held with accused persons, but in the case before them, the accused had admitted that in the really important matters, the statements of the officers were accurate.*[50]

The other police officer mentioned was Detective Sergeant Arthur Caldwell Sawtell.

During the trial, Archer's counsel objected to what was viewed as inappropriate questioning by Sawtell and Roche after Archer's arrest, and to Archer's wife being called as a witness to give evidence against her husband.

While passing the sentence of death, it was observed that Innes *was several times at the point of breaking down.*[39]

One does not expect the Judiciary to be without feelings but what happened was extraordinary and has a bearing on what one will say later with respect to another hearing conducted by Innes.

June 16, 1893 – an appeal lodged against the conviction was heard in the High Court at Sydney.[51]

Sir Frederick Darley, Ashley Westby's friend, and Sir William Charles Windeyer, another name to be remembered, were two of the three justices who ruled against the points reserved by Archer's counsel and upheld the conviction.[51]

July 11, 1893 – before the death sentence was carried out at Darlinghurst Gaol, Archer read the following statement:

Before my Maker, I declare my un-guilty conscious. For being in this position, I have to give my worthy thanks to Sergeant Sawtell and Detective Roche. If they had not told lies and spoke the truth, I would not have been where I am now. I have also to thank one or two other friends, Mrs Halliday. I have been nearly five weeks waiting for what I am to meet now. They are taking my life, but I have a pure and un-guilty conscience. They are not only killing me, but they are taking the life of those that are near and dear to me, that of my wife and child. God bless them.[52,53]

Prepared to meet his death, Archer's last moments became a dreadful scene when the hanging was bungled.

Dangling from the rope, thrashing about wildly and vainly with his legs and arms for around ten minutes, Archer was *gradually choked* or *garrotted*, as some described, life slowly and painfully ebbing from his body.[53]

One expected that police would have conducted a thorough search of the stables to locate the silver open-faced Geneva's watch numbered 14104 and gold mourning ring inscribed with the words "Oh, my brothers and my sisters" stolen from Emma during the murder, but apparently that was not done.

More than two years later, it was reported in *The Australian Star* that a groom by the name of P. Lawler *came across a lady's watch and a ring in the rafters of the Harris Street stables, above the peg on which Archer's bloodstained shirt was found.*[28]

Which peg, on the wall where it was left by Archer or from the *manger* where it was hung up by Delaney?

One suspects that Day or Burgess might have worked at the stables and secreted the watch and ring in the rafters, having in mind that Burgess later provided his occupation as a *groom* when arrested on another matter in Victoria.[54]

It was inferred also in *The Australian Star* that the finding of the watch and ring in the stables confirmed not only Archer's *guilt* but also removed *the slur of a dying man on the behaviour of the two police officers to whom he referred in his speech on the scaffold.*[28]

There is no denying that a jury found Archer *guilty* of Emma Harrison's murder, but was it a fair trial? The extraordinary comments made by Innes to the jury, and the fact that Innes was visibly upset during the sentencing, suggest that it was not.

In the absence of official documents, based on the reports in the newspapers which, admittedly, were not always accurate, one believes, on the *balance of probability*, that the Darlinghurst killer was Thomas Day, alias *Jack the Ripper*.[18]

3

SINS OF ANOTHER

The principle espoused by Sir William Blackstone, an eminent jurist, judge and politician of the 18th century in England, was that *it is better that ten guilty persons escape than that one innocent suffer*.[1] One agrees with Blackstone, but obviously the authorities in New South Wales did not, if, in fact, it was Day and not Archer, who murdered Emma Harrison at Darlinghurst.

September 20, 1893 – Florence Alfred Healey took over from John William (Jack) Phillips as manager of the City Bank of Sydney at Carcoar in the Central West region of New South Wales.[2]

Built on ground that sloped from the front toward the rear, there were two floors of the bank premises at the front and three at the rear of the building.

The front entrance, hallway, dining room, manager's office and banking chambers were on the ground floor of the building, bedrooms for the manager and his family on the top floor, and the servant's quarters, kitchen and basement were at the rear on the lower ground floor.[3]

After the formalities of the handover, it was expected that Jack Phillips and his family would vacate the premises and depart on transfer to Young, which is where the two suspects were seen after the Paddington murder.[2]

September 23, 1893 – discovering that the 10.30 pm train terminated at Cowra, south-west from Carcoar, Jack Phillips changed his plans and decided to take the 5.30 pm train two days later that went all the way to Young.[2,4]

If Jack had not changed his plans at the last moment, only the servant, Agnes McVicar, was expected to be on the bank premises that night.

While waiting for Jack to vacate the premises, Healey, who had possession of the manager's keys, took up residence at the Victoria Hotel in Carcoar, the duplicate keys being in possession of the accountant, Joseph George (Joe) Derwin.[2]

Around 9 pm, the Reverend Francis William Clarke drove Jack Phillips in his buggy to Blayney, north-east of Carcoar. After picking up Susan Jane (Susie) Stoddart, sister of Jack's wife, Annie Dorothy Phillips, their daughter, Gladys Mary Phillips, and Annie's friend, Letitia Frances (Fanny) Cavanagh at the railway station, the party went back to Carcoar.[2,5]

September 24, 1893 – around 2 am in the morning, Jack Phillips and Fanny Cavanagh were brutally murdered inside the bank.[6]

It was outlined in *The Broadford Courier* that with a *razor-edged tomahawk*, the killer *cut the manager down, and then with a ferocity and bloodlust, which was more like that of a baboon than of a man, he hacked the body to pieces as it lay on the floor.*[4]

Fanny's throat was cut *on the left side, in an oblique direction, extending from one inch on the right side of the throat to the angle of the left jaw, severing the skin, the windpipe, the main arteries and veins, and laying bare the spinal column.*[2]

Before the murders, an enterprising young man, Edwin Hubert (Bertie) Glasson, owned a butchery at Carcoar where he employed Thomas Graham (Thomas) Furner as the manager of the butcher's shop and a brother, Edward James (Ned) Furner, as the overseer of a property known as *Woodstock*.

Bertie speculated unsuccessfully in his business dealings and *more than once got into monetary difficulties from which he was relieved by members of his family.*[6]

When he lost heavily at the races, for the sake of the family's reputation, the debt of £1200 Bertie owed to some very shady characters in Sydney was settled. From thereon, however, it was made clear to Bertie that he was on his own.[4,7]

Without family and friends to support him, Bertie ran into further financial difficulties culminating in the butchery being sold off by the Sheriff's Office first for rent owed and then for overdrawing by £49 on his account with the City Bank of Sydney at Carcoar.[2,8]

A *horse and cart* saved from the first but not the second sale provides a correlation between the Carcoar and Gatton murders in that five years after the Carcoar murders, Thomas Day used a *horse and cart* at Clarke's butchery to convey meat to the butcher's shop and collect firewood for the coppers.[2,9]

One assumes that Thomas Day was employed in the same capacity at Glasson's butchery until the stock-in-trade of the butcher's shop was sold by the Sheriff's Office.[10]

During the frenzied attack inside the bank, Annie Phillips suffered horrific injuries. Of the belief that her death was imminent, Doctor Alfred Winter Hawthorne and Police Magistrate Nathaniel Connolly obtained a Dying Declaration from Annie, as follows:

I, Annie Dorothy Phillips, wife of John William Phillips, late manager of the City Bank of Sydney, Carcoar branch, being aware that I am in danger of death and may shortly die, make a solemn declaration connected with the tragedy which occurred at our residence after midnight at the Carcoar branch of the City Bank on the 24th instant. I retired to rest after receiving some friends who arrived a little after ten by train on the night of the 23rd inst. I and my husband retired to bed at about a quarter to twelve. The baby, Gladys, somewhat disturbed our rest. My sleep was a little uneasy, and after I had been in bed some time, I thought I heard a noise on the stairs like someone walking. This was about two o'clock, and I awakened my husband. Both of us noticed a glimmer of light in the dining room, and we got up and went downstairs together. My husband took his revolver in his hand, and as the light came from the dining room, we entered it. When we got into that apartment, I saw by the candle which I had brought from the dining room that there was a man behind the door with a half axe in his hand. The lower part of his face was covered with a black mask. It looked to me like leather, but I can't swear to the substance. The man at once knocked the candle out of my hand, and I believe he at once struck my husband, as he fell and carried me with him. At once, he moaned quite pitifully, and I endeavoured to get out of the room. After some little fumbling, I found the door, and almost at the same time the man in the room whistled. Mr Phillips then seemed to be struggling with him, and fell on the floor, moaning fearfully. I said to him, 'Why don't you use the revolver to him? Give me the pistol. If you can't shoot him, I will.' After that I don't know how I found myself at the foot of the stairs where I called Miss Stoddart, my sister, who had come from Sydney on Saturday, and Miss Cavanagh, who accompanied her, I next managed to scream out that someone was killing Jack in the dining room and called out 'murder.' Then I thought of my baby and went up to my bedroom to look for her. I heard a scream about this time. At first, I thought it was my husband, but I think now it must have been one of the girls. I tried to strike a match which I had in my hands but did not at first succeed. Eventually, however, I did get a light, but before I could do anything, a man came into the bedroom, and I saw him. He had not his mask on, as when he blew out my candle in the dining room and struck my husband, I pulled off his mask. I saw the man had the same axe in his hand, and immediately felt a blow on my cheek, but did not see any blood, but while the man was trying to pull the tomahawk out of my cheek, I struggled with him. Just at this time my sister, Miss Stoddart, came into the room and said, 'Oh, Annie, you are hurt,' and held something to my face. I said, 'I must go to Jack. He will be killed.' My sister said, 'You are dreadfully hurt. You must lie down.' She persuaded me to lie down, but I had not been on the bed five or ten minutes when the man without the mask came back and said, 'Give me keys, give me the keys of the bank safe, or I'll shoot you.' My sister said, 'Oh, do not kill us. You have a wife and relatives.' He said, 'How do you know?' But at the same time, my sister said to me, 'Give him the keys,' and I got up and got some keys out of my husband's trousers pockets. He took the keys and went out, but returned soon after and said, 'What do you mean? You have given me the wrong keys.' I said, 'Mr Phillips is not the manager. We have not got the keys here.' He said, 'Who has them?' I said, 'The new manager.' He said, 'Where is he?' I replied, 'He is at one of the hotels.' My sister added, 'I don't know where he is. I only came up to town tonight.' He then said, 'Let me get away, and none of you make a noise and scream, or I will shoot you.' Then he went away, and I feel sure that I knew him, as he was like Bertie Glasson in height and size, and since then, I am sure that he is the man. Some little time after the man left, I screamed out, 'Are you gone?' As I got no reply, assisted by my sister, I went downstairs to the dining room where my husband was lying in front of the door. He was not dead, but was speechless, excepting for a moment when he mentioned my name. I put his head on my lap, but I was soon unable to bear his weight, and was taken away from him."[11,12]

Bertie Glasson was arrested on suspicion of murdering Jack Phillips and Fanny Cavanagh. While in custody, he confessed to Constable Charles Augustus Prior about his involvement with a *dark man* and *rough-looking Irishman* in the murders, which the constable gave in evidence at the trial, as follows:

He said, "The man I met in Sydney told me he knew where there was gold up country and asked me to go with him. He said he had been in a bank, and a box of sovereigns had been planted in a tree. He wanted someone to go with him, and said if I would go, he would give me some money. He said it was near Cowra or Orange. The man declined to reveal his name or where the money was. I believed him and promised to meet him at Orange in three weeks, and to take with me a tomahawk, brace and bit, lantern, and an old suit of clothes. On the 22nd September, I pawned some things and purchased the tomahawk, brace and bit, and lantern. Next morning, I left for Orange, but got out at Blayney where I saw the man. He told me to get my things out of the train and meet him on the top of Red Hill. After I was there a little, the man I saw in Sydney and the other rough-looking Irishman came up. They laughed at me and called me a fool for believing what they said about gold in a tree. Then I heard a trap coming along and recognised Clarke's voice. I called out, but the men bade me to be quiet or they would shoot me. We started to walk, and after we had been journeying for some time, they made me change my clothes. Then they gave me something to drink. We came to a place where there were a lot of briars, and the men told me to draw plans of the City and Commercial Banks at Carcoar. They threatened to shoot me if I didn't do what they wanted. They took off my boots and put on a pair of slippers I had with me. The dark man also changed his boots. We went towards Carcoar, and when opposite Hades' place, the dark man went towards the creek. The Irishman and myself stopped in front of the City Bank. After we had been there an hour, I heard struggling inside and screaming. This was followed by a whistle, and the Irishman became excited and rushed towards the side door which was open, and the dark man came out and said, 'My God, I have done it! I have killed a man and two or three women, and my keys are no good. There are some people upstairs, but they are only women.' The dark man said to me, 'You go upstairs, keep those women there, tell them if they move you will murder them and ask them who the man is downstairs, and get the keys of the safe.' I refused to go. The dark man struck me over the eye and inflicted an abrasion and dragged me to the foot of the stairs and said, 'Remember, we know where your wife is. If you don't do what I tell you, we will kill her.' He then thrust something into my hand and told me to go upstairs. I went into the room where there was a light. Two women were in. One of them had a cut on her face and was all covered with blood. She came towards me and said, 'My God, has it come to this.' She caught hold of my arms and dragged them down. I felt a sharp pain in my foot, and it must have been then that I cut my leg with the tomahawk. I asked for the keys of the bank. One woman gave me some keys, and I went downstairs and gave them to the dark man. He went into another room, taking me with him. He tried to do something with the keys, and said, 'What do you mean? These are the wrong keys. Go upstairs and demand the keys. If they don't give you any, search the men's pockets, and tell them you must have money.' I returned to the room and said what I had been told to. Then another woman came in. One of the women asked me if I had taken any life. I said, 'No.' She also asked me if I had a wife and children of my own. They said they had no keys, the new manager had them. I noticed a man's trousers, and took them out of the room, but found no keys in the pockets. When I got outside, I saw the Irishman, who caught hold of me and said, 'For God's sake come away, or we will be caught.' We went to a small creek, where I washed my face and hands. On returning to the road we met the dark man with a horse. He told me to get on it and ride away for my life. If they were caught it would be through a fool like me. I galloped away, but don't remember where I went to, but sat on a log in the scrub and wrote a letter to my wife on the back of a programme. I remember passing Canowindra and coming to the rocks outside Cowra. I took the saddle off the horse and changed my clothes. I next went to Tasker's Hotel and lay on a form in front of it."[10]

At the Royal Commission, when Chairman Arthur Baptist Noel asked for a description of Thomas Day, William Burnett replied, "He was dark, about the build of Christie here."

"Somewhere," said Noel to Burnett, "about that build?"

"Somewhere about the build of Christie," replied Burnett, "a man of about 14 stones."[13]

The person referred to as *Christie* was Constable Robert George Christie, who gave evidence at the Royal Commission that Robert (Bob) King of Clarke's butchery at Gatton told him that Thomas Day was 30 years of age, contradicting what Inspector Urquhart and Acting Sergeant Toomey said about Day being a *beardless boy*, aged *20 or 21 years*.[14]

When Richard Burgess was arrested the year after the Carcoar murders and found *guilty* of assault at Maldon in Victoria, he was described in police records as a *groom* by occupation, about 5 feet 6 inches high, and a native of Ireland.[15]

Before the Gatton murders, when asked for his place of birth by Frederick Ross of the Salvation Army's shelter, Brisbane, whose statement can be found at the end of this Chapter, Burgess said that he was born in Ireland, corroborating what he told the authorities in Victoria.[16]

One assumes that the *dark man* described by Bertie to Prior was Day, and that the *rough-looking Irishman* was Burgess, so from here on they will be referred to as such.

Woken by the sound of the struggle between Jack and Annie with the perpetrator going on down below in the dining room, Susie and Fanny heard the cries of an infant.

"Oh, it's Gladys," said Fanny, who rushed to the main bedroom while Susie peered over the balcony to ascertain as to what was happening below.

Unable to see what was going on in the dining room, Susie was considering what to do next when Fanny ran past her with Gladys cradled in her arms.[2]

Leaving Jack alone in the dining room, Annie escaped the onslaught and was on her way up to the main bedroom when she was passed by Fanny going down the stairs with Gladys.

Soon after passing Annie on the stairs, Fanny let out a blood-curdling scream, her life coming to an end, fulfilling in part a dream that she had the night before and told to her father at breakfast that she saw a man murdered inside the bank.

Back in the main bedroom, before collapsing to the floor, Annie said to Susie, "Jack is being murdered."[2,17]

Plucking up the courage to do so, which was immediately after Fanny was murdered, Agnes made her way upstairs, passing Thomas Day going down the stairs.

Agnes then saw Gladys, who was crying, cradled in the lifeless arms of Fanny lying prostrate on the second landing, her throat cut from *ear to ear*.

Outside the main bedroom, Agnes saw Bertie talking to Annie and Susie inside the room.

While speaking to Bertie from the doorway, which was prior to Agnes brushing past Bertie to put Gladys back in the cradle, Agnes *heard other heavy footsteps down below*, confirming that the other she passed on the stairs, was still inside the bank.[2,18,19]

At 3.15 am, when Joe Derwin arrived at the bank, he checked the dining room and found bloodstained footprints on the floor and windowsill, indicating that someone without footwear had exited through the dining-room window.[5,7]

In the kitchen, Joe found the window raised with the blind in a lowered position and prints on the windowsill, indicating that a second perpetrator with footwear had exited the bank through the kitchen window.[5,7]

It appears that no bloody *foot* or *boot* print was found in the main bedroom, so one assumes that it was Bertie, still wearing the *slippers*, who exited the bank through the kitchen window, making good his escape through the garden.[7,20]

Bertie told Constable Prior that the *dark man* replaced his boots before entering the bank.

One assumes, consequently, that after disturbing Agnes on his way upstairs from the kitchen to the banking chambers, Thomas Day removed his footwear, possibly a pair of *silent shoes*, leaving the bloody footprints on the windowsill as he made good his escape through the dining-room window.[2,20]

At 4 am, when Florence Healey arrived at the bank, he inspected the safe and found it undamaged, the plates being in their rightful position over the keyholes.

Confirming that no money had been stolen, Healey then examined the windows at the front of the bank and found no entry there but saw where a third perpetrator, apparently, had jumped over the front fence, possibly Richard Burgess.[2]

One assumes that Thomas Day stole the horse once the property of Glasson's butchery and sold at auction, and that Day was leading a horse stolen from Bertie's brother-in-law, the Reverend Clarke, when he took up with Bertie and Burgess at a small creek.[10]

Day's horse was unsuitable for riding long distances and was abandoned south-east from Carcoar. The pair then rode double-banked from there to Cowra, a contention supported by a report in *The Town and Country Journal* that *there is every reason to believe that the horse found at Neville was ridden by one man, and the horse taken from the stables at the vicarage by another.*[7]

That being a fact was corroborated by another report in *The Daily Telegraph* that Mounted Constable Grainger tracked the horses of the fleeing suspects in a circuitous route, first to Blayney, north-east of Carcoar, around to Newbridge and then to Neville. Grainger formed the opinion there that the intended destination of the fugitives was Cowra, south-west of Carcoar.[7,21]

When advised of the murders, the Inspector-General of Police at Sydney, Edmund Walcott Fosbery, dispatched two of his experienced criminal investigators, Detective Sergeant George Edwin Goulder and Plain-Clothes Senior Constable John Fullerton, to assist local police with the investigation.[22]

September 25, 1893 – while Bertie was at the Tasker's Hotel in Cowra, which is where he was arrested on suspicion of committing the murders, Day was spotted acting suspiciously in the rocks outside Cowra.

The witness, who was the wife of Doctor William Richard Cortis, saw Day hide a pair of bloodstained white trousers under the back of his coat.

When police arrived, Day was seen in the Lachlan River, escaping northwards in New South Wales.

A bloodstained sack covered with horse hair was found during the search, confirming that Day and Bertie rode double-banked from Neville.[23,24,25]

While Day was escaping northwards in New South Wales, it appears Burgess made his way southwards to Wagga Wagga where he was known, apparently, to James Tracey whose letter can be found at the end of this Chapter.

It also appears that Burgess went over the border from Wagga Wagga to Maldon in Victoria, only to be arrested the year after in that town, as alluded to before, on a charge of assault.[15,26]

More will be said later about Tracey suggesting to Parry-Okeden that an undercover police officer should get Burgess to tie some *sailor's knots* to see if they were same as the knots found in the handkerchiefs securing the hands of Norah and Ellen Murphy behind their backs at Gatton.

September 26, 1893 – an inquest into the deaths of Jack Phillips and Fanny Cavanagh was opened by Coroner James Lithgow Cobb, assisted by Sub-Inspector Thomas Cameron. After the jury was empanelled, Cobb granted Cameron an adjournment so that inquiries could be made with respect to a *suspected accomplice*.[18]

Thomas Furner empanelled in the jury was then interviewed by Goulder and Fullerton.[5]

Same as the denial five years later, which was about Day not being the Gatton murderer, the authorities advised the public soon after the interview that there was *no second man to be sought* for the Carcoar murders.[27]

Resuming the inquest, acting on further advice from Cameron, Coroner Cobb discharged the jurors and excluded Thomas Furner from being empanelled in a second jury.[20]

September 27, 1893 – after consulting with Inspector-General Fosbery, who was involved six years later in the *shadowing* of Burgess from Queensland into New South Wales to keep him apart from Day, which can be found in his report at the end of this Chapter, Goulder and Fullerton returned to Sydney.[27,28,29]

Coroner Cobb's summing up to the jury was extraordinary, to say the least, part of which was published in *The National Advocate*, as follows:

There is no alternative but for you to bring in a verdict of wilful murder against the man to whom the evidence points alone all through, and who has been sworn to as the man whose hands, face and tomahawk, were seen steeped in blood, and were recognised in the City Bank.[30]

Going against Cobb's opinion, about Bertie acting alone, which conflicted with the evidence of Annie Phillips, Agnes McVicar, Joe Derwin and Florence Healey, and witnessed by others, such as Mrs Cortis at Cowra and Reverend Clarke's horse being double-banked, the jury found that:

John William Phillips and Letitia Frances Cavanagh came to their deaths at the City Bank, Carcoar, on the morning of Sunday, September 24, 1893, through being wilfully murdered by Edwin Hubert Glasson, commonly known as Bertie Glasson, and that another, or others, entered the bank with him, with a view to rob it.[30]

Pointing a finger at Thomas Furner in the courtroom, Bertie shrieked, "Who said wilful murder," leaving one in no doubt that Furner was involved in some way with Bertie and the others going to the bank to rob the contents of the safe.[18,31]

Jack the Ripper

Coroner Cobb committed Bertie to stand trial for wilful murder at the Bathurst Circuit Court on October 11, 1893.[32] The trial, however, was postponed to a later date, owing to the delicate state of Annie Phillip's recovery.[23]

October 22, 1893 – in the Circuit Court at Bathurst, Bertie was found *guilty* of committing the murders.

Same as what happened when he sentenced Archer, it was reported in the *Goulburn Evening Penny Post* that Justice Innes was *profoundly affected* when he sentenced Bertie to be hung by the neck until dead.[32,33,34]

Why was that so?

Those in the jury at Glasson's trial were John Morgan, John Burton, Henry Harris, George Madden, Michael Looby, Ross West, Thomas Quinn, John Phillip Cornwell, William Henry Marriott, William Hutchinson, Edmund Thomas Webb and William Thomas Stonestreet.[35]

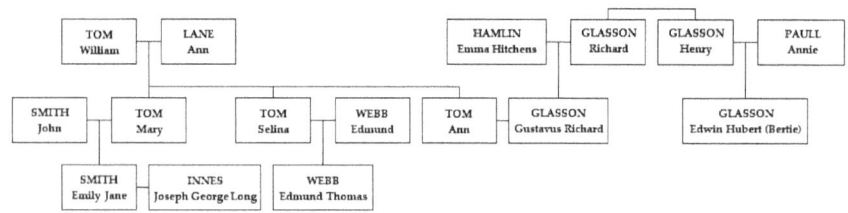

Glasson, Innes and Webb families

If you look at the above chart, you will see that Innes and Edmund Thomas Webb, a member of the jury, were *related by marriage* to Gustavus Richard Glasson, Bertie's cousin.[35]

November 29, 1893 – before the sentence of death was carried out at the Bathurst Gaol, Bertie read the following statement:

My dear friends, I have a few words which I would like to say to you before I die. I would like you to hear them. My words are not many. I would like to ask all who have been so kind to me, all my friends and relatives, not to grieve for me when I leave this world, for I have every assurance and faith that I will ascend to a brighter and happier home of which you, and they, yet know nothing and no one has yet experienced. I say as I stand here during the last few seconds that are given me to live, and I say before my God, that I am an innocent man, am innocent of the crime for which I am suffering. I admit that the evidence is strong and wholly against me. The defence prepared by my friends was wholly against my own wishes, but I do not blame anyone for this. I know my friends, my solicitor and everyone did all they could to save me from this terrible death. I do not blame them for anything. There are truths and statements, which have not been made known. I would have liked these statements to have been made public, for if they had been known and other evidence had been brought forward before, my life would have been spared. These statements will I hope in time be made public. I am dying for the sins of another. My last thoughts are of my Maker whom I love and adore. It is with the utmost comfort and assurance that I now go to meet Him. My last word is of my beloved and devoted wife, and now Goodbye.[36]

What was Bertie's motive for the murders? When the plan was hatched, it is obvious that Bertie and the others expected only the servant, Agnes McVicar, would be inside the bank. Bertie's motive, therefore, was to steal the contents of the safe and not to commit murder. If it had been murder, why did he leave witnesses alive so that they could identify him later?

In just over three months, two men sentenced to death in New South Wales by Justice Innes pleaded their innocence on the gallows, one saying that he was dying for the *sins of another*.[36]

June 2, 1894 – six months after Bertie's hanging, Edmund and Ashley Westby departed from Adelaide, South Australia, onboard the French mail steamer *Ville de la Ciotat* for England.[37]

While Edmund remained in England for the remainder of his life, residing at 50 Rutland Gate, London, Ashley returned to Australia to maintain the brother's interest in *Pullitop* and *Buckaginga* stations at Wagga Wagga.[38]

September 14, 1895 – Ashley Westby was a guest of Sir Frederick Darley at the Lieutenant-Governor's ball in Sydney.[39] If you do not remember, Darley and two other High Court justices dismissed Archer's appeal, resulting in Archer being hung for the murder of Emma Harrison.[40]

June 18, 1894 – the Prince of Wales and his family took up residence at Coworth House placed at their disposal for the Ascot Races by Sir William Farmer.[41]

It was a long-standing arrangement, but this one occasion serves the purpose of highlighting the relationship between Sir William Farmer and the Royal Family.

Furthermore, apart from Farmer and Prince Albert Edward being involved in the United Grand Lodge of England, Prince Albert Victor was appointed by his father in 1889 as the Principal Grand Master of Freemasons for Surry.[42,43,44]

October 30, 1894 – after an absence of 20 years, Sir William Farmer returned to Sydney, *purely on business*, so it was reported in *The Sydney Morning Herald*. Seventeen days later, Farmer was the honoured guest at a picnic for 538 employees of Farmer & Co in Correy's Gardens at Cabarita.[45,46]

Upon his arrival, Farmer made an extraordinary statement, possibly on behalf of the Royal Family, published in *The Clarence and Richmond Examiner*, as follows:

No doubt church disestablishment will come, but it won't come yet. Changes are affected very slowly in England. Agitation has its birth, and grows and continues for years, and when the change comes, the country is generally ripe for it. England is not a home of revolutionary movements. You have no sudden and violent alterations there. It takes a long time before people allow the old institutions to disappear. Just now, the public sentiment is being stirred up by the Welsh Radicals. They believe that if they can get the thin end of the wedge in Wales, the influence will extend. My own idea is that if the people of Wales were polled tomorrow, the voting would be in favour of establishment. There is no national feeling on the subject, it is a party move. I do not believe that in Wales or in England, any national desire exists for disestablishment. The Church was never doing a greater work in the history of Wales than it is doing today.[47]

One assumes Thomas Day was an illegitimate child, that his father was Sir John Charles Frederic Sigismund Day, Chief Justice of England and Wales, and that his mother, as alluded to before, was Edith Westby.[48]

While he was Sheriff of London, one assumes Farmer would have had a working and social relationship with the Chief Justice and that there also might have been a business aspect to the relationship, having in mind that both were successful merchants in London.

Moreover, during their business lives, Edith's father, Edmund Westby, as well as James Dickson, father of James Robert Dickson, Premier of Queensland at the time of the Gatton murders, were merchants of London.

One assumes that all were well-known to each other!

March 27, 1895 – in company of a lady visitor from Australia, Farmer returned to his estate of Coworth Park, being greeted there by 40 employees and parishioners, the Union Jack flying at full mast above the house.[49]

Same as Archer, one does not believe that Jack Phillips and Fanny Cavanagh died at the hands of Bertie Glasson.

That being so, the principle espoused by Sir William Blackstone that *it is better that ten guilty persons escape than that one innocent suffer* was thrown out the window by the authorities who hung Bertie Glasson for the murders committed by another, who, in my opinion, was Thomas Day.[1]

Received at Gatton on 24 April 99

Police Department
Criminal Investigation Branch
Brisbane 11th January, 1899

Report re Richard Burgess, suspected murderer.

Frederick Ross states I am the Officer in Charge of the mens shelter, Salvation Army, Ann street, Brisbane.

I remember Wednesday the 30th November last. At about 9 p.m. on that night I was in the office at the shelter when a man came to the office and said to me "Why did not your cart meet the boat for discharged prisoners" I replied "we have not been advised of any person coming up that wished to go to the Home". The man replied "You are paid to look after us and you ought to do your duty" I then said have you got your discharge. He replied "I have destroyed it, as I did not think it was of any use to me" I replied "very well we can easily find out by applying to the Comptroller. I then said "Do you wish to go to the Home" He replied "No" I can stop here I suppose for the night" I replied "Yes" I then said to him "What is your name" He replied "John Byrne" I then said "what is your age" He replied "36 years" I then said "What Country do you belong to He replied "Ireland" I then said have you any trade. He replied "No; I am a general labourer" He then paid me sixpence for a shelter ticket and he went to bed.

On the following morning he went out at 3 a.m. and returned at 6 p.m. same night. He remained in the shelter that night, and went out the following morning as usual He left at 3 a.m. on the 3rd December ult. and did not return until Tuesday night the 6th ultimo, and slept in the shelter every night up to Saturday the 10th ultimo, when he left at 3 a.m. and I have not seen him since. On looking at the Photo of Richard Burgess now shown me I identify it as that of the man known to me by the name of John Byrne.

(Signed) F.E. Ross.

Frederick Ross' statement dated January 11, 1899

(Courtesy of the Queensland Government (Queensland Police Service))

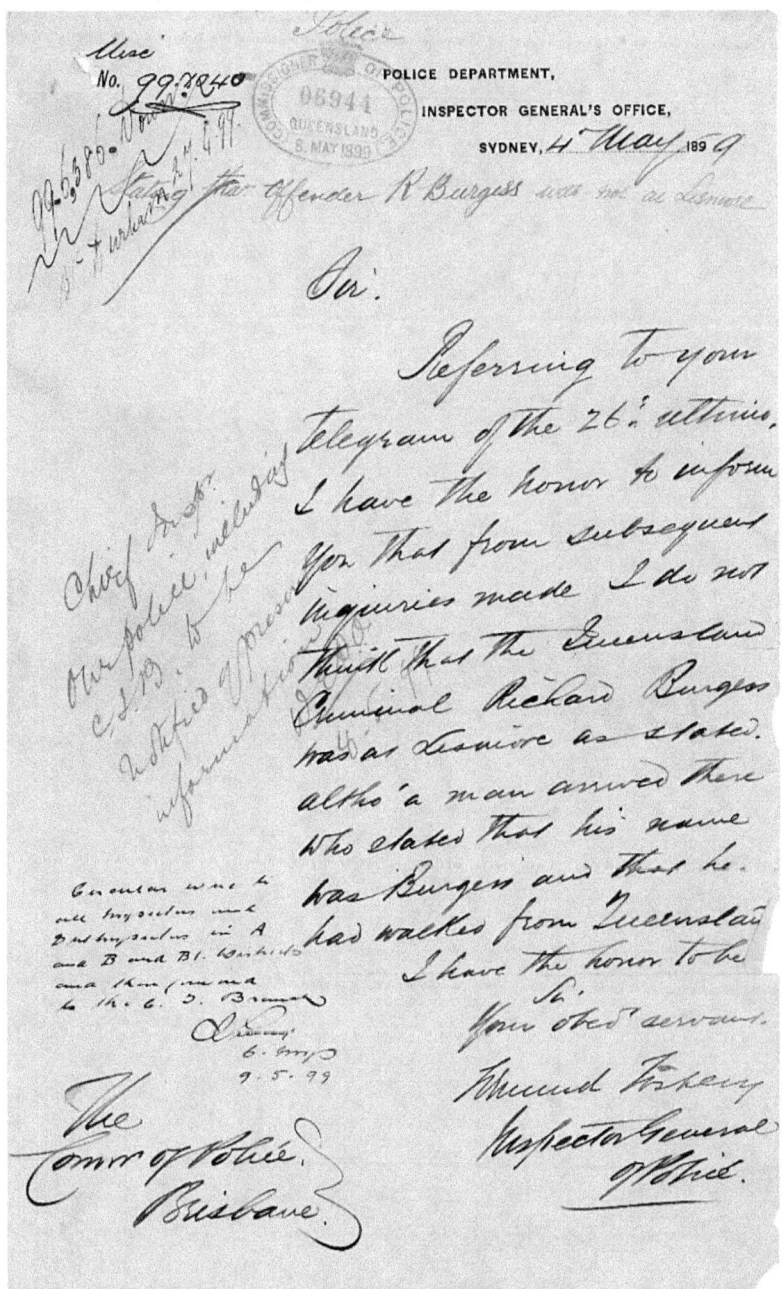

Fosbery's report dated May 4, 1899
(Courtesy of the Queensland Government (Queensland Police Service))

Jack the Ripper

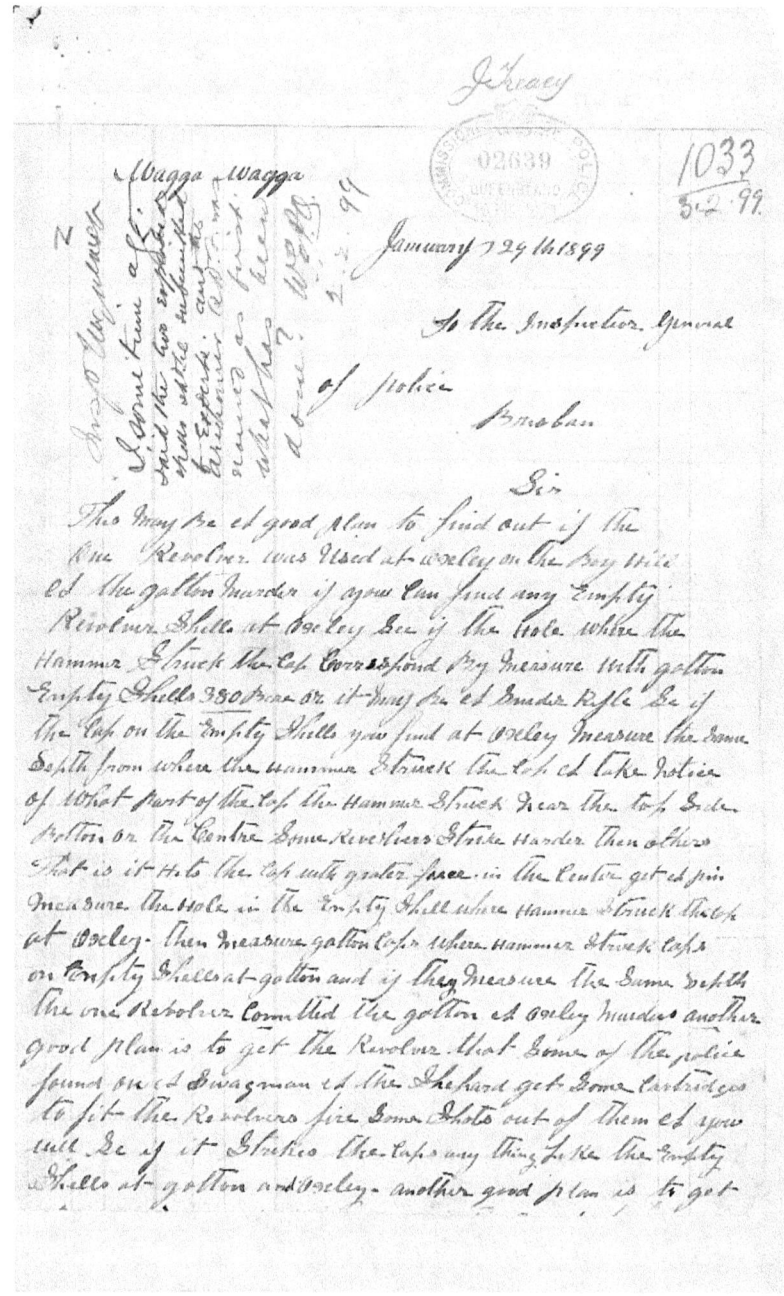

James Tracey's letter dated January 29, 1899, page 1
(Courtesy of the Queensland Government (Queensland Police Service))

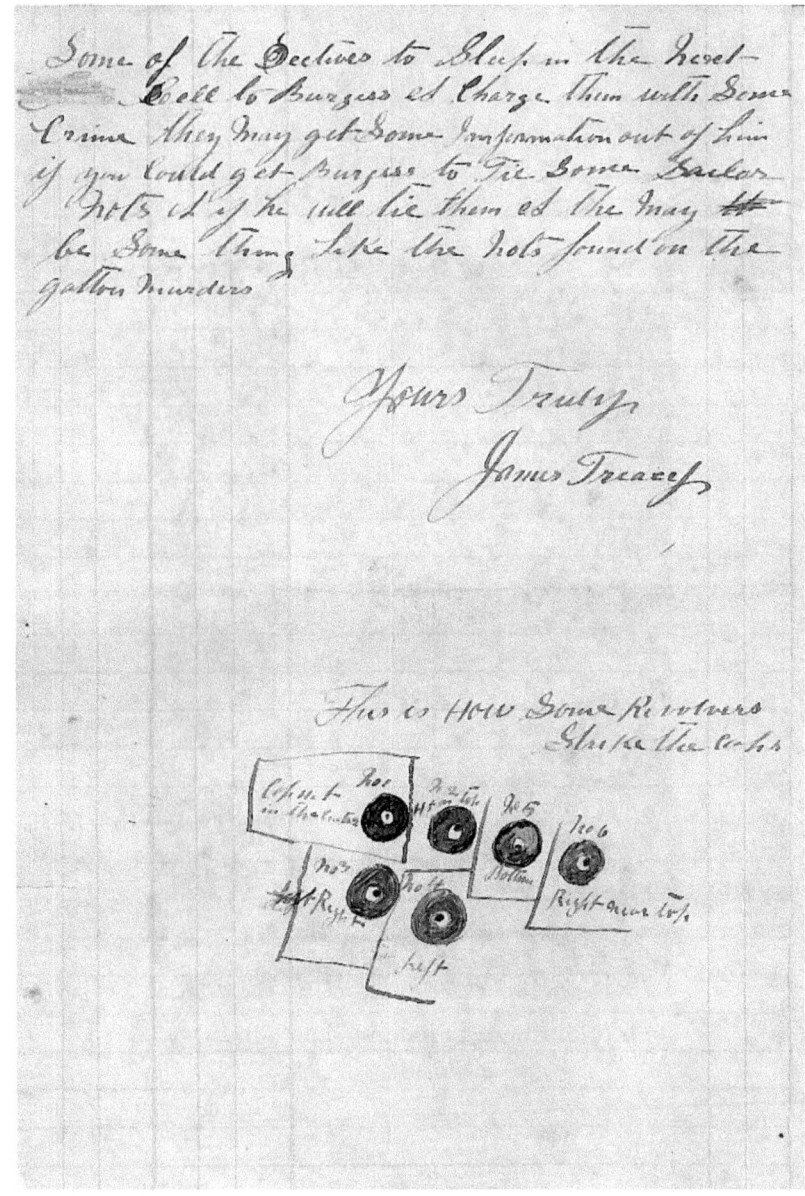

James Tracey's letter dated January 29, 1899, page 2
(Courtesy of the Queensland Government (Queensland Police Service))

Sir John Charles Frederic Sigismund Day
(Courtesy of Wikimedia Commons)

4

OLD JACK COMES "HOME" AGAIN

An English-born Australian, Frederick Bailey Deeming, was suspected of being *Jack the Ripper*. Deeming's hanging at Melbourne on May 23, 1892, confirms, however, that he could not have been the serial killer as another credible *Jack the Ripper* letter was received in England after his demise.[1,2]

April 9, 1896 – Charles Wallace Alexander Napier Cochrane-Baillie, Lord Lamington, became the 19th Governor of Queensland.[3] The Governor's son, Victor Alexander Brisbane William Cochrane-Baillie, being the *godson* of Queen Victoria, and Lady Lamington holding *the post of lady-in-waiting to the Prince of Wales*, identifies the family's close relationship with the Monarchy.[4]

October 14, 1896 – a letter beginning with the words "Dear Boss," which can be found at the end of this Chapter, was received at the Commercial Street Police Station from *Jack the Ripper*, announcing he had been abroad, that he was back in London, and that the Whitechapel murders would start again.[5,6,7]

Detective Inspector George Payne of H Division, Metropolitan Police, advised in a report, which can be found at the end of this Chapter, that the letter *was similar to those received by police during the series of murders in this district in 1888 and 1889*, and that *police have been instructed to keep a sharp lookout*.[7]

It is obvious from Payne's report that the Whitechapel murders began in 1888 and ended in 1889, coinciding with the suspected arrival of Thomas Day at Sydney during 1890, and the return of *Jack the Ripper* to London in 1896.[8,9]

December 27, 1896 – just over two months after the return of *Jack the Ripper* to London, a young woman, Edith May (May) Cook, 18 years of age, died at Lower Tent Hill, near Gatton, possibly from complications of an illegal abortion, the cause of death, however, was recorded as *typhlitis peritonitis*.[10]

Following the discovery of the bodies of the Michael, Norah and Ellen Murphy in Moran's paddock at Gatton, an "In Memoriam" notice relating to May Cook's death was found about 200 yards east from the sliprails of the paddock.

At the Royal Commission, "There was a piece of paper found," said Dickson to Toomey, "tied up in a strap?"

After saying that the strap belonged to the harness of the horse, "It was an 'In Memoriam' notice about a person who died in the district," replied Toomey. "I questioned everybody about this notice, and they all said they knew nothing about it, but they knew the girl referred to in it."

A younger sister, Catherine (Katie) Murphy, told Toomey that Norah cut the notice out of the newspaper, and that the notice was missing from the box where Norah put it in her room.[11,12]

What Katie said, however, was contradicted in the report of Constable Michael Carew that John Lunny, a former resident of Tent Hill, *knew the girl May Cook and was fond of her and possibly cut the notice out of the newspaper*.[13]

Two letters addressed to Lunny were found by an Aboriginal tracker known as Norman in Wiggin's paddock on the opposite side of Moran's paddock to Clarke's butchery.[14,15]

"How far was this paper found," said Dickson to Toomey, "from where the bodies were found?"

"About 800 yards."

"In what direction?"

"Towards the sliprails."[11,12]

It is reasonable to suspect that May Cook's demise had everything to do with *Jack the Ripper* not carrying out his threat to commit further atrocities in London, the serial killer returning to Australia to avenge the death of his *one good friend*.[16]

One is no expert but based upon some experience as a police officer, after comparing the *Jack the Ripper* letter with the statement of Tobias (Toby) Burke, which can be found at the end of this Chapter, one is of

Old Jack Comes "Home" Again

the opinion that there is some similarity between the handwriting of the letter and the signature on the statement.[6,17]

Interestingly, Toby Burke commenced his employment with John Campbell of Rosewood Station at Laidley, south-east from Gatton, during July 1890, which was the year after the last Whitechapel murder, and which was the year that one suspects Thomas Day returned to Australia.[8,9,17]

Toby Burke was described as being 28 years of age, *an Irishman, Roman Catholic, speaks with a strong Irish accent, well educated, farm labourer, 5 feet 10 inches high, weight about 10 stones 11 pounds, blue eyes, fair hair and moustache only, long features, eyes rather deep-set, sharp nose and chin, fair complexion, delicate constitution, slightly lame on right leg, the knee being injured in 1895.*[18,19,20]

One assumes that Toby Burke was known to Thomas Day and Richard Burgess, possibly in England and Australia, and that Burke might have written the *Jack the Ripper* letter prior to Day going back to England.

January 1897 – Edward Litton Carus-Wilson, charged later with the murder of Alfred Stephen Hill, was employed as a master at the All Saints College at Bathurst, north-west from Sydney.

During a game of cricket played at the college in October of the same year, Frederick George Davies, a clerk in the Bathurst Mercantile Company, became acquainted with Carus-Wilson.

When asked if he would like to earn some extra money, Davies agreed to run messages for Carus-Wilson.

Producing a revolver thereafter in the study of the college, Carus-Wilson ushered Davies into a bedroom where he behaved improperly towards Davies.

Davies' complaint resulted in Carus-Wilson being dismissed by the college.[21]

At the Royal Commission, when questioned about Thomas Day's antecedents, "Did he tell you he had been working for a man named Wilson," said Dickson to Toomey, "in New South Wales?"

Despite having a hyphenated surname, Carus-Wilson was often referred to as Wilson.

"That was some time after," replied Toomey, who added, "I was present when his statement was taken and heard that."

"Was his statement correct according to what he had told you before?"

"Yes, but I did not ask him if he had been working for a man in New South Wales."

"Was there anything inconsistent," said Commissioner John Sadleir to Toomey, "with his former statement?"

"There was nothing inconsistent about it."[22]

It is obvious from those questions that Dickson and Sadleir knew Day worked for Carus-Wilson in New South Wales but, surprisingly, Dickson and Sadleir did not pursue that line of questioning with Toomey, leaving the public in the dark as to the identity of the man named Wilson.

Their paths intertwining throughout Australia, and with the knowledge of Richard Burgess telling Charles O'Brien of Moggill, south-west from Brisbane, that Bathurst was *one of the places he had visited* before the Gatton murders, one speculates that Burgess was with Day when he worked for Carus-Wilson at Bathurst.[23]

June 2, 1897 – Frank Burns, alias Paddy Meo, a person of interest during the investigation into the Gatton murders, appeared in the Southern District Court at Warwick on a charge of stealing.

On being found *guilty*, Burns was sentenced to two years' imprisonment with hard labour at Boggo Road Gaol, serving out his time on St Helena Island.[24]

In 1898 – Carus-Wilson took up his appointment as a non-resident master at the Ipswich Boys' Grammar School at Ipswich, Queensland, living at first with Claude in a cottage that was off campus.

Moving from the cottage, Carus-Wilson and Claude took up residence at a boarding house where Carus-Wilson provided evening classes for boys in the top-floor parlour.

Convincing others that he was unable to care for his son, at a time when Carus-Wilson was, in fact, interfering with other boys at the boarding house, Claude was taken in by Isabella McInnes Betts at Ipswich.[25]

May 1898 – seven months before the Oxley and Gatton murders, Duncan Robert McGregor, a traveller and collector for the Singer Sewing Machine Company, who knew Richard Burgess for about 12 months, and whose statement can be found at the end of this Chapter, saw Burgess in company of another on the Howard Smith and Sons' wharves at Brisbane.[26]

One assumes, as alluded to in the Introduction, that the other seen by McGregor was Thomas Day.

May 5, 1898 – around midnight, Richard Burgess broke and entered the house of Mary Barry, 69 years of age, at Leyburn, south-west from Brisbane.

Woken by the noises made by Burgess, Mary went to investigate and was surprised by Burgess, who punched her on the head and neck, same as what happened to the Whitechapel victims, forcing Mary to the floor where Burgess indecently assaulted his victim.

Mary's son-in-law, John Rutsch, after arming himself with a loaded rifle, responded to the screams and was entering through the front door when Burgess brushed past him on the way out of the house. Firing a shot at the fleeing target, John heard a grunt, confirming that the bullet hit the mark.

After confirming that Mary was all right, John went back to the front of the house and saw Burgess running towards a gully. John fired another shot but was not successful in hitting the target on the second occasion.

Constable M. A. R. Becher of Leyburn took out a warrant for the arrest of Burgess for attempted rape.[27]

Shedding some light on his antecedents, an article in *The Warwick Examiner and Times* referred to Burgess by the aliases of *Yank* and *Dick Burgess*, and *The Kalgoorlie Miner* inferred that he was *a native of America*.[28,29]

After the Gatton murders, Robert McGrory of Esk, north-west from Brisbane, alleged that Burgess, alias Patrick Malone, worked on and off for him during 1894 and 1895, corroborating what Burgess told Charles O'Brien of Moggill that he was from Esk.[23,30]

On the last occasion that Burgess worked for McGrory, when McGrory said, "You are not an Irishman," Burgess replied, "I know I am not. I am a native of America!"[30]

It will be stated, time and time again, such as the report in *The Kalgoorlie Miner* that Burgess was a *native of America*, and another instance being what McGrory said about Burgess, that Day and his associates were from or had worked or lived in a country other than Australia.

Consider that aspect with the suspicion of police in England that *Jack the Ripper* was a *drover or butcher*, periodically appearing and disappearing with the *cattle boat* on which he was employed, and you have the likelihood of Day and his associates being involved in the Whitechapel murders.[31]

May 18, 1898 – Burgess was located at Ballandean Creek, south from Leyburn, by Mounted Constable John Wilson of Toowoomba, assisted by the Aboriginal tracker, Norman, who later found the Lunny letters at Gatton.[27,32,33]

Wilson arrested the fugitive and conveyed him to Stanthorpe, north-east from Ballandean Creek, where Burgess was charged with attempted rape.[34]

During a search prior to Burgess being placed in the lockup, it was found that the bullet from the first shot fired by Rutsch entered near the elbow and emerged close to the right shoulder, leaving a tear in the upper arm of the coat, which can be found in the photograph of Burgess at the end of this Chapter.[35]

May 20, 1898 – when Burgess appeared before Police Magistrate Frederick Hamilton Hyde in the Stanthorpe Police Court on the attempted rape charge, Sergeant Alexander McDonald applied for and was granted a remand to Warwick, north-east from Stanthorpe.[35]

May 26, 1898 – Burgess appeared before Police Magistrate Major Richard Albert Moore in the Warwick Police Court on the attempted rape charge.

Durham, who, after the Gatton murders, was instrumental in having Burgess sent to prison for vagrancy, withdrew the charge and substituted it with indecent assault.

After hearing the evidence, Moore committed Burgess to stand trial for indecent assault at the next sittings of the Southern District Court at Warwick.[27]

June 1, 1898 – Burgess appeared before Judge George William Paul in the Southern District Court at Warwick on the indecent assault charge.

On being found *guilty*, Burgess was sentenced to six months' imprisonment with hard labour at Boggo Road Gaol, serving out his time on St Helena Island.[36]

"I got off light," said Burgess to Constable Wilson, after he was sentenced, "but I will give you all a run for it when I come out again, I was born to be hung!"[14]

That statement supports a suspicion that Richard (Dick) Burgess, who was born in 1829 at Hatton Gardens, West End of London, England, and whose sketch can be found at the end of this Chapter, was the father of Richard Burgess.[15]

The mother of Dick Burgess was a lady's maid at Grosvenor House for the family of Lord Robert Grosvenor, 1st Marquess of Westminster, and his father, whom he knew briefly, was *someone connected with the Horse Guards*.[15,37]

At 12 years of age, Burgess and his mother *removed to the east end of London, to a place called Milk street, Commercial road*, which has relevance to where the Whitechapel murders were committed.

When expelled from school, Burgess and his mother moved elsewhere, Burgess quickly falling into a life of crime with *youths more advanced in years* than himself.[15]

At 18 years of age, then a convict, Burgess was transported to Australia.

Being granted a conditional pardon, Burgess set out on a life of crime in Australia before migrating to the South Island of New Zealand where he was arrested on the Otago goldfields and executed at Nelson on October 5, 1866, for murder.[15,38]

Prior to going to New Zealand, Burgess lived in Melbourne with a woman known as Anne, surname not provided, whom he described as being *a Magdalene of the better sort of unfortunates*.

Burgess sending her money *from the Weatherstone diggings* suggests that Anne had a child one assumes was Richard Burgess, possibly raised in England or Ireland.[39]

Richard Burgess, who was friendly with Thomas Day, as alluded to before, was also known as Dick Burgess.[28]

Furthermore, if one's assumption is correct, Richard Burgess might have been brought up by his paternal grandmother in England at the location referred to by Dick Burgess as *Milk street, Commercial road*, close to where the *Jack the Ripper* murders were committed within the Whitechapel district of London.[15]

September 13, 1898 – Constable Barber saw Edith McPherson, who was described as a *respectable-looking young woman*, just several months before the Gatton murders, *pulling a young man about in a violent fashion* in Bourke Street, Sydney.

When Edith allegedly turned on the constable, Barber arrested her for insulting behaviour.

Upon Barber inferred in court that Edith *was not right in her head*, "I am very right, perfectly right," replied Edith. "This man I was with last night in Bourke Street is the Whitechapel murderer, he's Jack the Ripper, and it is not right that he should be at large. He has treated me shamefully. You can do what you like with me."[32]

After that outburst, Edith explained to the court that she had written to Doctor Robert Anderson, head of the Criminal Investigation Department, Scotland Yard, England, and was prepared to show the response received from him.[33]

Uninterested in what Edith had to say, the magistrate asked the prosecutor, "What is known of her?"

"She was discharged for drunkenness in 1895."

"Yes, it was over this same case," replied Edith. "It was in connection with the Whitechapel murders, and Detective Dungey knew all about it."

After saying to Edith, "You may fancy you have a grievance against some person, but that is no reason why you should insult the public by such conduct," the magistrate imposed a fine of 20 shillings in default seven days' imprisonment.[32]

One assumes, having in mind that he arrived at Brisbane two months later from New South Wales, that Thomas Day was the young man involved in the incident with Edith McPherson in Bourke Street, Sydney.

October 14, 1898 – Frank Burns, the person of interest alluded to before, was released from St Helena Island with the condition that he was to report regularly to police.

Burns, apparently, was friendly with Burgess while he was imprisoned on the island.[40]

November 10, 1898 – Thomas Day's other associates, John Miller, alias *Frisco*, *Yank* and *York*, a cockney from London, England, who claimed that he had been to Frisco, obviously meaning San Francisco in America, and William Charles Chaston, left their employment on the Howard Smith and Sons' and Dalgety's wharves at Newcastle, northeast from Sydney.

After Newcastle, Miller and Chaston found employment at Sydney on the steamer *Peregrine*.[34]

One assumes that Day was also employed on the *Peregrine*, and that Day, Burgess, Miller and Chaston hatched a plan, either in Sydney or at Brisbane, to murder Norah Murphy and avenge the death of Day's *one good friend*, May Cook, on the second anniversary of May's death.[10,16]

> Dear Boss
>   You will be surprised to
> find that this comes from yours
> as of old Jack-the-Ripper. Ha. Ha
> If my old friend Mr Warren is dead
> you can read it. You might
> remember me if you try and
> think a little Ha Ha. The last job
> was a bad one and no mistake
> nearly buckled and meant it to
> be best of the lot curse it.
> Ha Ha I'm alive yet and you'll
> soon find it out. I mean to go
> on again when I get the chance.
> Won't it be nice dear old Boss to
> have the good old times once
> again. You never caught me
> and you never will. Ha Ha

1896 "Jack the Ripper" letter, page 1
(Courtesy of The National Archives, United Kingdom)

Old Jack Comes "Home" Again

> you police are a smart lot, the lot of you couldn't catch one man. Where have I been Dear Boss you'd like to know, abroad, if you would like to know, and just come back, ready to go on with my work and stop when you catch me. Well good bye now wish me luck. Winters coming "The Jewes are people that are blamed for nothing" Ha Ha have you heard this before
>
> your truly,
> Jack the Ripper

1896 "Jack the Ripper" letter, page 2
(Courtesy of The National Archives, United Kingdom)

> No. 6.
> Special Report.
> Metropolitan Police.
> Commercial Street STATION.   H. DIVISION.
> 14th Octr. 1896
> Reference to Papers. Attached
>
> I beg to submit attached letter received per post 14th inst. signed Jack the Ripper, stating that writer has just returned from abroad and means to go on again when he gets the chance. The letter appears similar to those received by police during the series of murders in the district in 1888 and 1889. Police have been instructed to keep a sharp lookout.
>
> Geo. Payne, Sergt.
>
> Submitted. I caused a telegram to be sent to surrounding divisions upon receipt of letter 14th inst. asking that direction be given to police to keep a sharp lookout, but at the same time to keep the information quiet. Writer in sending the letter no doubt considers it a great joke at the expense of police.

Report of Metropolitan Police, London, dated October 14, 1896
(Courtesy of The National Archives, United Kingdom)

Old Jack Comes "Home" Again

Tobias Burke. states – I am a farm labourer and have been in the employ of Mr John Campbell Snr of Laidley since July 1890 as a farm hand. On the 4th December 1895 I was admitted as a Patient in the Ipswich Hospital suffering from an injury received to one of my legs, while undergoing treatment from Dr Thornton I became acquainted with a man named John Lunny, an old man, who was also a Patient in another Ward suffering from "Calculous" or Stone in the bladder. Lunny was always talking to me about a legacy which was left him by a relation who died in British Demerara. South America. Lunny told me the documents in connection with the legacy were in possession of Mr William Draper Armstrong Member for this District, and he Lunny had asked Mr Armstrong to get the money for him but as Mr Armstrong failed to do so Lunny asked for the documents and was told by Mr Armstrong that they were in Possession of Mr Armstrong's Solicitor's Brisbane cannot remember the name of Solicitor. Lunny said he went to Brisbane to get the Papers and was told by Solicitor that before he (Lunny) could get Possession of Papers he would have

Tobias Burke's statement dated February 8, 1899, page 1
(Courtesy of the Queensland Government (Queensland Police Service))

(2)

to pay five or six hundred Pounds expenses &c attached thereto. Lunny said as there was no chance of his getting the Papers he would instruct Mr Summerville Solicitor of Ipswich to get them. A short time after first seeing Lunny in the Hospital. I was discharged, and re admitted as a Patient suffering from Dengue fever about April of 1897. I again saw Lunny in the Hospital. who was very anxious for me to assist him to get the legacy. I said I could not Possibly assist in the matter. I was only a few days in the Hospital the second time when I was discharged, and have never seen Lunny since. Some time after I was discharged from the Hospital I called to see Lunny and other Patients and heard that Lunny had died there.

Tobias Burke

Tobias Burke's statement dated February 8, 1899, page 2
(Courtesy of the Queensland Government (Queensland Police Service))

Below is a comparison of the *Signature* on the statement with the *Handwriting* of the letter

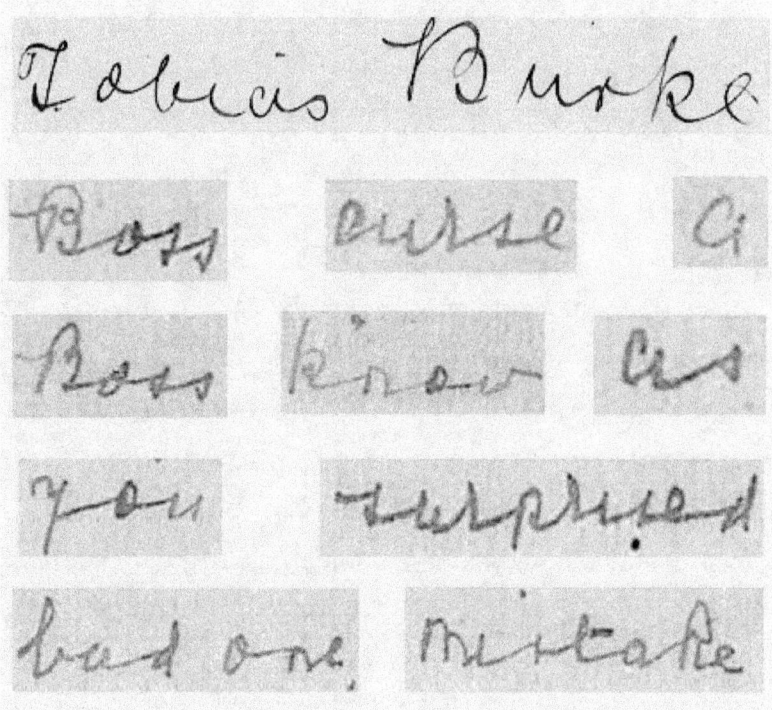

The letters "a" and "u" appear to match, and there is some similarity between the letters, "B" "e" "k" and "o."

Police Department
Criminal Investigation Branch
Brisbane 11th January, 1899.

Duncan Robert McGregor states I reside in Ethel street, Fortitude Valley, and am a traveller and collector for the Singer Sewing Machine Company.

I have known Richard Burgess for about twelve months.

I saw him about Messrs Howard Smith and Sons wharf in May last in company with a man whose name I do not know but can identify.

The man whose name I do not know came to me and asked for money which I refused to give. Burgess was standing near and could have heard all that was said but he did not speak. I then left them.

I have seen the unknown man about town several times since but did not speak to him. I did not see him in company with Burgess after May last neither did I see Burgess in Brisbane since that time.

At the time I saw Burgess in Brisbane in May last I did not know his name was Burgess. The photo' now shown me of Richard Burgess is identical with the man who was in company with the man, name unknown, who spoke to me at Howard Smiths wharf in May last.

On Tuesday the 6th December last I was coming in from Moorooka to Brisbane when I passed Burgess at the junction of Yeronga and Ipswich roads. He was by himself at the time and had a swag on his back which I think had oilcloth over it.

I did not speak to him. He was then wearing a soft felt hat (colour uncertain) brown tweed sac coat and light coloured trousers. I did not notice the colour of his shirt.

About 500 yards further along the road I passed the man who spoke to me at Howard Smiths wharf in May

McGregor's statement dated January 11, 1899, page 1
(Courtesy of the Queensland Government (Queensland Police Service))

May last in company with Burgess. I did not speak to him.

This man would be about 23 years of age, 5 feet 3 inches high, black hair, and moustache and slight side whiskers shaved on chin, dark complexion, high cheek bones, round forehead, wearing dark shabby half dress coat, dark vest and trousers, and dark soft felt hat. I look at the photo' of Frank Burns. He is not identical with this man.

On the following day (7th ult.) I was going to Oxley when I passed Richard Burgess at the Oxley Creek bridge and said to him "Are you going to have a rest" He replied "No" and went on. He had the same swag with him as when I saw him the previous day.

Just before Burgess passed another swagman passed going in the same direction but he was not the same man whom I had seen on the previous day on the Ipswich road and in May last.

I have not seen Burgess since.

(Signed) Duncan R. McGregor.

McGregor's statement dated January 11, 1899, page 2
(Courtesy of the Queensland Government (Queensland Police Service))

(L-R) Richard Burgess and Richard (Dick) Burgess
(Courtesy of the Queensland Police Museum and National Library of Australia)

5

OXLEY MURDER

After a visit to Brisbane in 1895, the well-known Irish home-ruler, Michael Davitt, declared that *whenever my fifth imprisonment comes along for opposition to England's anti-Home rule in Ireland,* his preferred place to do the sentence was on St Helena Island. Davitt found that all prisoners on the island were *engaged at useful labour tasks and worked mainly in the open air at agricultural, dairy, or gardening employment,* and with the warders standing at a distance, the *men worked by themselves in the fields, and are permitted to talk.*[1]

One assumes that the circumstances on St Helena Island were such that Thomas Day, even John Miller or William Charles Chaston, whether in a note or by word-of-mouth, would have had no difficulty passing a message on to Richard Burgess.

November 30, 1898 – after serving his term for the indecent assault, Burgess was released from St Helena Island.[2]

At about 9 pm, arriving at the men's shelter of the Salvation Army in Ann Street, Brisbane, Burgess said to Frederick Ross, whose statement can be found at the end of Chapter 3, "Why did not your cart meet the boat of discharged prisoners?"

"We have not been advised," replied Ross, "of any persons coming up that wished to go to the home."

"You are paid to look after us," said Burgess, "and you ought to do your duty."

"Have you got your discharge?"

"I have destroyed it as I did not think it was of any use to me."

"Very well, we can easily find out by applying to the Comptroller," said Ross, who then questioned Burgess, "Do you wish to go to the home?"

"No," replied Burgess, who queried, "I can stop here I suppose for the night?"

"Yes," said Ross, who asked Burgess, "what is your name?"

"John Byrne."

"What is your age?"

"Thirty-six years."

"What country do you belong to?"

"Ireland."

"Have you any trade?"

"No, I am a general labourer."

After paying six pence for a ticket, Burgess was provided with a bed at the shelter.[3]

Leaving the shelter at 8 am the following morning, Burgess returned at 6 pm that night, did the same the day after, which is when he worked for Charles O'Brien at Moggill, then left at 8 am on December 3, and did not return until the night of December 6.[3,4]

When shown a photograph, Ross identified that Byrne and Burgess were one and the same person.[3]

Early December 1898 – Miller and Chaston terminated their employment with the *Peregrine* at Brisbane.

Miller, a vegetable cook, found work at the Globe Restaurant in Albert Street, Brisbane, whereas Chaston joined A Battery of the Queensland Permanent Artillery at Lytton Fort, Brisbane.[5,6,7]

December 3, 1898 – Lord Lamington and his family, seven days before the Oxley murder and 23 days before the Gatton murders, took up residence in the whole of the Blue Mountain Hotel at Harlaxton, near Toowoomba.[8]

The Governor, consequently, was not far from the scene of the Gatton murders, so close, in fact, that he was strategically located to visit the town or, alternatively, to carry out any request on behalf of Queen Victoria.

December 6, 1898 – Thomas Day *arrived in Brisbane from New South Wales*, possibly on the *Peregrine*.[9,10]

At the Royal Commission, when questioned by Dickson about Thomas Day's background, "He came over from Sydney in a boat," replied Toomey, "but came from Brisbane by road."[10]

Burgess was at the Salvation Army's shelter on the day that Day arrived in Brisbane.

During the four days that he was absent from the shelter, Burgess possibly had a meeting or meetings with Day as well as Miller and Chaston.

After Day's arrival in Brisbane, Duncan Robert McGregor, whose statement can be found at the end of Chapter 4, passed Burgess alone near Oxley.

While he did not speak to Burgess, McGregor noticed, however, that Burgess was *wearing a soft-felt hat, colour unknown, brown tweed sack coat, and light-coloured trousers.*[11]

About 500 yards further along the road, McGregor passed the other seen with Burgess during May 1898 at the Howard Smith and Sons' wharves in Brisbane.

McGregor described the other as being about *23 years of age, 5 feet 8 inches high, black hair and moustache, and slight side whiskers shaved on chin, dark complexion, high cheek bones, round forehead, wearing dark shabby half-dress coat, dark vest and trousers, and a dark soft-felt hat.*[11]

Day obviously changed his appearance, giving others the impression that he was older or younger, taller or shorter, had black or dark-brown hair, dark or light-coloured moustache and whiskers, and was of fair or dark complexion.

It will be remembered that Bertie Glasson told Constable Prior that a *dark man* and *rough-looking Irishman* were involved in the Carcoar murders.

Furthermore, William Burnett gave evidence at the Royal Commission that Day was of *dark* complexion and an entry in the Queensland Police Gazette after his death, all of which will be outlined later, described Day as being of *sallow complexion.*

One assumes, consequently, that the other described by McGregor, who was seen not far from Burgess at Oxley, was Day, pinpointing at

Jack the Ripper

least on one occasion that Day and Burgess got together to discuss the *affair* at Gatton.

December 7, 1898 – when McGregor again came across Burgess at the Oxley Creek Bridge, McGregor said to Burgess, "Are you going to have a rest?"

Without stopping, "No," responded Burgess.[11]

December 10, 1898 – at 8 am, Burgess left the Salvation Army's shelter in Ann Street, Brisbane.[12]

Around 11 am, drawing Claude in the goat cart, Carus-Wilson began his journey from Ipswich to Brisbane.

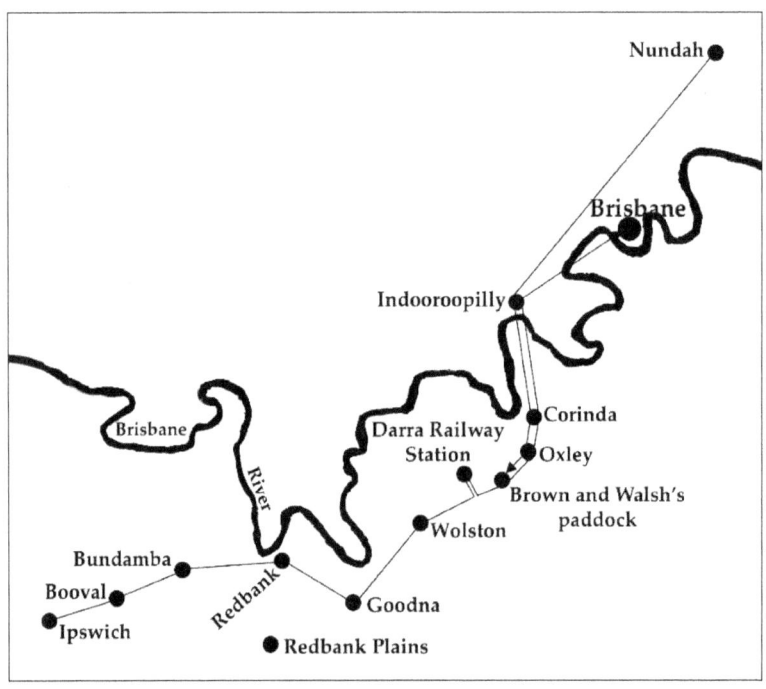

Brown and Walsh's paddock at Oxley
(map not to scale)

Three and a half hours later, 15-year-old Alfred Stephen Hill set out on a pony from his father's saddlery business at Nundah for his uncle and aunt's house at Redbank Plains.[13,14,15]

At 4.07 pm, after passing through the towns of Booval, Bundamba and Redbank, Carus-Wilson and Claude stopped at Goodna where

Carus-Wilson had a bottle of beer at the Royal Mail Hotel, confirmed in part by Benjamin Ford, who saw the empty goat cart outside the hotel.[14,16]

Before leaving Goodna, Carus-Wilson purchased some postage stamps at the railway station from Francis Fox, son to the station master. Francis, who knew Carus-Wilson as a master at the Ipswich Boy's Grammar School, saw the shape of a revolver in the right-hand pocket of Carus-Wilson's trousers.[17]

At 5.20 pm, James Bielby and his mother, Agnes, saw Carus-Wilson at Wolston, drawing Claude in the goat cart along the Ipswich Road towards Oxley.[18]

At 5.30 pm, after delivering a letter to Maria Catchpole, who lived opposite to the Oxley Hotel at Oxley, Alfred mounted his pony and started out on the ride of about six miles from Maria's cottage to Wolston.[17,19]

After Wolston, Carus-Wilson left the Ipswich Road and went down a side-road to the Darra Railway Station.[20]

Failing to locate anyone there, Carus-Wilson returned to the Ipswich Road and pushed Claude in the cart up and over the top of Quarry Hill, coming across Alfred and the pony on the Oxley side of the quarry.[18,21,22]

Claude admitted 50 years after the murder that Alfred *had dismounted and was tightening the saddle girth* at a rocky hollow near the fence along Brown and Walsh's paddock.[18,21,22]

This late admission explains why Alfred did not vault onto the pony and escape when confronted by Carus-Wilson.

Soon after passing Alfred, Carus-Wilson placed *a large flat stone across the end of one of the shafts* so that Claude *could sit upright without tipping the cart.*

Carus-Wilson then accosted Alfred, who was shot and killed in the paddock, the bullet entered at the base of the skull and exited just above the left eye.[21,23]

While his father was away for *about a quarter of an hour*, Claude heard *a shot rang out*, which would have been the shot fired obviously by Carus-Wilson that killed Alfred, leaving one in no doubt that Claude knew more than what he admitted in the Brisbane courts during 1899.[21]

Between 6 pm and 6.30 pm, Walter Bowler drove a buggy along the Ipswich Road from Oxley to Goodna.

Near the quarry, about one and a half miles from the Oxley Hotel, Bowler passed Carus-Wilson drawing Claude in the goat cart towards Oxley.

Bowler, however, did not see Alfred or the pony anywhere between Oxley and Goodna, which means that Alfred was already dead in Brown and Walsh's paddock.[17]

Not long after Bowler was out of sight, Carus-Wilson and Claude came across a man with a swag *slung across his left shoulder, a billycan dangled from his waist, and a clay pipe, bowl downward, protruded from his lips*.[21]

Going back to the Elizabeth Stride murder in England, the taller of the two suspects was seen by Israel Schwartz, lighting a *clay pipe* under a street lamp.[24]

Furthermore, after the bodies were found at Gatton, a small piece of official notepaper from the Gatton Agricultural College, apparently used as a *pipe stop*, was found about ten feet from where the strap from the horse's harness and the "In Memoriam" notice for May Cook's death were found in Moran's paddock.[25]

The above evidence, in my opinion, establishes a connection between the murders in England and Australia.

Moreover, Claude saw *his father passed him (the swagman) something* which, according to what Christie told the Royal Commission, was the revolver used in the Oxley and Gatton murders.[18,21]

William Heavingham Cushing told police that Burgess was the *suspicious-looking swagman* seen by him near Oxley, which was found to be incorrect.[20,26]

At 7.30 pm, Carus-Wilson called at the residence of Noah Wood, a dairy farmer at Oxley, where he was provided with directions to the Oxley Hotel.[18]

At 8 pm, Carus-Wilson and Claude were provided with accommodation at the Oxley Hotel.[14,18]

December 11, 1898 – after breakfast the following morning, Carus-Wilson told Annie Rumpf at the Oxley Hotel that he was going to Southport.

Carus-Wilson did not, however, take the train from Corinda to Southport, drawing Claude in the goat cart instead to Brisbane where they booked into the Metropolitan Hotel on the corner of Mary and Edward streets.[14,18]

At 4 pm, a reporter from *The Queensland Times* saw Carus-Wilson in the Botanical Gardens, drawing Claude in the goat cart across the cricket ground towards the exit at the corner of Alice and Edward streets.[27]

Cushing again saw the *suspicious-looking swagman* coming out of the scrub at Oxley, observing him afterwards walking in the direction of Wolston.[20,26]

Either before or on this date, Burgess went by train from Ipswich to Dugandan, south from Ipswich, walking thereafter through the Condamine Valley to Killarney.

That being so, the *suspicious-looking swagman* seen by Cushing, as alluded to before, more than likely was Day.[2,28,29]

December 12, 1898 – during the morning, Carus-Wilson allegedly took a shirt to the dry cleaners. On his return, "I have sold my revolver," said Carus-Wilson to Claude, "at the nearest shop to the hotel."[14]

Located diagonally opposite to the Botanical Gardens on the corner of George and Alice streets is the Queensland Parliament.

Rather than take his shirt to the dry cleaners and sell his revolver, one assumes that Carus-Wilson instead had a discussion with a politician, even a clergyman, about what happened at Oxley and his chance meeting with Day.

At 1 pm, Carus-Wilson told others at the Metropolitan Hotel that he was going to Southport.[30]

One hour later, Carus-Wilson and Claude left Brisbane on the steamer *Rockton* bound for Melbourne.[14]

December 13, 1898 – a boy at Ipswich confessed to his mother that Carus-Wilson committed an *unnatural offence* on him.

The mother made a complaint to Senior Sergeant Edward Johnson of Ipswich police who took no action as he considered the information was insufficient for a warrant to be issued.[30,31]

December 13, 1898 – then known as Joseph (Joe) Ryan, Richard Burgess arrived at Killarney where he went prospecting for gold with Thomas John Mattingly.[2,29]

December 13 or 14, 1898 – accidentally tipping over a pail of hot milk on the stove at the Globe Restaurant, Miller suffered burns to the back of the head, neck and shoulder.[7]

Chaston admitted that he visited Miller at the restaurant on at least two occasions, confirming that Miller and Chaston did, in fact, kept in touch with each other.[6]

December 14, 1898 – upon receiving further complaints from concerned parents, one of the fathers leaving the room during the interviews when he found the details too revolting, Johnson this time took out a warrant and sent a telegram to Stuart, as follows:

> *Edward Litton Carus Wilson, lately teacher in the Boys Grammar School here, is charged on warrant by this bench with having committed an unnatural offence on a boy. Description Englishman, about 50 years, about 5 feet 6 or 7 inches, dark hair and moustache only, turning grey, rather large straight nose, limps when walking, has a son with him 11-years-old paralysed in both legs. Left here by train for Brisbane Saturday last. May go by steamer, Melbourne or Adelaide.*[13,30]

Afterwards, during a conversation with another whose name was withheld for some apparent reason, a reporter from *The Queensland Times* questioned the other, "Do you think Burgess committed the Oxley deed?"

"No," was the emphatic response, "you will hear all about it in Ipswich in three or four weeks' time."

"Do you think, then," said the reporter, "that [Edward Litton Carus-Wilson] committed the deed?"

"Yes," responded the other, "and if he did not shoot the boy, then, in my opinion, it was an accident."

"An accident," exclaimed the reporter. "How could that possibly be, and by whom? Why was the horse shot?"

"Well," replied the other, "if Burgess wanted money, he could have easily got whatever the boy possessed without shooting him. Therefore, I do not think for a moment that Burgess committed the murder. [Carus-Wilson] is the most likely of the two to have shot both boy and animal, in order, possibly, to conceal another offence."[20]

The name of the person spoken to by the reporter was withheld, in my opinion, to protect the identity of a police officer who made those comments.

Based on Claude's admission many years later, it appears that Alfred stopped near the quarry to give his pony a rest as Claude saw the *saddle girth* was loose.

Seizing the opportunity, Carus-Wilson surprised Alfred and led him at gunpoint into the paddock, the revolver accidentally discharging, in my opinion, when either Carus-Wilson stumbled, or Alfred tried to escape.

At the Royal Commission, Dickson said to Parry-Okeden, "There was never any trace of the swagsman found?"

"No."

"They never fixed Burgess," said Commissioner Thomas Garvin to Parry-Okeden, "in that locality?"

"No."

"You see," said Dickson to Parry-Okeden, "it might have been Day?"

"Yes," conceded Parry-Okeden, who added, "by the later evidence, I see it is possible that it just could have been."[32]

Claude heard only one shot, so it must have been someone other than Carus-Wilson, who shot the pony and hid Alfred's body in the paddock. More to the point, because of the location of the brain in the head, euthanizing a horse with a single shot from a revolver is not a simple or easy task.

How to Euthanize a Horse

(Courtesy of the National Library of Australia)

After visualising diagonal lines drawn from an ear to the eye on the opposite side of the head, the location to do so on the forehead will be found in the above sketch.

It would have been highly unlikely for Carus-Wilson to have that knowledge. Someone, therefore, with stock experience or a horse-slaughterer, such as Henry Tomkins at Whitechapel, England, would have shot the pony.

One is in no doubt that the ponies were killed at Oxley and Gatton by Thomas Day, alias *Jack the Ripper*.

There also is no doubt in my mind that if the authorities had done something about the complaint made by Edith McPherson, the Murphy siblings might have lived beyond Boxing Day night, December 27, 1898.

Staff and Trustees of Ipswich Boys' Grammar School
(**Back row**) Edward Litton Carus-Wilson (second from the left)
(Courtesy of the Ipswich Library)

Crime scene in Brown and Walsh's paddock at Oxley
(Courtesy of the Queensland Police Museum)

6

BURGESS' ALIBI

It is obvious to me and so too should it be for you that there was a collusion between Day, Burgess, Miller and Chaston to murder Norah Murphy on the second anniversary of May Cook's death. While Day and Burgess separated at Oxley and took different routes to Gatton, Miller and Chaston apparently remained together throughout the journey from Brisbane to Gatton.

December 14, 1898 – arriving by train at Gatton, Day camped in the showgrounds and was employed two days later by Arthur George Clarke at his butchery on the Tenthill Creek Road, close to where the Murphy siblings were murdered in Moran's paddock.[1]

At the Royal Commission, "You told us on Friday that you were so satisfied yourself that you never made any inquiries into Day's history," said Noel to Urquhart. "Would you be surprised to hear that when joining the Permanent Artillery, he gave a false birthplace?"

"I am aware of that," replied Urquhart. "I am not sure it is false."

"You are not?"

"No, I know he said his birthplace was Cunnamulla."

"You did not, I believe, trace his previous record?"

"What previous record?"

"That there is no trace there of a man called Thomas Day? He either gave a false name or a false birthplace?"

"He gave the same name as at Gatton."

"And tells a lie about the reference?"

"No."

"That he had a reference from Clarke?"

"No, he named Clarke as a person whom the Permanent Artillery authorities might refer to if they so desired. He did not say he had any reference. I did not understand it so."[2]

When Clarke gave evidence at the Royal Commission, "I understand you wish to give us some information with regard to this man Day," said Noel to Clarke, "who was in your employ at the time these murders were committed?"

"I have no information to give," replied Clarke, prompting Noel to say, "I understood that you desired to give information?"

"No, I never desired to give information. Day was in my employ."

After some further questioning, "How long," said Garvin to Clarke, "was Day in your employment?"

"A little over a fortnight."[3]

An amended description of Thomas Day, two years after he deserted from A Battery of the Queensland Permanent Artillery, was provided in the Queensland Police Gazette.

It was outlined clearly in the Gazette, which would have been done on instructions from Urquhart at the Criminal Investigation Branch, Brisbane, that Day *had references from Mr Clarke, Tent Hill, Gatton, Queensland.*[4]

More to the point, it was not just a reference, but two or more references received by Thomas Day from Arthur George Clarke, confirming that Day worked for Clarke at Tent Hill before Day was employed again by Clarke at the butchery in Gatton.

The Royal Commission could have done more to establish Day's previous employment with Clarke at Tent Hill, but the Commission did not pursue the matter, once again leaving the public in the dark as to what Clarke knew about Day before employing him just prior to the Gatton murders.

December 17, 1898 – failing to recover from the injuries suffered in the incident at the restaurant, Miller was admitted to the General Hospital in Brisbane where his burns were treated.[5,6]

After a disagreement with Mattingly, Burgess left Killarney and travelled north-west by train to Warwick, setting out from there on foot northwards to Allora.[7,8]

December 21, 1898 – recovering from his injuries, Miller was discharged from the General Hospital where records described him as *30* *years of age, 5 feet 7 or 8 inches high, slight build, thin features, small moustache only inclined to be ginger, ruddy complexion, active appearance, dressed in a dark coat, tweed trousers, cotton shirt, brown soft-felt hat.*

Miller also told hospital staff *that he was from London, a Roman Catholic, and that he had been four years in the Colonies and three weeks in Queensland.*[5]

Upon Miller's burns being treated with *picric acid*, the hair on the back of his head turned a yellow colour which, when combined with him being taller and having a ginger beard and ruddy complexion, would have made it easy for others to identify Miller apart from Burgess.[9]

When he was last seen at the hospital, Miller was *dressed in a dark coat, tweed trousers, cotton shirt*, and a brown soft-felt hat, which can be found in Urquhart's memorandum dated February 8, 1899, at the end of this Chapter.[10]

At the restaurant, Miller wore *dark clothes and black hard-felt hat*, which places him at the sliprails before the Gatton murders.[11]

December 24, 1898 – at 6.30 pm, Burgess arrived at the property of Edward and Annie Sparksman known as Glengallan station at Goomburra, east from Allora and south from Gatton. Provided with directions along the track from there to Gatton, Burgess camped that night near the residence.[12]

At 8 pm, while Burgess was at Goomburra, several young men were at the Gatton Railway Station when Edwin Andrew (Ted) Chadwick said, "What about a dance on Boxing Day night?"

"All right," replied Stephen (Steve) Jordan. "I will help you to make the arrangements for it."

"We will hold the dance," said Chadwick, "in the Divisional Board hall."[13]

After deciding they would hold a dance, Chadwick and Jordan made their way to the shooting gallery operated by William Marsh near the Wilmott Hotel. Meeting up there with Patrick Joseph (Pat) and Atoise Jeremiah (Jerry) Murphy, Chadwick asked as to what they were doing on Boxing Day.[13]

Burgess' Alibi

Pat replied, "I am going to the Mount Sylvia races."

"We are going to hold a dance in the Divisional Board's hall on Boxing Day night," said Chadwick to Pat. "Will you come?"

"I will be going to the college that night," replied Pat, "and will call in and see the dance."

"I am going to the Mount Sylvia races," added Jerry, "but I will try to get back and bring my sisters in."[14]

If everything had gone to plan, Jerry and not Michael would have been killed on Boxing Day night.

December 25, 1898 – during the day, Frank Moran removed several unshod horses from his property known as Moran's paddock, the sliprails on the Tenthill Creek Road at Gatton being the main entry to the paddock.

There was, however, a loose rail at the back of the property through which access could be gained to the paddock.

Frank *put up the rails again* when he exited the paddock with the horses.[15,16]

After telling the Sparksman family that he was going to Allora, Burgess set out with a noticeable limp.

Doubling back to conceal what he was doing, which was his usual *modus operandi*, Burgess was seen walking freely along the Gatton track until he realised that he was being watched by the family, forcing him to do an about turn, last seen walking towards Allora.

If Burgess had continued along the Gatton track, he would have been in Gatton when Thomas Day carried out his revenge for the death of May Cook.[12]

Around 9 am, Burgess had breakfast at a farmer's house, 14 miles from Allora.

Between 10 am and 10.30 am, Burgess left the farmer's house, went past Pilton station, then headed due west.

At 8 pm, being provided with water by William Henry and Mary Christina Siebenhausen, Burgess set out for Greenmount, north from Allora.

About four miles from the Siebenhausen residence, Burgess passed the Presbyterian minister, John Smiley, who was described as wearing a white helmet and driving a sulky.

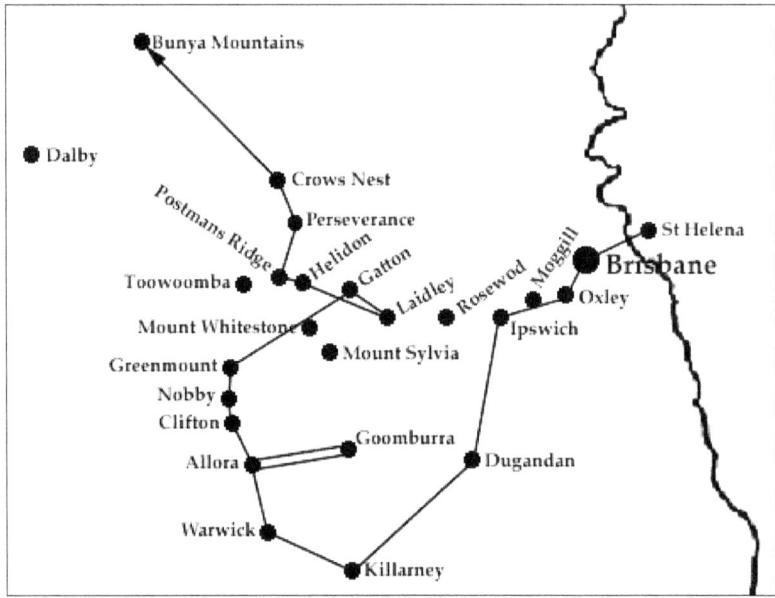

St Helena Island to the Bunya Mountains
(map not to scale)

At 10 pm, about two miles further on from where he met John Smiley, Burgess camped for the night near Nobby, south from Greenmount.[12,17,18]

December 26, 1898 – around midday, Burgess, who was seen *wearing tweed pants and coat, and an old straw hat, and blue striped cotton shirt*, accepted the hospitality offered and was provided with lunch by a Danish woman, Christina Pearson.[12,17,18]

Between 2 pm and 2.30 pm, Burgess walked past the Irvine farm and saw a man ploughing a field.

At 4.30 pm, Burgess walked past a cricket match played in a paddock on the Forsyth's farm, Burgess having a conversation afterwards with a boy named Michael Fallon.[17,18,19,20]

Around 6.30 pm, while resting on a couch on the front veranda of his home near the Brian Boru Hotel in Gatton, Sidney Joseph Hallas, a railway employee, was disturbed by a swagman. Without looking at the visitor, Sidney called out for someone inside the house to give him some matches.

Sidney's wife, Lucy, responded and handed a *cardboard matchbox with some matches in it* to their daughter, Beatrice, who went out onto the veranda and saw a man standing on the steps.

Beatrice did not see his face as *he had his hat well down over his forehead*. She noticed, however, that he was wearing *a greyish coloured coat* which was *dirty and greasy about the front* and *was broken in front of the right arm near the shoulder* that was *stitched up roughly with coarse cotton* and had *broken out again in the same place*.[21]

Beatrice's brother, Frank, who was going out through the front gate when the swagman entered the yard, described the man as *about 5 feet 7 or 8 inches high, brown moustache and very little beard, wearing a greyish coloured coat, and blucher boots*.[22]

Sidney and Lucy were unable to provide police with a description as neither looked at the swagman.

Toomey misleadingly outlined in his report dated February 14, 1899, which can be found at the end of this Chapter, that the evidence of Beatrice and Frank located Burgess in Gatton on the Eve of the murders, both selecting him later from a line-up arranged at the lockup of the Toowoomba police station.[23,24,25]

Cutting to the chase, Beatrice and Frank incorrectly identified Burgess as the swagman.

That is where the matter could end but a younger brother, Sidney Henry Hallas, gave some vital evidence to police in a statement, which can be found at the end of this Chapter, as follows:

I am 11 years of age. I reside with my parents in Spencer Street, Gatton. I remember Boxing Day the 26th December. Between a quarter past six and seven o'clock on that evening, I was in the garden in front of my father's house at that time. A man came in the gate and went up to the veranda steps. My father was lying on the couch on the veranda and I heard the man ask for a few matches. My sister, Beatrice, gave him the matches, and he left the yard. I believe I would know the man if I saw him. He was not a tall man. He was about 5 feet 8 inches high. He was not stout build. He had a reddish kind of moustache and beard which was short and was wearing a soft brownish hat.[26]

If you go back to the description for Miller provided on December 21, 1898, the above statement, in my opinion, identifies that the swagman at the Hallas residence on the Eve of the Gatton murders was Miller wearing Burgess' coat.[9,10]

Furthermore, as outlined in *The Facts Against Richard Burgess* dated January 15, 1899, which can be found at the end of this Chapter, Beatrice and Frank first identified Burgess as the swagman from a photograph shown to them by Toomey.[27]

Consider that with Parry-Okeden's telegram of January 4, 1899, which can be found at the end of the Introduction, and which identifies that the Government and police were, at the time, protecting Thomas Day from arrest for the Gatton murders, then you have prime evidence of coercion, albeit of a minor nature.

Nine days after Toomey showed them the photograph, Beatrice and Frank identified Burgess from the line-up at the Toowoomba police station as the swagman seen at their home on the Eve of the Gatton murders.

This is exactly what was done to other witnesses, such as John Carroll, who was coerced into saying that Burgess *looked something like the man* to detract from his original statement that the man he saw near the sliprails was *Clarke's butcher.*[28]

Either before or after Miller visited the Hallas residence, two men were seen at the Brian Boru Hotel.[29]

One assumes that it was Miller and Chaston, so the two men will be referred to as such.

Bert Johnson, who was at the hotel, described Miller as being shorter, thickset, and older, and Chaston as being tall and thin, and about 35 years of age.

While Miller was with others, Chaston allegedly told Johnson that he had been on a long tramp, had met up with Miller, and that he was making for Sydney if suitable work could not be found.[29]

Burgess' Alibi

Around the time when he was incorrectly identified by Beatrice and Frank as being at Gatton, Burgess had a meal with the Beck family, about four miles from Nobby.[17,18,20]

During the night, Burgess was camped, allegedly, about two miles from the Greenmount Railway Station.[17,18,20]

If that part of his *alibi* was correct, which one does not believe it was, a report in *The Darling Downs Gazette* outlined that the distance for Burgess *to have walked to Gatton and back would have been about 36 miles, and that it would have had to be done from about six pm on Boxing Day till eight am on the 27th.*[30]

A historical map outlining the routes from Greenmount to Gatton, excluding bush tracks, which gives some idea as to what was meant by the report in *The Darling Downs Gazette*, can be found the end of this Chapter.

Based on the estimation provided, Burgess could have arrived on foot in Gatton at about 1 am the day the bodies were found in Moran's paddock. If he made his way by horse, however, he would have arrived much earlier, but not before the murders.

Around 6 pm, instead of returning with the others to Lower Tent Hill, Jerry Murphy stayed behind at Mount Sylvia after the races and went to the dance there on Boxing Day night.[31,32]

That is the reason for the earlier comment that if he had not changed his plans, it would have been Jerry and not Michael, who lost his life in Moran's paddock on Boxing Day night.

Back on the family's farm at Lower Tent Hill, when told of Jerry's change of plans, Mary Murphy said to her daughter, Norah, "You had better go to the dance."

"No," replied Norah. "I will stay at home and look after the child."

"No, I will mind the child," said Mary. "You can go."

The child was the grandson, Daniel Joseph (Joe) McNeil, son of the brother-in-law, William McNeil, and his wife, Mary (Polly) McNeil, formerly Murphy.

"I am going to take the girls," said Michael to his mother, "to the dance."

"They had better stay at home," replied Mary, who obviously realised that Norah might have been unwell.

"Oh," scoffed Michael, "get ready and come!"[33]

At 7 pm, in company of his mother, Margaret, and a friend, Mary Callinan, John Carroll set out in a spring trap on the return journey from Mount Sylvia to Gatton, the countryside being well lit by moonlight.[34,35]

Between 7.30 pm and 8 pm, Steve Jordan and his brother, Joseph (Joe) Jordan, rode into Gatton for the dance. They met up with another brother, Thomas (Tom) Jordan, who was with Chadwick near Logan's shop. Soon after, Chadwick and the Jordan brothers, Steve and Tom, opened and lit the internal lamps of the hall.[36,37]

At 7.45 pm, Arthur Brooking was walking along the Tenthill Creek Road past Moran's paddock when he heard what sounded like a gunshot. More than likely, it was a firecracker going off during a fireworks' display at Clarke's butchery.

Brooking saw a man dressed in dark clothing near the sliprails, his hat pulled down over the face, which was same as the clothing worn by Miller at the restaurant and the wearing of the hat described by Beatrice Hallas, so one assumes that it was John Miller.[15]

At 8 pm, Pat Murphy left the farm at Lower Tent Hill and set out on his ride back to the Gatton Agricultural College.[32,38]

Norah and Ellen were dressed and ready to go to the dance, and Michael was harnessing Norah's pony known as *Tom* in a buggy owned by William McNeil.[32,39]

When McNeil saw Michael selecting a whip, which was more like a switch or small riding whip, "Oh," said McNeil to Michael, "this is the better one to take!"

A description of the whip was provided during the investigation, as follows:

> *An ordinary buggy whip with a black handle about two feet long with ferrules of white metal and butt of same. The butt has two tacks driven through it on each side into the whip. From the top of the metal butt for six inches up the handle it is bound round with common twine.*

The ferrules up the whip are probably six or seven in number and the keeper is of soft greenhide bound with common twine and has two tacks driven on each side through the keeper into the whip. The tacks in the keeper and the butt are not bright tin tacks but the ordinary small black iron tacks. The thong is about as long as the handle and is of plaited leather and has a greenhide fall about two feet long and there is no cracker.[40,41]

This whip was the one referred to by Parry-Okeden in his telegram dated January 4, 1899, which can be found at the end of the Introduction, being used, in my opinion, to rape Norah and Ellen in Moran's paddock.

Around the time that Pat Murphy left the family farm at Lower Tent Hill, as alluded to before, Clarke had a fireworks' display at his butchery on the Tenthill Creek Road, which can be found in the map on page 1.

The house and slaughter yards were about 700 yards from where the Murphy siblings were murdered in Moran's paddock, a narrow laneway separating Clarke's property from the paddock.[3]

At the Royal Commission, "Did you give a display of fireworks," said Dickson to Clarke, "on Boxing Night?"

"I did."

"At what time?"

"Between eight and nine o'clock. I know that, because I looked at the clock at ten minutes to nine, and called the children in."

"Was Day there?"

"No."

"Do you know where he was then?"

"No, I do not."

"Had you seen him before that?"

"Yes, having his tea."

"About what time?"

"I cannot say exactly, but it was about half-past six."

"Were all the others connected with the house at the fireworks?"

"Yes."

"Was Day the only one who was not there?"

"Yes, that is all."³

Not only did Day fail to give a proper account of his movements on the night of the murders, but also no one associated with Clarke's butchery, after the meal, saw him again until the next morning.

At 8.20 pm, about a mile on the Gatton side of the Murphy's home, Pat was overtaken by the buggy driven by Michael.

A quarter of a mile further along the road, Pat passed the sisters, Annie and Maude Wilson, daughters of the Head Teacher at the Lower Tent Hill School, riding in the opposite direction.³²,³⁸

After passing Pat, the Wilson sisters rode on to the residence of Annie Cook at Lower Tent Hill.

While the Wilson sisters were talking to his mother, Walter Albert Cook, brother of May Cook, heard the sisters say that they had just met Michael, Norah and Ellen on their way to the dance.⁴²

At Deep Gully, about nine miles from Gatton, Sergeant William Arrell and Michael (Mick) Connolly, who were returning to Gatton from the races at Mount Sylvia, came out of the gully and fell in behind Pat Murphy.

From there on into Gatton, Arrell and Connolly rode about a chain behind Pat.³²,³⁸

At 8.30 pm, about 100 yards on the culvert side of the sliprails, John Carroll was driving and sitting on the right-hand side of the spring cart when overtaken by the buggy driven by Michael.

With the Murphy's buggy about 50 yards in front of him, John saw a man on the left-hand side of the road, very close to the buggy as it passed him.

Wearing dark trousers, short blue coat or shirt and a grey felt hat turned down over his face, the man was observed by John from when the man was level with the buggy until John passed him in the spring cart, prompting John to say to his mother, "I believe that is Clarke's butcher."[35,43]

At the Royal Commission, Noel said to John Carroll, "You saw somebody?"

"Yes."

"Did you say anything to your mother with regard to it?"

"Yes. After we passed him my mother said, 'There is a man,' and I said, 'Yes, that is Clarke's man'."

"How did you know it was Clarke's man?"

"I thought it was by the clothes and hat he wore."

"Where had you seen him?"

"I had seen him several times in the cart."

"What was he?"

"He was working for Mr Clarke."

"Had you seen him often," said Dickson to John, "before driving in the cart?"

"Pretty often."

"Was it," said Noel to John, "a fine night?"

"A moonlight night."

"Did you tell the police?"

"Yes. I told Sergeant Arrell and McNeil that I saw the man," which was at the crime scene in Moran's paddock during the afternoon of December 27, 1898.[28]

When he was questioned, "Did you ever hear," said Garvin to Toomey, "that the boy had said on the ground before the bodies were removed, 'The man I saw at the sliprails on the night of the [26th] was Day'?"

"No, I did not," replied Toomey. "I may state that this boy is a boy who, I believe, will tell a yarn, as other boys will. He might tell a civilian whom he met in the street that it was Clarke's man, or some other man, he saw at the sliprails, but when he came to be tested by the police, he would not say in any shape or form that it was Clarke's man."

"Did you question Mrs Carroll?"

"Yes."

"What did she say?"

"She said she did not know the man, but that her son had told her that he thought it was Clarke's man."[44]

When she was questioned, "Do you know anything," said Noel to Margaret Carroll, "about the matter?"

"We were coming in from the Mount Sylvia races," replied Margaret, "and when we were near the sliprails, the Murphys were in front of us, and a man was standing in the road. Both carts were close together, and my son said, 'That is Clark's man'."

"Meaning whom?"

"He did not say his name," replied Margaret. "We did not say any more about it, but afterwards people said that blood was found on the man, and all that."

Dickson said to Margaret, "Who said?"

"It was said by Clarke, the butcher," replied Margaret, "and that he washed his clothes afterwards."[45]

At 8.45 pm, Florence (Florrie) Lowe rode through Gatton on her journey from the Gatton Agricultural College to her parents' home at Deep Gully.[15]

It appears that Lowe did not come across Michael, Norah and Ellen, as one did not find any evidence of her seeing them while she made her way through the town toward Deep Gully.

Near O'Leary's house on the Tenthill Creek Road, Lowe met Margaret and John Carroll, and Mary Callinan, on their way into Gatton.[46]

Shortly after at Logan's Hill, Lowe met Pat Murphy riding into Gatton.[32,38]

At 9 pm, when no one turned up for the dance, Chadwick and the Jordan brothers put the lights out and locked the hall.[36]

Riding past the sliprails around the same time, Arrell and Connolly did not see anyone lurking there.[47]

Burgess' Alibi

At 9.10 pm, while entering the yard to return the keys to the caretaker at his house next to the hall, Chadwick and the Jordan brothers saw Michael, Norah and Ellen drive past in the buggy.

Without stopping to speak to anyone, Michael turned the buggy around and commenced the return journey to the family's farm at Lower Tent Hill.[31]

At 9.15 pm, upon meeting Michael, Norah and Ellen on their way back to Lower Tent Hill, about a quarter of a mile from where he passed Lowe, Pat had a conversation with his brother and sisters for about two or three minutes.[38]

On Clarke's Hill, Arrell and Connolly passed Lowe riding in the opposite direction. They next came across the Murphy siblings conversing with each other near O'Leary's house, Connolly calling out, "Goodnight."[38,47]

When Arrell asked as to who was in the buggy, Connolly replied, "They are the Murphys."[47]

After leaving his siblings, Pat met Albert Murray, about 400 yards on the Gatton side of Logan's house.[38]

Around 9.15 pm, Thomas Drew and Michael Donohue, who *had a few drinks but knew what* [he] *was about*, rode past the sliprails to Moran's paddock.

About 70 yards past the sliprails, Donohue saw *a man on the left-hand side of the road.*

Seeing that he had *a big felt hat drawn over his face*, Donohue said to Drew, "Do you know that bugger?"

Drew did not, Donohue describing the stranger as *about 5 feet 8 or 9 inches* [wearing] *dark clothes.*[48]

This obviously was a third perpetrator, possibly Chaston, as Miller was somewhat shorter, and Day was seen by John Carroll wearing dark trousers, short blue coat or shirt and a grey felt hat turned down over his face.

After passing this third perpetrator, Drew and Donohue met *Florrie Lowe in the sandy flat at the foot of the hill.*[46,48]

Michael, Norah and Ellen were next passed by Drew and Donohue, about one mile from the sliprails, Donohue noticing that *Tom* was walking as the siblings approached Moran's paddock.[46,48]

Riding past the sliprails in front of Michael, Norah and Ellen, Lowe was confronted by a man with a moustache, dark clothing, and wearing a hat. Walking to within three yards on the left of Lowe, he said something to her that she did not understand. Concerned by his behaviour, Lowe prodded the ribs of the horse, making it walk faster until she lost sight of the man.[15,49]

At the Royal Commission, when told that Urquhart wanted to say something about his prior testimony, Noel said to Urquhart, "What do you wish to say?"

"I stated on Friday that the boy Carroll said that he did not recognise the man as Day, but he thought the clothes of the man resembled those worn by Day," replied Urquhart. "I afterwards got a statement from Carroll and questioned him closely. Afterwards various tests for identification were carried out under the superintendence of Mr [Sub-Inspector John Warren-White] in the courthouse at Gatton because he had similar tests to carry out in Toowoomba, and it was considered better that one officer should carry out the whole of the tests. It was reported to me by Mr [Warren-White] that Carroll had picked out Burgess as the man he saw at the sliprails."

"Was Day amongst the men when Carroll was brought in to make the identification?"

"No."

"Had the boy seen Day in the presence of the police?"

"I don't know."

"What was the note that Mr [Warren-White] made with regard to this identification?"

"Mr [Warren-White] has his own notes."

Noel said to Warren-White, who was present, "What was the note you made?"

"John Carroll identified Burgess."

"You noted that as a fact?"

"Yes."

"You did not note down what Carroll said?"

"No."

"Day was not there?"

"No."

"What was," said Garvin to Urquhart, "the date of this?"

"24th January [1899]."

"Was there any resemblance," said Noel to Urquhart, "between Day and Burgess?"

"Not the slightest. The next step was that Carroll gave evidence at the Magisterial Inquiry on oath where he stated he could not recognise the man."

"He said he could not," said Sadleir to Urquhart, "identify anybody?"

"Yes. He said he could not identify the man at the sliprails as anybody."

"Carroll still stuck to Burgess," said Noel to Warren-White, "as being the man at the courthouse."

"Yes."

"That was," said Garvin to Warren-White, "on the 24th January [1899]?"

"Yes."

"When was it," said Garvin to Urquhart, "that the police first showed Day to Carroll after the murder?"

"I don't know, he may have seen him in the presence of Acting Sergeant Toomey. I would like to read the report from the Courier of the 11th March of the evidence given by the boy Carroll on the 10th March. It states there that John Carroll, son of the last witness, aged 13 years and 9 months, corroborated his mother's evidence. He also said he noticed Michael with a whip, and that the man they passed had a grey slouch hat on, also that he wore a blue coat or shirt. He said he had recognised a man at the courthouse on 24th January as like the person he saw near the sliprails, but he could not swear positively he was the same."

Noel said to Urquhart, "The boy said, 'As like the person'?"

"Yes. When the tests took place, Carroll picked out Burgess as the man."

"Sub-Inspector [Warren-White] did not take down Carroll's words?"

"No. Mrs Carroll also picked him out, and said he looked like the man."

"It seems to me that the word 'like' makes all the difference?"

"Yes."

"But you say the word 'like' absolutely excluded Day, because he was absolutely unlike Burgess?"

"I do not go as far as that."

"How far do you go? The boy thought it was Clarke's man, because of the clothing – he could not see his face sufficiently?"

"Yes. There is another point to be brought into that. The man at the sliprails was seen by another witness, a girl named Florence Lowe, who passed close to him on horseback. The man stepped forward and spoke to her. She, in describing that man, said he wore a dark coat, rather long in front, came around in front. Of course, we made inquiries with reference to Day being possessed of such a garment, of ever having been seen with such a garment, and he had not. He never had."

"There is nothing to preclude two different men being at the sliprails at different times?"

"Oh, no."

"Both may be right, the boy and the girl Lowe?"

"Yes, of course. It is within the bounds of possibility they saw two different men."

"If there were two or more men engaged in this business, it might have been one was on the lookout at one time and another on the lookout at another time?"

"Yes."

"There is nothing to preclude that?"

"There is nothing to preclude that."

"Did you know at the time of the examination," said Dickson to Urquhart, "that the boy Carroll said to his mother as they passed the sliprails, 'That is Clarke's man'?"

"I think I did hear it. I do not know that it was officially before me. When the boy made his statement, he did not say so."[45]

Because of the questions asked, it is obvious to me, and so too should it be for you, that the Royal Commission had possession of John Carroll's statement dated December 31, 1898, which can be found at the end of the Introduction.

"You knew," said Dickson to Urquhart, "he had said so?"

"Yes."

"Did you know that," said Garvin to Urquhart, "when you took his statement?"

"I knew he had said so."

"Was that not a matter that you should have pressed him on, that he said to his mother, 'That is Clarke's man'?"

"Yes."

"That would be very important?"

"I pressed him very particularly on that point."

"That he was sure it was Clarke's man?"

"Yes, but he was not."

"Did you press him in such a way," said Noel to Urquhart, "as to frighten him?"

"No."[45]

That was a blatant untruth as Urquhart and Toomey coerced John Carroll into providing a second statement dated January 11, 1899, which also can be found at the end of the Introduction, removing all reference in the first statement to the man seen at the sliprails being *Clarke's butcher*.

"Did you ever hear that the boy said on the ground, after viewing the dead bodies, to McNeil," said Garvin to Urquhart, "that the man whom he saw at the sliprails when they passed on the night of the 26th was Clarke's man?"

"That he said to McNeil on the ground?"

"Yes, on the ground?"

"No. I have never heard that before. I do not think McNeil has ever informed anybody. It has never come to my ears."

"He informed McNeil?"

"It never came to my ears until this moment."[45]

In other questioning of John Carrol, Sadleir said to John, "Did you identify any other man as the man who was there?"

"I did not identify Burgess," replied John. "I said he looked something like the man."

"Did you say that he was the man?"

"No. I said Burgess looked something like him."[28]

Not only were Beatrice and Frank Hallas coerced into identifying Burgess as the swagman seen at their home on the Eve of the Gatton murders, but also the evidence of John Carroll was distorted to give others the impression that John had identified Burgess as the man seen at the sliprails before the murders.

Moreover, it appears that Carroll, Lowe, Donohue and Drew saw three perpetrators at the sliprails, obviously Day, Miller and possibly Chaston, joined in Moran's paddock, in my opinion, by another, or others, on horseback.

Three days after the discovery of the bodies in Moran's paddock, it was reported in *The Brisbane Courier* that *the head of a heavy hammer, and a small riding switch, were found* on the ground behind a stump near the sliprails. The *hammerhead was not stained*, and it was *supposed from the tracks that have been discovered behind the stump that one of the murderers was in hiding near the sliprails.*[50]

One assumes the *hammerhead* was taken there to pacify the victims, and that the *small riding switch* might have been the whip Michael was

Burgess' Alibi

going to use until handed the other by McNeil with the heavy brass-mounted handle which was used obviously by the perpetrators instead of the *hammerhead*.

Surprisingly, one searched but did not locate the *hammerhead* and *small riding switch* in the List of Exhibits found at the scene of the Gatton murders.[51]

There would have been fingerprints on the *hammerhead*, and possibly *boot prints* near the stump and sliprails, which appears to have been the case, as the *blucher boots* owned by Richard Burgess became the focus of considerable police attention until Burgess' *alibi* was proved.

Day wore *blucher boots* and so too did Miller.

If Urquhart and Toomey had been given a free-hand in the investigation, the Gatton murders would have been solved, and Day, Miller and possibly Chaston would have been hung.

Jack the Ripper

> Very Urgent
>
> Head Quarters Office
> Special Police District
> Gatton 8' February 99
>
> Circular Memorandum
>
> re Burgess' Mates.
>
> Referring to my Circular Memo of 2nd February instant, the following further description of a man believed to be identical with the man seen in Burgess' company at Postman's Ridge on 28th December 98 has now been obtained.
>
> Name - John Miller
> Age - 29 years
> Country - Native of London.
> Religion - Roman Catholic
> Height - 5 ft 7 or 8 in
> Build - Slight
> Features - Thin
>
> Small moustache only inclined to be gingery - Ruddy complexion - Active appearance - On 21st December 98 was dressed in a dark coat, tweed trousers, cotton shirt, soft brown felt hat. Had been four years in the Colonies and three weeks in Queensland. Came from Newcastle, N.S.W. - Worked at Green's Resturant, Albert Street, Brisbane, where he got scalded on the back of his head and neck with hot milk upset from a pail on the stove in the resturant kitchen and was treated at the General Hospital, from which he was discharged on 21st December 1898.
>
> He is a vegetable cook and resturant hand and is known by the nick-name of "York" and "Yank".
>
> WHUrquhart
> Inspector

Urquhart's memorandum dated February 8, 1899, page 1
(Courtesy of the Queensland Government (Queensland Police Service))

injuries such as above described and treated with Picric Acid

Every effort must be made to trace and locate these men

The greatest importance is attached to the finding of these men.

Urquhart
Inspector

Urquhart's memorandum dated February 8, 1899, page 2
(Courtesy of the Queensland Government (Queensland Police Service))

Gatton Police Station
February 15th 1899

Inspector Urquhart.

Sir,

Burgess' Photo has been shown to nearly every person in Gatton, a boy named Frank Hellas identified it as being a man that called at his Father's house for matches at about half past six o'clock on the evening of the murder. His Sister Beatrice also said that about half past six o'clock on the evening of the murder she saw a man at her parents house, he asked for matches. She did not look at the mans features but said he was wearing a tweed coat which was broken in front of the right shoulder.

These two children were afterwards taken to Toowoomba by Const. Head & they there identified Burgess from amongst a number of other men, the first named recognising Burgess by his features & the last named by the coat that Burgess was wearing, it was broken in front of the right shoulder.

These are the only two persons that located Burgess at Gatton on the evening of the 26th December last with the exception of the persons that have identified him

Toomey's report dated February 14, 1899, page 1
(Courtesy of the Queensland Government (Queensland Police Service))

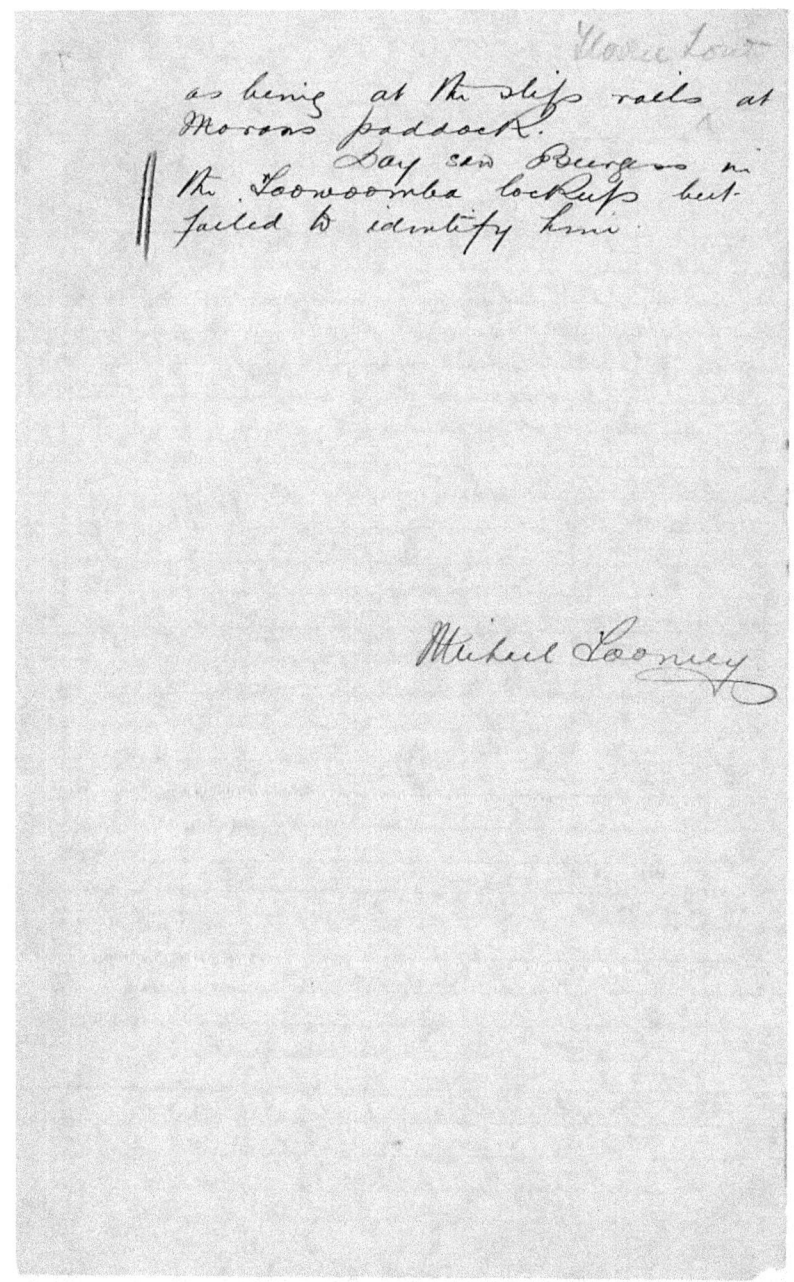

as being at the slip rails at Moroo's paddock. Day saw Burgess in the Toowoomba lockup but failed to identify him.

Michael Toomey

Toomey's report dated February 14, 1899, page 2
(Courtesy of the Queensland Government (Queensland Police Service))

COPY.

Gatton,
Head Quarters Special District,
January, 15th. 1899.

THE FACTS AGAINST RICHARD BURGESS UP TO-DATE.

After sentence for Leyburn outrage Burgess said to Constable Wilson, "I got off light but I will give you all a run for it when I come out again, I was born to be hung."
Discharged from St. Helena November, 30th. 1898.
Seen at Oxley by Duncan Mc.Gregor, December 7th. 1898. (Identified by photo.)
Photo identified by Ross as having left the Salvation Army Temple, Ann Street, on December, 10th. 1898.
Sub Inspector White reports, "Two reliable witnesses identify photo of Burgess as that of man seen on road between Goodna and Oxley on 10th. December, but this is doubtful.
Identified from photo by Mrs. Berry, Limestone Street, Ipswich, as having called at her house between 15th. and 20th. December, obtained food, and left in the direction of Rosewood.
Positively identified (by photo) by Frank and Beatrice Hellas as having called at their father's place in Gatton at about 6.30 P.M. on the evening of December, 26th. 1898. (Night of murder)
Positively identified (from photo) by Lizzie Lahinsky as having been seen in Laidley at 2 P.M. on December, 27th. 1898
Positively identified (from photo) by Robert Russell as having been seen near Flagstone Creek, two miles South of Helidon, on December, 29th. 1898.
Positively identified (by photo) by Mrs. Berg as having called at her house near Helidon on December, 29th. 1898, and while giving her her first news of the murder made the statement that "Michael Murphy was shot"; a thing that was not known at the time as a fact even to the Police, and even if it had been
.... is authority for the

"The Facts Against Richard Burgess" dated January 15, 1899
(Courtesy of the Queensland Government (Queensland Police Service))

Burgess' Alibi

Sidney Henry Hellas

States I am a 11 years of age I reside with my parents in Spencer Street Gatton. I remember Boxing Day the 26th of December last. Between a quarter past Six and 7 O'C on that Evening I was in the garden in front of my fathers house, at that time a man came in the gate and went upto the Veranda steps, My father was lying on a couch on the veranda and I heard the man ask for a few matches; my sister Beatrice gave him the matches and he left the yard. I

Sidney Henry Hellas' statement dated January 15, 1899, page 1
(Courtesy of the Queensland Government (Queensland Police Service))

> I believe I would know the man again if I saw him. He was not a tall man, he, was about 5ft 9inches high, he was not stout build, he had a reddish kind of moustache, and beard which was short. and was wearing a soft brownish hat

Sidney Henry Hellas' statement dated January 15, 1899, page 2
(Courtesy of the Queensland Government (Queensland Police Service))

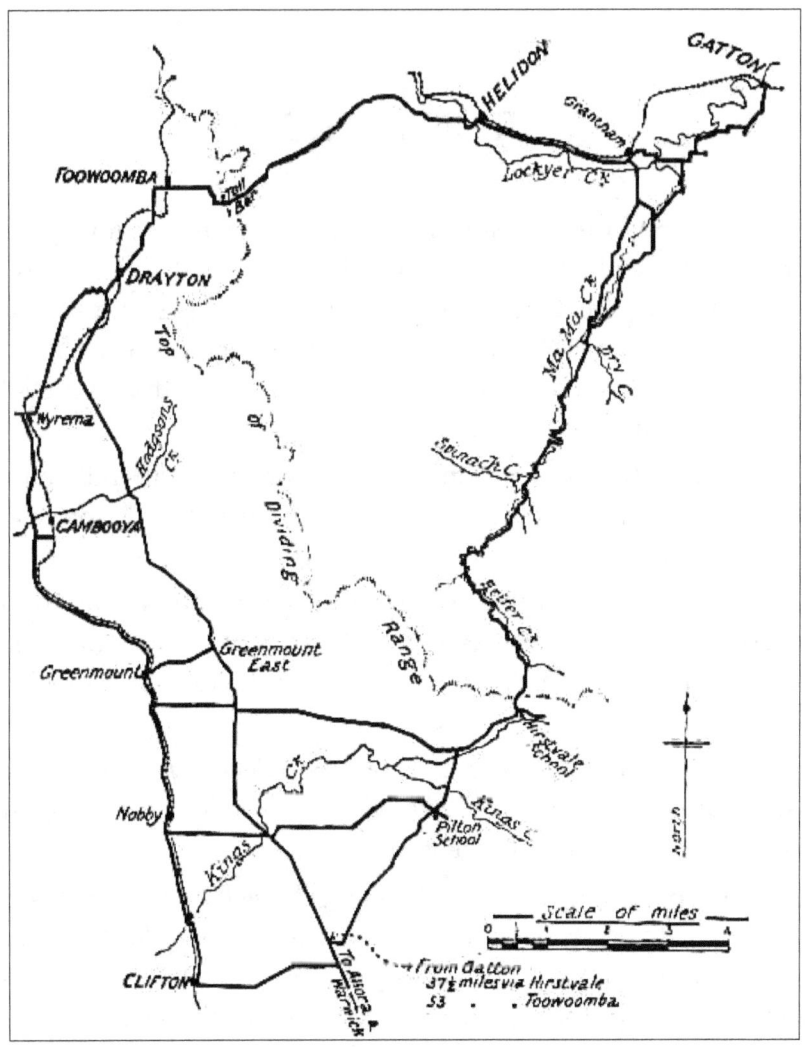

Greenmount to Gatton
(Courtesy of the National Archives of Australia)

7

GATTON MURDERS

One hundred and fifteen years after the Gatton murders, it was posted by the Queensland Police Media on the website of the Queensland Police Service that Inspector Urquhart wrote in his summary of the police investigation, "We have failed because from the very outset, we had no chance of success," which was the truth, as the investigation from the beginning was a *cover-up*.[1]

December 26, 1898 – around 9.30 pm when Arrell and Connolly rode into Railway Street, Pat Murphy was leaving Gatton for the Agricultural College.[2,3]

At 9.55 pm, Louisa Thuerkauf, a domestic servant at Clarke's butchery, was putting the cats out through the back door of the residence when she heard a revolver shot in the direction of Moran's paddock.

About three minutes later, Louisa heard *three or four screams* from the same direction, *loud at first but afterwards got faint*, sounding like a female who called out twice, "Father!"[4]

It was reported 15 days later in *The Telegraph* by Urquhart's good friend, Reginald Spencer Browne, that *Thomas Day, who lives in a humpy, about the same distance from the scene of the tragedy* as Louisa Thuerkauf, *also heard screams and shots*, and that *the police had questioned Day*.[5]

Around the time Louisa Thuerkauf heard the screams and a shot, Walter Albert Cook, allegedly, was looking for cows in Dwyer's paddock when he *heard a shot from the direction of Moran's paddock, a distance of two miles in a straight line*.[6,7]

One assumes that Cook's statement to police was untruthful, and that he was on horseback in the paddock, either before or after the murders.

Between 9.30 pm and 10 pm, Catherine Byrne, living with her parents at Lower Tent Hill, *about a mile and a quarter from the scene of the murders*, was on the back veranda when she *heard about five or six screams in the direction of Moran's paddock*. She could not say, however, if the screams, which were *louder and clear at first*, but *grew faint and died away*, were from a male or female.

Either before or after the screams, Catherine also *heard the report of firearms*, which was *sharp and quick*.[8]

During the investigation, after locating Constables Thomas Head and Joseph (Joe) Murphy in the Clarke's and Byrne's residences, Toomey and Arrell went into Moran's paddock to where the bodies were found.

Around the time when the screams and shots were heard, Toomey *fired two shots in quick succession from a bulldog revolver of "380" calibre, and about two minutes after he fired two "380" revolver cartridges out of a sporting rifle, and then screamed five times*.

Conferring afterwards with the constables, Toomey was told they *heard the four firearm reports and five screams distinctly*, Head adding that he recognised the Acting Sergeant's voice.[9]

At 10.30 pm, John Wiggins and his brother, William, were walking their dogs along the road past the sliprails when the dogs left them to investigate something on the ground around the rails and inside the paddock.

John was not sure, but William was adamant that the rails were up in their proper position across the gateway.

When the dogs came back to them, the brothers continued with their walk, returning afterwards to John's dairy farm on the opposite side of Moran's paddock to Clarke's butchery.[6]

December 27, 1898 – at 2 am in the morning after the murders, Frank Moran *was going through the sliprail opening* when he heard a noise *like someone rushing into the bushes near the culvert*.[10,11]

At 3 am, Jerry Murphy left Mount Sylvia and returned to Lower Tent Hill with a visitor, Robert (Bob) Smith.[10]

Around 7.30 am, McNeil saddled a horse and went in search of Michael, Norah and Ellen.[12]

About one and a half hours later, McNeil found the wheel tracks of his buggy leading from the road into Moran's paddock. Upon finding the bodies on the spur of a hill, McNeil rode into Gatton where he asked for directions to the police barracks at the Brian Boru Hotel before reporting the murders to Arrell.[12,13]

At the Royal Commission, Noel said to McNeil, "You went close to the bodies?"

"Yes, within two yards of the body of Norah."

"Had you any doubt that they had been murdered?"

"I had a doubt at the time, by the way the bodies were lying about."

"Why did you not say the three Murphys were lying murdered?"

"I don't know. At all events, they were dead, and I reported that."

"When you came in first," said Dickson to McNeil, "you went to the hotel, did you not?"

"Yes."

"The publican, what is his name?"

"Charles Gilbert."

"What did you tell Gilbert?"

"I said the same as to Arrell. I asked where the sergeant was and said the three Murphys were lying dead in the paddock."

"You saw the three of them?"

"Yes."

"Did you say anything about the horse lying dead?"

"I do not remember now. He asked me some questions, and I said, 'Yes, the horse is dead, too'."

"When you saw them first, did you not come to any conclusion as to how they were killed?"

"No, I thought they were murdered when I saw them."

"How? Murdered by what?"

"I did not wait to look."

"Did you look for any tracks?"

"No, I did not. I thought the murderer might be thereabouts, and the sooner I left the better."

"When you noticed the tracks of the buggy, or whatever vehicle it was, near the sliprails," said Garvin to McNeil, "were you on horseback?"

"Yes."

"You got down and took down the sliprails?"

"Yes."

"Did you follow the tracks in on horseback or on foot?"

"I did not follow any tracks at first. I rode into the paddock in the direction that the track went, expecting to meet a house."

"Did you look on the road," queried Garvin, who added, "How would you know what direction the track would go if you did not look for tracks?"

"Where I started from the rails, I went in that direction."[13]

After further questioning, more about what McNeil failed to do, or should have done, "Have you," said Garvin, "ever thought over this horrible matter, McNeil?"

"Yes, I have thought a lot of it."

"Have you come to any conclusion about it?"

"Well, no, I cannot say that I have. A certain man named Day has been mentioned a good deal lately. I was in company with Acting Sergeant Toomey when he took Day's statement, and Carroll said he thought it was the man Day who was met at the rails. He said to his mother that he thought it was Day they passed."[13]

It was quickly pointed out by Urquhart what was said at the Magisterial Inquiry by John Carroll and published in *The Brisbane Courier*. Urquhart did not, however, say anything whatsoever about Browne's report in *The Telegraph* that Day *heard screams and shots* coming from the direction of Moran's paddock. And neither did Day give evidence at the Magisterial Inquiry, even though he was easily contactable at A Battery of the Queensland Permanent Artillery at Lytton Fort, Brisbane.

In other words, the Government and police force *shielded* Thomas Day from giving evidence that might have incriminated him at the inquiry.

"Was Day," said Garvin to McNeil, "acquainted with the Murphy family?"

"No, he was a stranger."

"Did you," queried Dickson, "know Day yourself?"

"I never saw him to my knowledge."

"Did the Murphys get meat from Clarke's?"

"Yes."

"Who used to take the meat out, or did they go in for it themselves?"

"Clarke used to go himself."

"Did he ever send it out?"

"I do not know."

"Did Day ever take any out?"

"I do not think so, but I would not be sure."[13]

It appears that Thomas Day might have planned to kill Norah while delivering meat to the Murphy family. The dance on Boxing Day night, however, presented Day with a better opportunity to carry out his revenge.

When Arrell gave evidence, "At what hour on the morning of the 27th did you get information," said Noel to Arrell, "as to the murder being committed?"

"About a quarter past nine."

"Who gave you the information?"

"McNeil."

"Did he inform anybody else before he informed you, do you know?"

"He informed me, he said he had."

"Whom did he inform?"

"He said he had informed Mr Gilbert, the landlord of the Brian Boru Hotel. He said he had gone there first."

"How long before he informed you?"

"He came straight from the hotel and informed me. He came to the police barracks and reported the matter to me. They took him to the hotel first so as to inquire where the barracks were. He did not know where the barracks were."

"What did you do upon receiving the information?"

"I got ready as soon as possible. I saddled my horse and accompanied McNeil to the scene of the murder."

"You and McNeil arrived. Was anybody there before you?"

"No."

"You arrived on the scene first?"

"Yes."

"Did anybody follow you?"

"Yes."

"At what interval?"

"Just close behind us. They nearly arrived there as soon as us."

"How many?"

"Four."

"Who were they?"

"Charles Gilbert, Thomas Wilson, J.P., a man named [William Devitt], bootmaker in Gatton, and [Richard James], local chemist."

"You inspected the bodies?"

"I did."

"What did you do? Did you make any notes for reference?"

"Not just then."

"What did you do?"

"I examined the ground all round where the bodies were lying, to see if I could find any weapon or any sign of a struggle. I made a very careful search but could not see anything. I could not find any tracks or sign of a struggle."

"Was the ground in the same condition at that time as it was the day before yesterday?"

"No."

"In what way did it differ?"

"Then, it was all covered with grass and dead leaves."

"Thick grass?"

"Just like the other part of the paddock, not very thick."

"Was it high grass?"

"No, just like it was the other day, only thicker. There were a lot of dead leaves, broken twigs, and dead branches, but I could see no sign of a struggle."

"What did you do? How long did you remain there?"

"About twenty minutes or half-an-hour."

"Did you make any notes as to the appearance of the bodies, the way they lay, or anything of that kind?"

"Not then."

"Well, what did you do?"

"I asked Mr Wilson to remain in charge while I returned to town."

"Did you ask anybody else?"

"I asked the four but Gilbert, and James, said they could not stop, so Wilson and Devitt agreed to stop until I came back."

"Were you making an examination all the time you were there?"

"Yes."

"When you got into town, what did you do?"

"I wired to the Commissioner telling him of the occurrence."

"Where from?"

"The railway station."

"What was the time when you wired," queried Commissioner Theodore Oscar Unmack, who added, "have you got a copy of the telegram?"

"No, but the time I put on the telegram was 10.55 [am]."

"Did you send an 'Urgent' message?"

"No, an ordinary message. I asked the telegraph master to send it 'Urgent,' but he said the police had no authority to send 'Urgent' wires."

"Had you no authority under Regulation 6," said Noel to Arrell, "to send an 'Urgent' wire?"

"I believe there is such a rule, but I knew nothing about it then. I had got no instructions to that effect."

"If you had known of that Rule 6, you would have sent an 'Urgent' [wire]?"

"I certainly would."

"Then you went back to the scene of the murder?"

"I did not go back immediately, because the telegraph master told me that I could get the wire through immediately, and that it would go to Brisbane as soon as an 'Urgent,' so I thought I would get a reply in ten or fifteen minutes, and I waited, thinking I would get a reply."

"How long did you wait?"

"Twenty minutes, or perhaps half an hour. Then, as I had got no reply, I rode out again. I got out to the scene of the murder at about quarter-past twelve."[14]

Between 10.40 am to 12.15 pm, no police officer was in the paddock guarding the crime scene and many, including McNeil, who brought Mary Murphy to the bodies of her children, trampled over marks made by horses and boots, including signs of a struggle.

"When did you first get a reply," said Unmack to Arrell, "from the Commissioner or the Chief Inspector's office?"

"I did not get any message at all from the Chief Inspector's office."

"Did you get a message from any office?"

"I got a wire from Sub-Inspector Galbraith from Rosewood."

"That could not be in answer to your message to Brisbane?"

"No."

"I want to know when you first got an answer from Brisbane to your message?"

"If you will permit me, I would like to make an explanation. I wired to Sub-Inspector Galbraith at the same time that I wired to the Commissioner, as he was my immediate superior officer, and in reply, he sent me a wire from Rosewood, stating that he would make all possible haste to arrive at Gatton about five o'clock. When Mr Galbraith came up at five o'clock that night, he took charge of the case."

"Then you got no reply at all," clarified Noel, "from Brisbane?"

"I did not."[14]

One assumes, as alluded to before, that Norah was the intended victim, her body being found on a rug, about 30 feet from Michael's and 28 feet from Ellen's, both Michael and Ellen being positioned on the ground close together, back to back, the distance from the bodies to the sliprails being about 1,050 yards.[15]

After Arrell explained that he found many of the locals in the paddock near the bodies when he returned, Noel said to Arrell, "Were they walking around?"

"They followed the tracks of the buggy right down to the sliprails, and some of them were walking around the bodies."

"Close to the bodies?"

"Yes."

"Did you order them away?"

"I did. I ordered them away several times, and they went back a little, but would not leave the paddock."

"Would you not have authority to absolutely order them away on an occasion like that?"

"I did order them away."

"But have you no authority to enforce an order of that description?"

"I do not know if there is any law authorising me to do so."

"You say you ordered them away, and that they went back a little and afterwards came in again?"

"Yes."

"Were the four men who went out with you," said Dickson to Arrell, "Justices of the Peace?"

"One of them was."

"Did they assist you to keep the people back?"

"No, the Justice of the Peace I left there, went into town again shortly afterwards, but there were other magistrates there."

"Did you speak to them?"

"I did."

"Did you tell them to keep the people back?"

"Yes."[14]

During questioning about his failure to secure the crime scene, "Why didn't you stay with the bodies," said Noel to Arrell, "and ask the Justice of the Peace to go into town and send a wire?"

"I thought it was best to go myself."

"Why?"

"I thought the wire might perhaps go astray, or not get away."

"Didn't you think that a Justice of the Peace had sufficient intelligence to send a wire to the Commissioner?"

"That did not strike me."[14]

At 2 pm that day, Richard Burgess was at Laidley, south-east from Gatton, a sighting confirmed by Lizzie Labinsky, who subsequently identified Burgess from a line-up at the lockup of the Toowoomba police station.[16]

Having in mind what was alluded to in *The Darling Downs Gazette* that it would take roughly 14 hours to walk 36 miles, how did Burgess get from Greenmount to Laidley so early in the afternoon?[17]

It appears the answer to that question was provided by Burgess upon his arrest several days later at the Bunya Mountains, north-west from Gatton.

Burgess told Constable Gillies, allegedly, that he was camped at the culvert near Moran's paddock on Boxing Day night and *heard a horse gallop furiously along the road from the direction of Gatton*, which was supported by Frank Moran, who heard *a noise like someone rushing into the bushes near the culvert* around 2 am.[10,11]

At 2.30 pm, the bodies were conveyed from Moran's paddock to a room at the Brian Boru Hotel.[14]

While laying out the bodies, Thomas Bailey, whose statement dated December 31, 1898, can be found at the end of this Chapter, heard Mary Murphy say, "My cook, my washerwoman, and my all is gone, will I reveal it, or will I leave it to the Lord."[18]

Similarly, William Miller, whose statement also dated December 31, 1898, can be found at the end of this Chapter, heard Daniel (Dan) Murphy say, "I would sooner have my children, then have any more lives lost over the affair."[19]

One assumes the *affair* had everything to do with the sudden and unexpected death of May Cook, and that Norah did something, such as perform an illegal abortion, that resulted in May's death.

When Arrell was questioned about the post-mortem examinations, Dickson said to Arrell, "Who called in Doctor Von Lossberg?"

"When I sent the wire to Sub-Inspector Galbraith," replied Arrell, "I asked him to send up a medical man."

"It was at your request he came?"

"Yes."[14]

At 4.15 pm, First Class Constable James Murphy, who was not related to the deceased, advised Urquhart at his home that the murders at Gatton had been confirmed.[20]

It appears that there is truth in the police rumour passed on to me, which will be outlined in greater detail in due course, that Thomas Day confessed at Gatton to the Catholic priest, Father Daniel Walsh, who was threatened with excommunication if he went public with the confession.[21]

Upon his arrival at the Brian Boru Hotel, Doctor William Henry Von Lossberg, Government Medical Officer for the Ipswich district, found the room where the murdered victims had been placed was crowded.

After Arrell cleared the room, Von Lossberg had the bodies removed, one by one, to a more appropriate room at the back of the hotel where the post-mortem examinations were conducted.

Commencing with Ellen's body, Von Lossberg found that the face and upper part of the body were smeared with blood, the brain was protruding through a fracture on the right side, the hands were still tied with a *handkerchief* behind the back, there were numerous *fingernail marks* over the body, and *abrasions* on both hands.

"You opened," said Noel to Von Lossberg, "the skull of Ellen Murphy?"

"Yes, and I examined all the fractured bones, the membranes, the vessels, and the body of the brain. The skull was fractured in all the principal bones, that is, the frontal bone, the parietal bone, the occipital bones, were all fractured. All compound comminuted fractures."

"The head was battered to pieces," said Noel, who clarified, "The skull was battered to pieces?"

"Yes, battered to pieces, and the brain was in a state of pulp. I unloosened then the hands and saw that they were greatly swelled. The nails were black."

"May I ask whether that indicated to you a struggle, great struggling, on her part?"

"The swelling?"

"Yes?"

"No."

"It was the tightness of the [handkerchief]?"

"Yes. I then examined the lower portion of the body, and lifted the clothes, which were greatly spattered with blood, and the legs were scratched with fingernails and smeared with blood."[22]

If you remember the murder of Emma Harrison at Darlinghurst in New South Wales, you will recall that her underclothing was saturated with blood, and that what appeared to be *water mixed with blood* was smeared over the bedclothes.

"Was Sergeant Arrell present," said Noel to Von Lossberg, "when you did all this?"

"Yes."

"Did you make any remarks to him as you made your examination?"

"I did."

"Did you tell him what was indicated to your mind, what impression your mind received from these circumstances?"

"The impression on my mind was that it was caused by a heavy blunt instrument."

"You told him so?"

"Oh, yes, and by these fractures and injuries to the brain."

"Did you tell him what the scratches and marks conveyed to your mind?"

"Fingernails."

"What did you say?"

"I said, 'These are fingernails'."

"Did you see anything else that would indicate it?"

"Would indicate," clarified Von Lossberg, "that somebody interfered with the girl?"

"Violently," said Noel, "that she was outraged?"

"Yes."

"Did you tell him so?"

"I did. I examined her internally, and, at the same time, to get to the womb properly, I took one hand, and pressing the womb down, I put the other hand internally in the womb. That is the only way I could ascertain she was not pregnant. The womb in its fresh state is only about two inches to two and a half inches in length."[22]

It appears Von Lossberg established that Norah and Ellen were not pregnant at the time of their deaths.

"Did you find any marks," said Dickson to Von Lossberg, "on the loins – legs?"

"I did."

"What?"

"Scratch fingernails."

"On the legs?"

"On the thighs, inside the thighs."

"You saw blood on the clothes?"

"I did."

"On the petticoat, was it?"

"I think it was the petticoat, sort of petticoat."

"Spots of blood. Can you form any idea where these spots came from?"

"They came from the passage of the vagina."

"That is your opinion, where they came from?"

"Yes."

"You told," said Noel to Von Lossberg, "that to the sergeant?"

"Yes, and I asked him to take care of the petticoat. At the same time, I may mention that when I withdrew my finger, there were undoubtedly signs of semen, but certainly I had no microscope. But it was quite undoubtedly semen, male semen, on my fingers."[22]

In fact, based on the amount of semen found by Von Lossberg and subsequently by Doctor Andrew William Orr on Norah and Ellen's clothing, as well as Michael's clothing, it is obvious that Norah and Ellen were raped by more than one male.

The blood, however, on Nora and Ellen's thighs and clothing was the consequence, in my opinion, of them also being raped with a *blunt instrument*, namely the handle of the whip searched for but never found.

"Could the swelling you saw on the wrists," said Dickson to Von Lossberg, "have been caused by the tying before or after death?"

"Before death."

"If these [handkerchiefs] had been tied after death, you would not expect to find them swelled?"

"I would not. That was before death. After death there could not be swelling like that."

"Did you," said Noel to Von Lossberg, "inform any police officer, Sergeant Arrell or other, that, in your opinion, the [handkerchief] had been put on before death?"

"I think I did. I do not recollect. But I omitted to say that this body was very blanched, almost bloodless, quite in an anaemic state, just the reverse of the other girl."

"Have you any doubt at all," said Garvin to Von Lossberg, "about her having been violated?"

"Not the least."

"Can you say whether she was suffering from monthly sickness, or courses, at the time?"

"No, she was not suffering from her monthly courses."

"That blood you spoke of as having been on the petticoat, what would cause it?"

"That was just from the outraging of the girl, it was the effect of resistance. The labia of the vagina was very swollen and scratched. The finger-marks went right through to the anus. The blood came from the scratches on the labia."

"That might have come from the scratches on the legs?"

"I did not say legs – the labia of the vagina."

Noel said to Von Lossberg, "The lips?"

"Yes, the lips."

"Was this girl a virgin up till this time," said Sadleir to Von Lossberg, "can you say from your examination?"

"Which?"

"Was this girl Ellen a virgin up till the time this outrage was committed?"

"She was right enough."

"Was she a virgin?"

"No, she was no virgin. The hymen was broken."

"The hymen can be broken," said Noel to Von Lossberg, "and a girl still be a virgin?"

"Yes, certainly."

"Was it broken," said Sadleir to Von Lossberg, "sometime long before or at the time of this outrage?"

"I cannot say. I cannot answer the question."

"What was the blood to come from? You found blood coming from the vagina. What blood would that be?"

"From the injuries, scratches, on the side of the labia."

"Not from a ruptured hymen?"

"I do not think so. She was not a virgin."

"No, because she had been outraged?"

"Yes."

"Are we to understand," said Garvin to Von Lossberg, "she was not a virgin prior to the outrage?"

"It is very hard to say."

"Can you say, from the injuries you saw inflicted," said Dickson to Von Lossberg, "that she would have resisted violently, what you would have expected from violent resistance?"

"That she resisted violently."

"You would expect to see at the place where she was ravished marks of a struggle, would you not?"

"I would."

"Can you say she had not been shot?"

"If I can say that?"

"Can you say death had not been caused by a bullet?"

"I am sure it was not."

"Why?"

"Because I have had all the parts of the brain out, and I have examined all the bones, the neck, and all parts of the body, and I found no wound of such a description."

"Could not the bullet have gone through these damaged parts of the skull, and passed out without you knowing?"

"Not without my detecting it. I am absolutely certain she was not shot."[22]

He then examined Norah's body and found *a very plethoric state of the face and body*, resulting in Von Lossberg finding *a strap quite tight around the neck, so tight that it had stopped the circulation*, and *on the right side of the eye, a sharp cut* of about two inches.[22]

With respect to the cut on the face, "Did you come to any conclusion," said Noel to Von Lossberg, "as to how it was made?"

"It was made by some sharp instrument, very likely by a knife. It was a clean cut."

"Could it have been made," said Dickson to Von Lossberg, "by the piece of wood you saw?"

"It could not possibly have been made by that."

"Nor," said Noel to Von Lossberg, "by a fist?"

"No."[22]

The piece of wood referred to by Dickson, which was a dead limb that had fallen from a tree, about *four feet long* and *weighing eight pounds* with blood and hair attached thereto, was taken possession of as an exhibit.[22,23]

Von Lossberg found that Norah's clothes *were torn open from the neck right to the waist*.

There were numerous *fingernail marks* over the breastbone, hands, and arms, and *abrasions* on the hands.

Same as Ellen, all the principal bones of the head were fractured, however, in Norah's case, all the blood vessels were overfilled with blood.

"That was owing," said Noel to Von Lossberg, "to the strangulation?"

"I took it to be owing to the strangulation."

"Would you say that strap," said Dickson to Von Lossberg, "was put on before or after death?"

"Before death. It could not be seen."

"Had it," said Noel to Von Lossberg, "sunk into the flesh?"

"Yes. Nobody saw it until I made a very minute examination. If I had not found it, nobody would have known there was a strap round her neck at all."

"You called Sergeant Arrell's attention to this?"

"I did. Then, after exposing the brain in the same way as I did with the other girl and finding the same sort of fractures caused by a similar instrument as in the first case, I went to the examination of the privates as well."

"Before passing to that," said Dickson to Von Lossberg, "could you say positively that Norah had not been shot?"

"She had not been shot."

"You went on to examine the private parts?"

"After removing the clothes, I found, principally on the left thigh, great numbers of fingernail marks, and they went to the privates and right to the anus, in fact, right to the constrictor anus. The marks were more plentiful than with the first girl. I examined her likewise internally, and found a swelling, but no blood of any kind. The hymen was ruptured. I gave the opinion that she was not in a pregnant state."

"Did it appear," said Garvin to Von Lossberg, "to be a recent rupture?"

"I could not answer that question with certainty."

"Would you say," said Dickson to Von Lossberg, "she had been ravished?"

"Yes. I gave that opinion at the time, and I am still of the same opinion."

"She was a non-consenting party," said Noel to Von Lossberg, "struggling to prevent violation, and so received those injuries, in your opinion?"

"That is so."

"Would you say," said Dickson to Von Lossberg, "there must have been great struggling on her part?"

"I would."

"If she was lying on a rug, would you expect to see that rug all tossed about?"

"I would, but I would not expect that she would keep on a rug. I would expect that the rug be all disordered, and that she would roll off."

"Would you expect the ground to be torn up with the movements of her feet and her struggles?"

"Certainly. She had on a pair of quite new, strong boots, with high heels, and those boots would have made an impression somehow on the ground."

"And if the ground was soft and strewn with leaves, would you expect to find it greatly disturbed?"

"I would."

"Did you inform Sergeant Arrell," said Noel to Von Lossberg, "that she was outraged, and had struggled violently?"

"Yes, I said she must have struggled more violently than the other girl, because all her hands and face and everything were marked with fingernails. I forgot to say that on the left side of the throat there were the marks of three fingers of the hand just above the strap, a hames strap it was."

"Do you think it was possible," said Garvin to Von Lossberg, "for one man to have ravished both of those girls?"

"I do not think it was possible at all. I have said from the beginning that I did not think it possible for one man to have done it."

"Did you give your opinion," said Noel to Von Lossberg, "to the police?"

"I did."

"To whom, you recollect. Was it to Sergeant Arrell?"

"Yes. I said at the time to the gentleman who was present that it was not possible to outrage the girl, and at the same time to do this tying. If the tying was done after death it would have been another thing, but one man could not possibly tie the hands when alive, and at the same time outrage the girl."

"Do you think," said Garvin to Von Lossberg, "one man could have outraged both?"

"He could. A strong man could. I think so. He could do it, but I don't think it was one man."[22]

Moving on to the third and last post-mortem, "Now tell us," said Unmack to Von Lossberg, "about Michael Murphy's body?"

"Michael Murphy represented, when first looked at, the same picture, except that his hands were only bent back and not tied."

"Was there any mark on either hand," said Dickson to Von Lossberg, "to show that they had been tied?"

"No mark of being tied in Michael's case, but he had in one hand an empty purse. He had in one hand a quite loose purse, and between the two hands there was lying a strap."

"That you heard," said Noel to Von Lossberg, "but did not see?"

"I saw it. They were brought in and placed down as they were found. The purse I saw, and the strap too. On examination of the head, I found in his case, just behind the right ear, some blood that extended to the lower jaw and to the neck in a thin film, and quite dark and dry. I cleared this blood away. I dare say it extended about from three to three and a half inches. I washed it carefully away, and I found a wound behind the right ear. I said then to the gentlemen present, 'Hullo, there is a bullet wound,' and nobody said anything to that. I then commenced directly to probe the bullet wound with my finger. I went on for a considerable time, removed a few loose bones from the skull, and felt all at once a very sharp click on one of my nails. I went to a basin and washed my hands in a disinfectant fluid, after which I went on with the examination again. Then I felt a numbness going up my arm, and a swelling of the finger, so I asked the chemist who was present, Mr James, if he would be good enough to probe for the bullet.

He said, 'Very well,' and tried to find it, but did not succeed. As I felt more and more the effects of the poison, I did not proceed further with the examination, but left it in an incomplete state."

"What did you get," said Dickson to Von Lossberg, "blood poisoning?"

"I did. I was three months ill, and I have still the effects on my body in blotches on the skin, even my hands show still the marks of abscesses and all sorts of things. I felt regularly ill for three months from the blood poisoning. After that I got the bodies replaced. The police sergeant was present."

"Did you tell the sergeant you were unable to complete the post-mortem?"

"I said, 'I cannot go on'."

"You told him that?"

"I did not address him specially. I asked the chemist, who is a handyman, to try and find the bullet, but he could not, and then as I could not go on any more, I got the bodies replaced in the other room where I had found them."

"Do you know," said Noel to Von Lossberg, "that Sub-Inspector Galbraith says that neither of the two women showed any signs of having had a post-mortem examination made on the skull?"

"If he says that, he has no authority for the statement, as I had eleven bones out, which shows that there must have been an examination."

"How long were you occupied in making this post-mortem?"

"I was about two hours and twenty minutes."

"What was your opinion," said Dickson to Von Lossberg, "as to the cause of the death of Michael Murphy?"

"My opinion was that he was killed by a shot."

"Did you," said Noel to Von Lossberg, "express that opinion?"

"I did."

"To the people present?"

"I did. There were present the two women who have been referred to, and they wanted to go on washing the bodies and preparing them for burial. I said, 'Nobody must touch these bodies until a higher police officer gives an order for it.' Sergeant Arrell was present."

"What else did you find," said Dickson to Von Lossberg, "about the head besides this hole which you thought was a bullet wound?"

"I found fractures of all the principal bones. Some of the bones were detached from the membranes, and the cap of the skull was quite loose and bare."

"Could those fractures have been caused by the piece of timber shown to you?"

"Yes, they could."

"When would you say those blows were inflicted, when he was in a standing position, or lying down?"

"I dare say those injuries were done after death. I gave that opinion at the time, and I am still of that opinion."

"You did not come to the conclusion that they could be done while Michael was standing?"

"I do not think he was standing."

"Why do you think he was not standing," said Noel to Von Lossberg, "and that the women were?"

"The fractures in his case went more from the top to the right side where the shot was and did not extend as far to the left as the others did. The fractures in Michael's skull were in the same bones, but the fractures in the case of the girls extended more down to the left side underneath the ear."

"Would the post-mortem appearances be different if the blows were struck after death from what they would be if the blows were struck during life?"

"Oh, yes, if blows were struck after death there would be no exudation of blood, as there would if blows were struck during life."

"But you did not see the amount of exudation, did you?"

"There was nothing but that which appeared about the bullet wound, on the throat and neck, there was no blood in the brain."

"And that indicates to you that the injuries were done after death in the case of Michael?"

"Yes, that is, the injuries caused by a blow with a heavy instrument."

"Did you state that to the police, to Sergeant Arrell?"

"I do not think I did."

"You did not tell him that you thought the girls received the batteries during life, and that Michael received the battery after death?"

"No, I did not. He is a very quiet man and did not ask one question at all during the whole affair. He formed his own opinion from the first, and never asked me a single question, and when I spoke in his presence, I did not exactly address him, I addressed the four or five persons round the door. I addressed one as much as the other, and only when I said the bodies were not to be touched was he there alone. I said, 'These bodies have not to be touched till a higher officer of police comes and inspects them and takes charge of them'."[22]

It has been and is still my contention that too many were at the postmortem examinations, some possibly under the influence, even drunk, resulting in Von Lossberg withdrawing with an injury to a finger, allegedly, before completing Michael's examination.

"Did a higher officer," said Unmack to Von Lossberg, "come before you left Gatton?"

"Yes."

"Whom did you see?"

"I saw Sub-Inspector Galbraith."

"Did you examine," said Dickson to Von Lossberg, "the private parts of Michael?"

"I have seen the penis."

"Did you notice anything about it?"

"No."

"Did you notice any trace of semen about it?"

"No, I must say that I did not examine the parts to see if there was semen about. I had only a glance at them, but I saw that there was a swelling of the prepuce."

"In the case of death from a gunshot wound," said Noel to Von Lossberg, "is the emission of semen a common thing in the male?"

"It happens in cases."

"But is it a common thing?"

"I dare say it is, but I have not experience enough to give an absolute opinion on that point."

"Have you ever known," said Dickson to Von Lossberg, "of any cases of death by gunshot where at the time of death there has been an emission of semen?"

"Yes, I have seen that."

"So that it would not have surprised you," said Noel to Von Lossberg, "if semen had been found in Michael Murphy's trousers?"

"It would not. But understand this, I could not go on any further with my work, I ceased with my work there. You put yourself in my position, doing three post-mortems one after the other on a hot December day in a narrow room only a few feet wide, with all those people round, and standing there, feeling the effects of the poison, you are not inclined, and you cannot look for all those things. I had never taken the clothes off Michael Murphy. I had not taken his pants off, but they were open in front, and I could see that the prepuce of the penis was swelled. I had to leave the operation of the post-mortem in an unfinished state."

"How did you, account for the prepuce of Michael being swelled?"

"I did not account for it."

"Did you form any opinion about it?"

"I did not."

"You did not express any opinion?"

"No."

"What," said Garvin to Von Lossberg, "would cause it?"

"It could be caused by a great many things. A violent connection is a very common cause of it. Through violent connection this swelling frequently takes place, but it could be caused by a blow or anything else."

"From the way in which you saw Michael had been killed," said Dickson to Von Lossberg, "would you have expected to find an emission of semen?"

"I might. I say I would. But, as I say, I did not examine that."

"I am not asking if you examined that, but if in that case you would have expected to find it?"

"Yes, I would certainly have looked for an emission of semen."

"You say that when you got there the room was filled and packed with people?"

"Yes."

"Was there nobody in charge?"

"Nobody."

"There was nobody in charge?"

"No, I had to say to the sergeant, 'Here, out with all these people.' There were between twenty and thirty people counted in that room."

"Did the sergeant say anything about the people being there?"

"No, the room was not locked or anything, and the sergeant met me half-ways to the railway station."

"Was he trying to keep the people out?"

"Certainly, he helped me."

"That is when you told him to do so, and said, 'Out with all these people'?"

"Yes, I said, 'All out, I don't want any of you,' and he certainly helped to get them out."

"Your opinion is that those people should not have been allowed into that room at all?"

"Certainly not."

"The bodies," said Garvin to Von Lossberg, "ought to have been locked up in the room?"

"Yes."

"Those offences were committed at night. Do you think the person or persons committing them would have blood upon them?"

"I would expect that."

"You would expect that they would be splashed with blood?"

"Well, I would not say that, but I dare say there would be some spots of blood upon any persons committing such offences."

"On what parts of them would there be blood spots, can you form any opinion as to that?"

"Well, of course, I think the trousers would show some spots. Then in the case of Norah, where there was a sharp cut in the face, it is very likely there would be spots of blood on the upper garments of the offender."

"From the bashing of the head, what about that?"

"I would not expect it so much in that case, because the piece of timber I was shown was four feet long, or something longer."

"About what weight would it be?"

"I dare say it must have weighed eight or ten pounds, eight pounds, I will say. You see the blow would be executed from above, and the person struck falls down. The aggressor is not likely to go to the body, and he would very likely throw the stick away. On this stick, I saw some light hair, like that of the girl Ellen. The other girl had not exactly dark hair, but more brown hair."

"Did you find some dark hair on the stick as well?"

"No, I did not."

"Did you look for it?"

"I was shown only that one spot with hair on the stick. I looked over the whole piece, however, it was a crooked piece, and there might have been other hair on it without my detecting it."

"About the tracks, do you think any person committing those offences could have covered up the tracks so as to prevent persons coming thereafter from seeing them?"

"I do not think so. In fact, if it is not out of the way, when I was brought to the bodies, I said to the sergeant, 'How were those bodies brought in?' and he said, 'On a cart.' I said, 'Is there any blood on the cart?' He said, 'No, there is not.' I said, 'Is the ground much disturbed?' and he said, 'No, not much disturbed.' I never expressed that, because I was told in the inquiry to shut up."

"You," said Unmack to Von Lossberg, "were told?"

"I was told."

"Who," said Garvin to Von Lossberg, "told you that?"

"Mr Urquhart. He says, 'You are not to speak away, only to answer questions.' He told me not to speak anything, only to answer questions."

"What was this about," said Unmack to Von Lossberg. "What were you saying at the time?"

"It was about the post-mortem. When I gave the first statement, I was going naturally to the second statement of the second post-mortem, and he said, 'Nothing of that. We won't hear anything. You are to answer only the questions, nothing else,' in a very rough way. I weighed just in my mind at the time if I would answer any further questions at all, because it was quite unbecoming behaviour to a gentleman. There were several other higher police officers present."

"You say that before you left Gatton you saw Mr Galbraith?"

"Yes."

"What did you tell him?"

"As soon as I saw him, I was introduced to him, he said to me, 'Did you find a bullet?' I said, 'No, I did not, I found a wound. I traced the wound and I looked for the exit of the bullet, but there is no exit, and the bullet must be in the head, so I advise you to go to the hotel and inspect the bodies and take charge of them.' He said, 'Where was that wound?' I said, 'Behind the right ear.' This is evidence I could not give because I was closed up at the [Magisterial Inquiry] by Mr Urquhart."[22]

Locating a copy of the Royal Commission's report, which has been digitalised by the Queensland Parliamentary Service and made available online for all to see, provided many answers to questions that one did not have when *Oxley-Gatton Murders: Exposing the Conspiracy* was published.

That report, together with the historical documents found at the Queensland State Archives, exposes the *cover-up* that protected Thomas Day from arrest for the Gatton murders.

Furthermore, one now has a better understanding of what went on before and during the post-mortems, as well as the reason why Von Lossberg withdrew soon after his finger, allegedly, became infected with blood poisoning.

"You are not closed up here," said Unmack to Von Lossberg, who, as alluded to before, was not the only one to suffer at the hands of Urquhart and Toomey, "just tell us what you want to say?"

"After this was done he said, 'What about the girls?' I said, 'I did not find any wounds here, but in my opinion, they were outraged,' and I said, 'One girl was strangulated at the same time.' He did not ask any more, and I said, 'Sergeant Arrell there will show you the bodies.' I went then by train down."

"When you had decided that you could not go on with any further examination of Michael's head with the bullet wound," said Garvin to Von Lossberg, "did you express an opinion to any of the police there that a further examination should be made before the body was buried to find that bullet?"

"I did not, but I considered that as a matter of course, as I drew the attention of the sub-inspector to this, that he should take charge of the bodies. I certainly expected he would get another medical man to finish this post-mortem, and that he should find the bullet or prove the exit. The least he could have done would be to wire to the Department here for further instructions."

"You did not advise that?"

"I thought he knew his duty."

"Did you," said Dickson to Von Lossberg, "give a certificate of death of each?"

"I did not."[22]

When Galbraith was questioned, "Tell us all you know about the Gatton murders," said Noel to Galbraith, "and what you did?"

"On Tuesday, 27th December, about half-past three in the afternoon, I was in Rosewood, and I went to the police station to inspect it. Acting Sergeant Perry told me that he had heard a rumour that there had been a murder committed at Gatton. I asked him who gave him the information, and he said the telegraph master. I went over to the telegraph master and said, 'What about this murder in Gatton?' He said, 'Are you Sub-Inspector Galbraith?' I said, 'Yes.' He said, 'A wire has gone through to you about it, and also to the Commissioner of Police.' I asked him the purport of the wire, and he said, 'I just heard it going through, but I gathered that two girls and a man were murdered.' I then asked him when a train would go up, and he said, 'You have missed the train. There will be no train up now till later on in the evening.' I asked him if he would lend me a bicycle to go up by the railway, and he said he would, but he advised me not to go, as the Liverpool Range is rather steep. Eventually I got a police horse and rode to Gatton."

"How far is that?"

"I should say close on thirty miles. I had my little boy of three years old with me, and I left him at the police station. A Mr George Baines, who knew the country well, accompanied me. Sergeant Arrell makes a mistake with reference to the time I arrived at Gatton. We went the back track over the range and missed our way, so that we did not get to Gatton till about half-past seven o'clock in the evening. I had never been at Gatton before, and I rode straight down to the police station and saw Sergeant Arrell. I then questioned him with reference to the murder, and I asked him if the doctor was there. He said, 'Yes, Sir, he is just going away by the train.' I said, 'Come on to the station with me and we will see the doctor, and you can tell me all about it as we are going.' He gave me the heads in a short time, and what he had heard about the murder. I met Doctor Von Lossberg at the station. I think I was introduced to him by Mr Baines. I asked him if he had performed the post-mortem examination, and he replied, 'Yes.' I said, 'What was the result, doctor?' He informed me that the heads of the girls were literally smashed in, and the occipital bone was broken. I said to him, 'Were the girls ravished?' and he said, 'Undoubtedly they were. The elder girl fought fiercely, as she was covered with scratches.' So, I said to him, 'Have you got any of the semen, doctor?' and he said, 'What is the good of my getting the semen, the clothes are literally covered with it?' Just to show you how very short the conversation was, I may mention that there was one train in waiting for the other train to pass, and by the time I had got to this stage, the other train came in, and he got into the train and went away."[24]

Before Galbraith arrived at the hotel, going against the instructions given by Von Lossberg, Caroline Lee Eames and Elizabeth Selby removed the clothing and washed and dressed the bodies in their shrouds, ready for burial.[24,25,26]

With respect to semen found on the clothing of Michael, Norah and Ellen, as alluded to before, the clothing was examined by Doctor Orr, the findings of which were outlined in his report of March 1, 1899, as follows:

- **Exhibit "A"** No. 7 and No. 3 [Norah's flannelette singlet and drawers]. Two pieces removed from each. Was successful in satisfying myself as to the presence of semen in the first pieces removed from each on 8th January 1899. An examination of the second pieces removed from each allowed me to discover the presence of spermatozoa, which is proof positive of the presence of semen in the stains;
- **Exhibit "B"** No. 5 [Ellen's cotton chemise]. One piece removed; presence of spermatozoa – semen in stain;
- **Exhibit "B"** No. 6 [Ellen's drawers]. Two pieces removed; spermatozoa – semen in stain;
- **Exhibit "C"** No. 4 [Michael's shirt]. Two pieces removed presenting stains. (1) Hemin crystals; blood in stain of one. (2) Spermatozoa – semen in stain of the other; and

- **Exhibit "C"** No. 1 [Michael's trousers]. Inside on left side of fly was a milky white stain. Examination showed spermatozoa – semen in stain. Scraping from inside of left leg of trousers where peculiar mark of trousers is to be seen. Hemin crystals found; blood in stain.[25]

Continuing with the questioning of Galbraith, "You heard what Doctor Von Lossberg says," said Noel to Galbraith, "that on the 28th of December, he filled in his form in the police magistrate's office in Ipswich, on the 27th, rather, how did you get the order for burial, and from whom did you get it?"

"I got no order for burial as far as I can remember. I was not present at the post-mortem the doctor held. When I saw the doctor at the railway station, he informed me he had completed the post-mortem. Therefore, I did not bother any more about it."

"Who gave the order for burial?"

"Mr Wiggins, the Justice of the Peace."

"Who got the order?"

"Sergeant Arrell would have got the order from him."

Unmack said to Galbraith, "What is the date of it?"

"I do not know," admitted Galbraith, who added, "I will look and see."

"It is," confirmed Noel, "the 27th?"

"Yes," agreed Galbraith.

"That is only the certificate of burial," declared Noel, who added, "We will ask Sergeant Arrell."[26]

"Who," said Noel to Arrell, who was present, "got it?"

Arrell replied, "The undertaker."

"Did you see it?"

"Yes."

"Who asked for it?"

"I believe it was the undertaker."

"He would not bury," declared Galbraith, "without it."[26]

"How did you," said Noel to Clement Batstone Wiggins, a Justice of the Peace, "come to give the order for burial?"

"The bodies had been there 40 hours when I gave the order for burial, and I was under the impression the post-mortem was finished. Doctor Von Lossberg had not led us to believe any other way, and never did. He took evidently no steps to complete the post-mortem up till that time."

"When," said Unmack to Wiggins, "did you give the order for burial?"

"About two o'clock, on the 28th."

"Without any certificate," said Noel to Wiggins, "as to the cause of death?"

"Well, of course, it was the first case I had ever been on, of the sort, and I did not know, what was the proper procedure, but I was under the impression the post-mortem examination had been concluded that evening."

"Who gave you that impression?"

"Doctor Von Lossberg."

"Did you not know, as a Justice of the Peace, that you had no right to give an order for burial until you got the actual certificate as to the cause of death?"

"I was placed in a very awkward position. I did not know what to do. The bodies had been out in the sun for about 12 hours. They had lain there for about 40 hours. What was to be done? They could not be left in the hotel. It was an impossibility."

"And you took on yourself a responsibility, you see, which is reacting. Doctor Von Lossberg distinctly says he did not give a certificate of the cause of death to you?"

"I expected he would do that in Ipswich. In fact, I do not think Doctor Von Lossberg knew what he had come out to do at all. I do not think he had the certificates with him to give."

"It is certainly very mixed up," concluded Noel, who added, "He certainly took no steps to complete the examination."[26]

From the beginning, the investigation into the Gatton murders was *very mixed up*, but that is not what Urquhart meant when he wrote, "We have failed because from the very outset, we had no chance of success."[1]

Thomas Bailey Carpenter residing 6 miles from Gatton, working at Gatton at present. I have been into Gatton every day for last month. I know Mrs Selby she lives in Gatton she washed the bodies of the Murphies. Mrs Hames assisted her. Mrs Selby told me on the day of the funeral when I was coming back at her house she said I laid out the bodies and the bodies were terrible. Mrs Selby said that Mrs Murphy was there when I laid out bodies, and she (Mrs Murphy) said "My cook, my washerwoman and my all is gone, will I reveal it, or will I leave it to the Lord. I then said to Mrs Selby, Mrs Murphy must know something about it. Mrs Selby little girl was at the window but I don't know if she heard. Thomas Bailey

Thomas Bailey's statement dated December 31, 1898
(Courtesy of the Queensland Government (Queensland Police Service))

> Oct 31st
>
> William Miller I live with my parents my age is 20. My Father made two of the coffins for the Murphys. On Tuesday 27th inst at 12.30 p.m. I helped to take the coffins down to Gilberts Hotel. Mr Murphy, sen! Mr Gilbert, Mr Taylor were there on the verandah of Gilberts Hotel. Mr Murphy & Gilbert were 2 verandah post away from me. Gilbert said to Murphy have you any idea who did the deed. Mr Murphy said I could go straight to them: or say who it was. I am not sure which remark it was, but it was one of them. Gilbert said are you not afraid to say that, and Murphy said. No. ~~When that was~~

William Miller's statement dated December 31, 1898, page 1
(Courtesy of the Queensland Government (Queensland Police Service))

said Taylor came up to them and they all talked together. And I think while Taylor was there, Murphy said I would sooner have my children, then have any more lives lost over the affair. As soon as I got home I told my Father. I thought Murphy had a little drink taken but not drunk.

W. Miller

What my son has stated in the within paper, is word for word what he told me, when we were driving home. I believe my son is speaking the truth

W. J. Miller
1-1-99

William Miller's statement dated December 31, 1898, page 2
(Courtesy of the Queensland Government (Queensland Police Service))

Jack the Ripper

Sliprails to Moran's paddock at Gatton
(Courtesy of the Queensland State Archives)

Crime Scene in Moran's paddock at Gatton
(**L-R**) Constable Daniel (Dan) Murphy, Paddy Perkins and Colquhan
(Courtesy of the Queensland Police Museum)

8

DON'T ARREST JACK!

Many *mistakes* and *blunders* were made by Arrell, and the failure of Von Lossberg to complete the post-mortem examinations was *inexcusable*, but behind the scene was an even greater threat to a successful investigation into the Gatton murders. Others can go on believing that the police force reacted slowly to information received and incompetently misplaced or failed to open telegrams promptly. What happened had everything to do with the *Defence of the Realm*, in my opinion, having in mind that Lord Lamington, the father of Queen Victoria's godson, Victor Alexander Brisbane William Cochrane-Baillie, was located not far away from the goings-on at Gatton.

December 28, 1898 – at 7.15 am, Urquhart and Toomey left Brisbane to take part in the investigation at Gatton. There was a train at midnight, but Urquhart delayed his departure until the following morning.[1]

One assumes the delayed was caused by Urquhart being briefed by Home Secretary Foxton that Thomas Day was not to be arrested, and that Urquhart did not, at first, include Toomey in the *conspiracy*.

If he had been involved from the beginning, Toomey would not have included *Clarke's butcher* in the first statement taken from John Carroll. Removing those words from the second statement identifies that Toomey became involved in the *cover-up* between December 31, 1898, and January 11, 1899.

At 11.30 am, during the funeral service, Father Daniel Walsh declared that what was done to Michael, Norah and Ellen was *the most atrocious outrage ever perpetrated in Australia*.[2,3]

Michael and Ellen *were buried side by side*, whereas Norah's grave was *about eight feet away*.[2]

Once again, it is obvious to me, and so too should it be for you, that Norah was the intended victim, and that Michael and Ellen were in the wrong place at the wrong time.

Threatened with excommunication if he went public with the confession, as alluded to before, rather than appeal to others to come forward and reveal the identity of the perpetrators, what Father Walsh no doubt wanted to say was that *a secret entrusted to him under the seal of the confessional, which, if revealed, might have thrown light upon the crime.*[4]

Walsh did not go public with Day's confession. He, however, suffered a mental breakdown and went back to his native Ireland where he recovered, returning afterwards to Gatton where he is buried in the same cemetery as the Murphy siblings.[5,6]

Around 2 pm, after the sighting at Laidley by Lizzie Labinsky, Burgess was observed again in company of Miller on the Toowoomba Road at Postman's Ridge, west from Helidon.[7]

December 29, 1898 – during the night, three Aboriginal trackers dispatched from Fraser Island by Archibald Meston, the Southern Protector of Aboriginals in Queensland, arrived at Gatton to assist in the search for evidence.[8]

One was known as Barney, who, along with Thomas Orten Irvine (Tom) King and his brother, Nathaniel Irvine (Nat) King, and other trackers from Queensland, participated in the 1880 capture of Edward (Ned) Kelly and his gang at Glenrowan in Victoria.[9]

That being a fact was known by the ex-Superintendent, Commissioner Sadleir, who will be found along with Barney in the photograph at the end of this Chapter.

At the Royal Commission, "When did you," said Noel to Meston, "go to the scene?"

"On Friday," replied Meston, which was the day after the trackers arrived at Gatton from Fraser Island.

"Three days and a half, roughly," said Noel to Meston, "had elapsed?"

"Yes."

"Did you put those boys on to try and trace tracks?"

"No, I had nothing to do with the trackers beyond sending them to the Commissioner. I took one of the boys out with me to the scene."

"For your own guidance?"

"Yes."

"Those you sent," said Sadleir to Meston, "were there before you?"

"Yes, the day before."

"Did this boy," said Noel to Meston, "point out anything to you?"

"Yes, the boys all had a very decided theory of their own about who committed the murder and how it was done."

"Did they state that they found any tracks?"

"Yes."

"All three?"

"Two of them, one of the Fraser Island men and a boy from Crow's Nest named Norman (the latter being responsible, as alluded to before, for tracking Richard Burgess to Ballandean Creek after the Leyburn outrage)."

"What did they tell you, and did you convey that information to any member of the police or officer of police?"

"I understood the information given to me by the trackers of course would be given to the officers of police. I had nothing to do with them. I did not interfere with them in any way. It was merely for my own information that I took the boy out, because I had a very decided opinion of my own."

"We want to see whether the police refused to do anything after getting information of any value. Theory is of no particular value unless based on some facts. Did you yourself see any tracks about the scene?"

"One track, which was quite distinct, because it was outside the trodden area."

"Track of what?"

"Track of a horse."

"There were, horses running in the paddock?"

"This was one particular track the boys knew of which had not been interfered with. It was not trodden over at all. It was away, it was back on the ridge, it went from the rails round to the scene of the murder, and round the ridge."

Sadleir said to Meston, "Round the ridge?"

"To the left. As you go on the cart track to the scene, this track was away to the left, round the ridge."

"Looking towards Clark's place?"

"Clark's place," said Garvin to Meston, "is the other way."[8]

One assumes that this track was made by the horse ridden by Walter Albert Cook, who might have entered through the loose rail at the back of Moran's paddock.

"Did you convey any information to Inspector Urquhart," said Noel to Meston, "with regard to what you had seen and what the trackers had told you?"

"I told Inspector Urquhart on Saturday who I thought committed the murder, and how I thought it was done, and also called his attention to several significant facts in connection with it, and I told him before leaving, 'If you go outside that you will be wasting valuable time and throwing cruel suspicion upon innocent people, and find yourself in a worse position than you were in at the starting point'."[8]

Not included in the *cover-up*, Meston became involved in a personality clash that played right into the hands of Urquhart.

"Did you ever," said Noel to Meston, "put anything in writing?"

"I did. On my return to Brisbane I wrote my belief as to how the whole thing occurred, and got it typewritten, and showed it to the Home Secretary, who alone had the right to see it from me and also to the Commissioner of Police. Outside of that I am not responsible for any statement. I was credited by the public with many statements I had nothing to do with."

"Inspector Urquhart says you stated to him, as you were leaving, something to this effect, that you were completely baffled?"

"That is utterly untrue. I never had a shadow of a doubt from the start up to the present time. Mr Urquhart makes some statements in his evidence which are utterly untrue. He says, in answer to question

13870, that I was there a week afterwards. I was there four days afterwards. He was asked whether I gave him any information, and he said, 'No, I heard that he announced on the railway platform that he could solve the mystery in twenty-four hours.' I did nothing of the kind. I am not in the habit of talking on a railway platform on a subject of that kind in that way."

Sadleir said to Meston, "Or anywhere else?"

"No, all I stated is in my written statement, which I gave to the Home Secretary. He was asked if he thought it would be possible for a tracker to pick up tracks a week after an occurrence, and he said, 'Such a suggestion would be ridiculous.' One of the finest pieces of tracking ever done in Queensland was where the tracks were picked up three weeks afterwards. That was out west from Charters Towers."

"That might be under different circumstances?"

"The tracks all around the bodies would be effectually smothered on the day the crowd went out, but there were tracks outside of those. He says, 'The trackers sent up were of a very inferior type'."

"He is speaking of the first, possibly?"

"The three trackers I sent were three picked men out of fifty, and one was the best of those that went after the Kellys in Victoria, and one of Sergeant King's favourite men. I was not likely to send any but good men."

"Who is the tracker that was in Victoria?"

"Wooranalie, or Barney, as he is known amongst white men. He is a specially good tracker, and the other two were excellent boys and able to track anything anywhere if they got a fair chance and were properly worked. I pointed out to Urquhart that he was starting in a wrong direction altogether. The blunders he made seemed to me to be so stupid as to amount to infatuation. He had good men, excellent men, with him, but unwise instructions were given. Take the Queensland Police Force as a body, you will not find a better force in the world."

"You allege blunders generally," said Noel to Meston. "Can you give one instance of a blunder?"

"He did not do one wise thing from start to finish. When I went there on the Friday, I asked him where was so-and-so, and so-and-so, at the time of the murders, and he said they had all proved alibis. He took their statements without hesitation and took no action on them. He was not even acquainted with human bloodstains. He did not even know that blood dries from the edge to the centre, in a concave form."

"You spoke about a solitary track," said Garvin to Meston. "Was that a horse track?"

"Yes."

"On the ridge on the right-hand side from Clarke's?"

"No, on the left side."

"It was near Clarke's fence?"

"On the Gatton side of the track, going out. The [buggy] tracks skirted round on the right-hand side."

"How far," said Sadleir to Meston, "did you follow the tracks?"

"Only from the centre, just about the centre."

"Did you follow them from the scene of the murder?"

"You could not follow them from the bodies."

"How did you know," said Noel to Meston, "that Urquhart did not do that?"

"I don't know."

"We want information," reiterated Noel, "regarding the efforts of the police in this matter."

"I want to know," said Sadleir to Meston, "what was the theory of your boys?"

"Four of the boys were unanimous in their theory."

"What was their theory?"

"That would be hardly fair to make public. The boys were unanimous about one man."

"Tell us how their theory led to one man?"

"Well, it involves others."[8]

The following year, a young man died at Sydney from a self-inflicted gunshot wound to the head, which will be expanded upon late.

Same as what happened at the Royal Commission, the names of several people associated with the Gatton murders provided in a note left behind by the young man were withheld from the public on instructions of City Coroner Woore, who, it will be remembered, conducted the inquests into the deaths of Annie Morrison and Emma Harrison.

The suicide note, which was passed on from New South Wales to the authorities in Queensland could not be found, unfortunately, in the Gatton murder files at the Queensland State Archives.

"Well, I won't press you," said Sadleir to Meston. "You indicated that theory to the Minister?"

"Yes. The Minister has it, and I have it."

"What action did the Minister take?"

"It was only given to the Minister for his own information."

"It was," said Noel to Meston, "given to the Commissioner, too?"

"Yes."

"What action," said Sadleir to Meston, "was taken?"

"No action. He did not agree with the theory at the time."

"The Minister, the Commissioner, and Mr Urquhart disregarded your theory?"

"Well, they did not act on it. The Commissioner was in doubt as to what action should be taken, but he was very anxious to arrive at the truth."

"And yet he disregarded your theory?"

"Yes, he said there was not sufficient evidence to take action on."

"You are not helping us," said Sadleir to Meston, "with this evidence."

"We can," suggested Noel, "see his report."

"I will place my report at your disposal," responded Meston. "I may say that the police did all they could. Urquhart's mistake is the whole mistake."

"There is no reason for saying that," said Sadleir to Meston, "and we have no evidence in support of that."

"Did the trackers tell you," said Garvin to Meston, "they had examined the tracks of a hoof?"

"Yes."

"What was the result of that examination?"

"Two of the boys said they knew the horse."

"Did they tell you whereabouts in the paddock they saw the tracks?"

"Yes, coming down from the scene, near a waterhole, and going back on to the road again from the gates."

"That is contrary," said Sadleir to Meston, "to what you told us just now?"

"No, I spoke about a different track."

"You did not say," said Noel to Meston, "anything about another track."

"There was a second track."[8]

One assumes, as alluded to before, that the first track mentioned by Meston was made by the horse ridden by Walter Albert Cook, and the second, in my opinion, was from a horse ridden by Burgess, who double-banked Day out through the sliprails along the road to Clarke's butchery.

It will be remembered that Burgess told Constable Gillies at the Bunya Mountains that he was camped at the culvert and *heard a horse gallop furiously along the road from the direction of Gatton.*

One assumes that Burgess told Gillies the truth, and that the horseman was Cook.

"Did you ask the trackers," said Garvin to Meston, "if they could trace that track of the hoofs of a horse any distance?"

"No, that track was lost on the road."

"You spoke of a waterhole [location can be found in the map on page 1]?"

"Yes, that was between the road and the scene of the murder."

"Did you find any tracks there?"

"No."

"Did you ask them if they looked round outside the fence to see if they could see any tracks there?"

"They looked all round."

"All this," said Noel to Meston, "is in your report, is it?"

"Not about the tracks."

"That is the most important part of it. If you gave no information to the police, how can you blame the police?"

"This information the police should have had from the trackers. I was not acting as a medium of communication between the trackers and the police. The boys simply volunteered the information to me on account of my knowing them."

"We are not inquiring into who committed the murder, except incidentally while inquiring into certain facts?"

"The theory of the murder, of course, you will get in my report."

"At any rate, your theory was not acted upon?"

"No, it is a difficult theory to act upon, except in one particular direction, which can be acted upon now just as easily as then."[8]

This evidence given by Meston at the Royal Commission on October 17, 1899, combined with other incriminating evidence at the inquiry, should have resulted in a warrant being taken out for the arrest of Thomas Day, in my opinion, same as what was done by Parry-Okeden with respect to Carus-Wilson.

If it was good enough to arrest Carus-Wilson and bring him back to Queensland from Albany, Western Australia, the same also should have been done with respect to Day.

Instead of that happening, rather than arrest Day and Chaston as deserters from the Queensland Permanent Artillery, police in other colonies were acting at the time on a request from Parry-Okeden to make inquiries *of such a nature as not to alarm* Day and Chaston, advising Parry-Okeden immediately by *wire* if they were located.

"Is there anything else," said Noel to Meston, "you want to say?"

"I think not. Inspector Urquhart said that the trackers came from Deebing Creek. There were two aboriginals came from Deebing Creek, but they certainly were not trackers. He seems to have included the whole of the trackers in one condemnation, which is most unfair to the boys. I had no intention of coming here, in fact, I was especially desirous of not being included in the examination at all, until my name was brought into it the other day, when I was absent in Rockhampton. Some of Inspector Urquhart's statements were not true, and it is only fair I should make an explanation. Any information the Commissioners wish to obtain privately, I shall be only too happy to afford them."

"Your report will give that?"

"I am very sensitive about anything being made public where people are concerned, and, however certain I may feel about it, there is always a doubt, and it is only fair they should have the benefit of it."

"Then," said Sadleir to Meston, "there is some doubt?"

"I have not the slightest doubt in my own mind. I never had from the beginning. I may say, in regard to what I said previously about the tracks, that the track going down on the triangle was the same as the track on the ridge to the left. I was thinking of another track when I made my previous statement."[8]

Without identifying them as such, at the Royal Commission, Meston named three of the conspirators – Foxton, Parry-Okeden and Urquhart, who were involved in the *cover-up* that protected Thomas Day from arrest for the Gatton murders.

December 30, 1898 – adding credence to the later evidence given by Meston, Toomey questioned Day on this date and took possession of a bloodstained jumper. Clarke confirmed that no *spots* of blood were on the jumper when he last saw Day wearing it on December 24, 1898, and that there was no work at the butchery on Christmas Day and Boxing Day. Instead of having it expertly examined, as alluded to before, Toomey returned it to Day.[10]

Don't Arrest Jack!

December 31, 1898 – it was on this date that John Carroll gave his first statement to the effect that he believed the man at the sliprails was *Clarke's butcher*.[11]

On the same day, Frank Burns, who was with Burgess on St Helena Island, was seen, allegedly, in company of Burgess and Miller at Perseverance, north-east from Murphy's Creek.[12]

At the Royal Commission, when Noel asked Galbraith as to when he first visited the crime scene, "It was a little before six," replied Galbraith.

Sadleir queried, "On the morning of the 28th?"

"On the morning of the 28th, I set two trackers to work under Acting Sergeant Murphy. They got to work. I let him work the trackers. I then examined the spot."

"When," said Unmack to Galbraith, "did they get there?"

"They got there sometime early in the morning, about one or two o'clock."

"On the morning of the?"

"Twenty-eighth."

"They were there before you went out at six o'clock?"

"Yes. I examined the spot, and noticed certain things, and all that sort of thing. Then I ran the gully down to a fence and ran the waterholes down myself, taking care, of course, naturally, that I did not go over any ground that would obliterate tracks. I may mention that when I came to the paddock early in the morning I stopped and examined the rails and the approaches into the paddock and made a fairly minute examination of about seven to ten minutes there. All traces of any given track were obliterated, that is, there had been, in my opinion, scores of horses over the tracks. I certainly did notice wheel tracks. On the route where McNeil and Sergeant Arrell had followed down to the scene of the murder there was a wheel track quite perceptible, the wheel track of a buggy quite perceptible. It was a specially beaten track to the beaten track. Another thing that I noticed at the scene of the murder was that the ground was in no wise disturbed. It was a thing which struck me forcibly. I then went right round the chains of waterholes and down to the culvert. You know the culvert. I then from there went back to Gatton and went into Gilbert's backyard and examined certain spots in the backyard where I had water that had been thrown out covered over. Afterwards I came out, and, going down the main street from Gilbert's backyard towards Gall's Hotel, it was I first met young Murphy. I spoke to him and questioned him in reference to certain things he mentioned about names and all that sort of thing. I also questioned him and let him talk in reference to the matter. I was actually questioning him as to certain family business, how long his married sister had been sick. I understood she had been paralysed. I also questioned him with reference to certain things about a brother-in-law, and how long he had been in the district, and questions like that. I went into considerable detail with him about it."

"What time," said Sadleir to Galbraith, "was this?"

"I really cannot say, I am giving the events as they consecutively come. I did not take much notice of the time I went out to the paddock about six."

"Nobody had arrived from Brisbane up till this time?"

"No. I can tell you when they arrived from Brisbane."

"Yes, go on?"

"I had also sent Covell, I think it was Covell, towards Tent Hill to make inquiries. I was a great stranger to the locality, I did not know it. After I had this long talk with Murphy, I went and had my breakfast. It was late, I remember. Breakfast was cleared away at the hotel. I then went down and forwarded a long wire to Inspector Stuart."

"What time," said Unmack to Galbraith, "was that?"

"It would be after nine."

"On the 28th?"

"On the 28th. I sent a long wire to Inspector Stuart. As I was writing the wire Inspector Urquhart came into the office. He had arrived by the ten o'clock train at Gatton, and when he came into the office, I abruptly ceased my wire in which I would have given more information had he not arrived."

"You did not send that wire?"

"Oh, yes, I sent the wire, but I would probably have added something to it if Mr Urquhart had not arrived. I then informed Mr Urquhart of everything I had done and of the results of my investigations."[13]

One does not suspect that Galbraith was involved in the *conspiracy*, but it is obvious that he was aware Urquhart had been sent to Gatton to *cover-up* the involvement of Day in the murders, prompting Garvin to say to Galbraith, "When did you first hear about Day?"

"I think it was the day of my arrival, or the day after, that I heard about the man Day at Clarke's butcher's shop."

"That he was the man the boy Carroll saw there?"

"Carroll never told me that he saw Day there," denied Galbraith, who added, "It was with the greatest difficulty that we could get any person to say anything like that. I only wish that he had said so in a way."[13]

This fear spoken about by Galbraith was extraordinary, to say the least, suggesting that Day was not an ordinary person, as alluded to by Urquhart and Toomey at the Royal Commission, and that some very powerful people did whatever they could to protect Day from arrest for the murders he committed in England and Australia.

Was he of Royal blood, or did he know something extremely incriminating about a member of the Royal family?

After placing Urquhart in overall command, Parry-Okeden dispatched Galbraith and others to locations outside Gatton to ensure that police with good intentions did not thwart the efforts to protect Day, which was noticed apparently by Noel, who said to Galbraith, "When did you take up your quarters at Tent Hill?"

"I could not say exactly."

"When," said Dickson to Galbraith "did you leave Gatton?"

"On the 7th or the 8th January."[13]

Galbraith was one of many sidelined during the investigation, another being Christie, who said to Toomey at the Royal Commission,

"I shall bring another constable tomorrow to show that you tried to bring off that man."[14]

When he used the words "bring off," Christie, in effect, alleged that Urquhart and Toomey protected Thomas Day from arrest for the Gatton murders.

During the questioning of Arrell, "Were you of the same opinion as Christie," said Dickson to Arrell, "that there was only one man in it, and that was Day?"

"I have already stated in my evidence that I consider one man could do it."

"Were you of opinion that there was only one man in it, and that man was Day?"

"I have had a strong opinion that Day had a hand in it, I will admit that."

"And that there was only one man in it?"

"One man could do it, but I would not like to say there was only one man in it."

"Can you point to any defects in the police inquiries," said Sadleir to Arrell, "as regards Day being the murderer?"

"Well, nothing further than that he might have been detained while inquiries were made as to the statements he made. I do not know that there is as much evidence as would convict the man at any time. I do not think there is."

"Suppose he had been telling lies, and that was discovered, that would not convict him?"

"It would be evidence against him so far."

"Is it a fact," said Dickson to Arrell, "that you were as frightened as Christie of Mr Urquhart?"

"I am not frightened of Mr Urquhart now in the least."

"Did you state to Christie, 'I have a good mind to chuck my uniform over the fence the way Urquhart treated me, just like a blackfellow'?"

"I believe I did make use of those words. I was angry at the time."

"Were you frightened to say any more about Day to Inspector Urquhart?"

"I had a certain amount of fear. I made up my mind not to say any more about Day to him, because I considered after he cautioned me, it would be an act of insubordination. Of course, when Mr Urquhart told me he had cleared up the man, I thought it was all right."

"You were serving under my orders," said Urquhart to Arrell, "all the time I was at Gatton, were you not?"

"Yes."

"For a period of nearly seven months, was it not?"

"About that time, I should think."

"Had you anything to complain of in my treatment of you or of any of the other men?"

"I was away a good part of the time."

"But when you were there, did I ever treat you unreasonably or harshly?"

"I cannot say that you did with the exception of that once."[15]

When he appeared at the Royal Commission, "What do you," said Noel to Andrew Stevenson Smith, a storekeeper and baker at Gatton, "want to tell us?"

"Just a few words in reference to this man Day. On the morning of the murder, this man came into my store and bought a razor. A few hours afterwards, he came back shaved and in clean clothes, and he paid a quarter's subscription to the School of Arts, which my daughter was looking after. Within two or three days after this, I was speaking to Carroll in reference to the man he saw at the sliprails. I said, 'John, who did you take the man to be?' and he said it was Clarke's man. Of course, I told detectives Toomey and Head, and Sergeant Arrell."

"Did they take action?"

"I expect so. I have no complaint to make against them."

"The police knew about it?"

"Yes."[16]

When Garvin suggested to Urquhart, words to the effect, that he protected Thomas Day from arrest for the murders, "Oh, no. I think I can make that clear to you," replied Urquhart. "What you apparently wish me to say is that but for Burgess, I would have pursued Day, but I tell you that I would not have pursued him."

"Then, I want you to tell us why you gave up following Day between the date the bodies were discovered and the 24th January?"

"Because there was nothing to follow, there had been no suspicious circumstances against Day."

"Had he not blood," said Noel to Urquhart, "on his arm?"

"Yes, he was a butcher, and had been carrying meat on his arm. Mr Clarke told us that."

"What sort of a stain was it?"

"It was a smudge on the sleeve."

"Do you know whether the persons who identified Burgess," said Garvin to Urquhart, "had seen Day, whether they were shown Day?"

"I do not know. I do not think they were."

"Did anybody suggest to you," said Noel to Urquhart, "that you should have the blood on Day's sleeve analysed?"

"No."

"And you did not think of it yourself?"

"No, I did not, and I do not think it would have been of any use if we had had it analysed."

"Why?"

"It would simply have been pronounced to have been mammalian blood."

"But analytical chemists can go further than that?"

"They can't here."

"I am told that there are several chemists here competent to do so?"

"They won't swear absolutely."

"But they will say probably?"

"But it can be done absolutely in some places."

"Did it not strike you as a reasonable inquiry to take possession of the man's coat and have it analysed?"

"No."

"His employer says now that he boiled his coat. I do not know whether he told you that at the time?"

"He did not. I have the statement here taken by Acting Sergeant Toomey, who interviewed Clarke. He was also supposed to have killed a sheep and burnt it on the top of his clothes, and several other little things. I might have arrested every butcher in the country and called him to account for blood on his clothes as reasonably as Day."[17]

Despite the evidence against Burgess being flimsy, Parry-Okeden sent a memorandum to Doctor Orr on January 16, 1899, which can be found at the end of this Chapter, instructing Orr to examine Burgess' clothing.[18]

"But there was a reason given," said Garvin to Urquhart, "why this man's clothes should have been microscopically examined?"

"What reason?"

"The mere fact that he was seen washing his clothes after he was spoken of as a suspect?"

"All these men wash their clothes occasionally."

"That is all very well, but in this case, it was a reason why his clothes should have been taken possession of?"

"I do not think the washing of the clothes was mentioned till long, long afterwards."

"Of course, it would be a different thing if you did not hear that till long afterwards?"

"It was never mentioned till it was mentioned by Sergeant Arrell about two months afterwards. That was the first I heard of it."[17]

At the Royal Commission, "Were you stationed at Gatton," said Noel to Sergeant Walter Stuart King, "at the time of these murders?"

"No."

"Were you sent out there?"

"Yes."

"When?"

"On the 28th – on the morning of the 28th."

"Who was there then? What other police officers?"

"Sub-Inspector Galbraith and Sergeant Arrell."

"And I presume you were told off for duty?"

"Yes."

"What were you told to do, shortly, not the details? Were you told to do any specific duty, or were you told to make general inquiries?"

"General inquiries in the town."

"And try to find out who might be the perpetrators?"

"Yes."

"And you made inquiries?"

"I did."

"Did you come to any conclusion or suspect anyone after your inquiries, or any person or persons?"

"I did."

"Do you object to give the names of those you suspected or the name?"

"Yes."

"You do object?"

"I do not see it will do any good to make it public."

"Did you make any report to your superior officer," said Noel to King, "as to any person or persons you suspected?"

"I did verbally."

"What officer?"

"Well, Sub-Inspector Galbraith and Inspector Urquhart."

"I will put a direct question? Did you give any information with regard to the man Day?"

"No."

"None?"

"None. I never heard of Day at the time."

"Or at any time afterwards?"

"No."

"Did you make any report in writing," said Garvin to King, "to your officer?"

"No, I did not."

"Have you," said Sadleir to King, "any statement to make?"

"No. I have no statement to make."

"We understood you wished to make a statement," said Noel to King, "or we should not have sent for you."

Before King had time to answer, "Were you removed," said Garvin, "from that district?"

"Yes."

"After?"

"Some four years ago."

"But on the occasion, you went out on this special business, how long did you remain there?"

"At Gatton?"

"Yes?"

"Well, I was there for some time."

"Several days?"

"Several days, not in the town, outside."

"Making inquiries in connection with these murders?"

"I did not apply to come here to make a statement."

"Have you anything to say?"

"No."[8]

One did not uncover evidence that King suffered under Urquhart at Gatton, same as what happened to Christie and Arrell, it is obvious, however, that he was unhappy with the *cover-up* and wanted to say something but decided at the last moment not to do so.

Often, it was better in those times to say as little as possible out of a fear that you, or those associated with you, might suffer at the hands of the unscrupulous and devious powers-to-be, King being a prime example.

Apart from serving for many years at Gatton, King was a member of the Gatton Masonic Lodge as well as *a grandson of the late Major W. S. King, nephew of the Reverend W. S. King, and cousin of Sir William Irvine, Chief Justice of Victoria.*[19]

Prior to the bodies being removed from Moran's paddock to the Brian Boru Hotel, John Carroll told William McNeil that he believed the man he saw at the sliprails was *Clarke's butcher*.

One assumes McNeil would have said something in that regard to Daniel and Mary Murphy, who, out of a fear that others might lose their lives if they did so, made it clear to others at the hotel that they would not say anything about Day or the reason why their children were murdered.

Many obviously knew Thomas Day, alias *Jack the Ripper*, but feared the consequences if they said anything incriminating about him to the authorities.

Don't Arrest Jack!

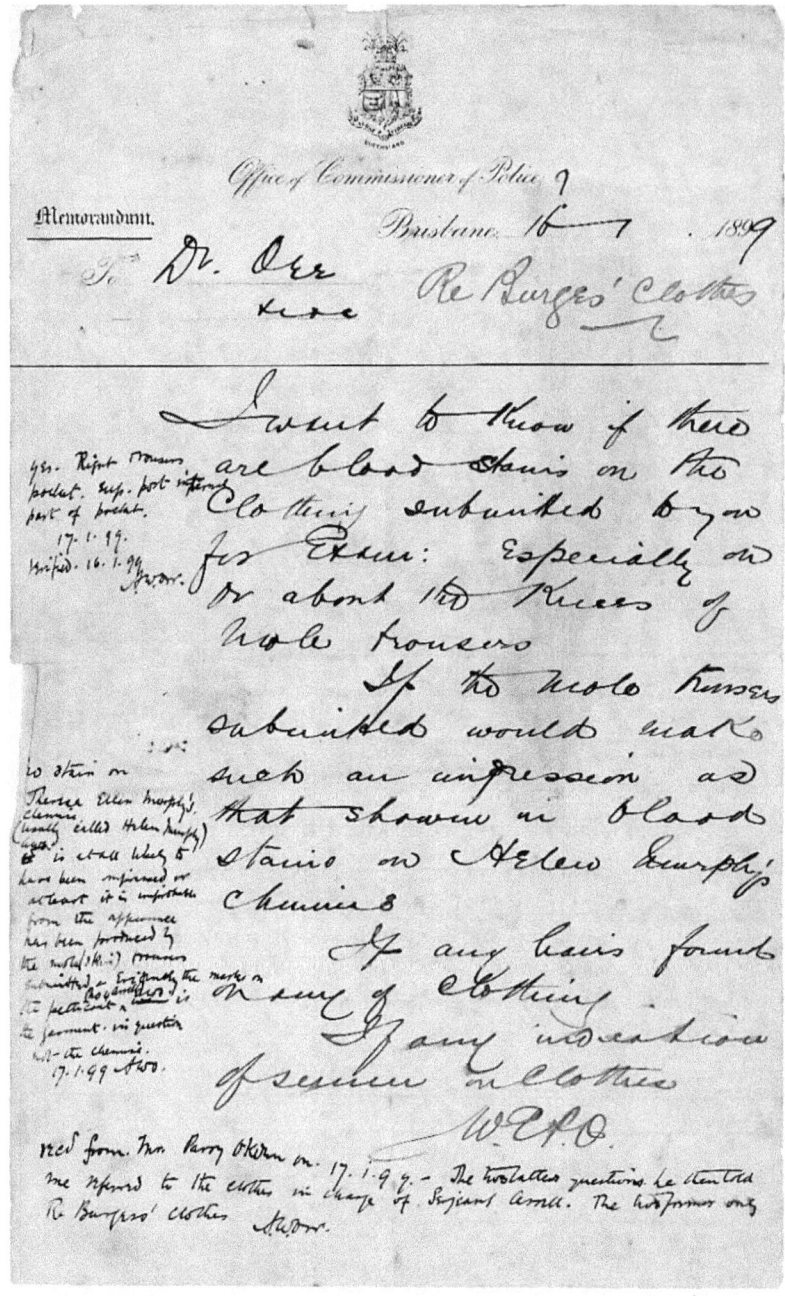

Parry-Okeden's memorandum dated January 16, 1899

(Courtesy of the Queensland Government (Queensland Police Service))

Queensland Native Police contingent, Kelly Gang

(**L-R**) Senior Constable Tom King, Sub-Inspector Stanhope O'Connor (seated), Troopers Jimmy and Barney (sitting on the fence), Trooper Hero (standing between Jimmy and Barney), Troopers Johnny and Jack (seated on the ground), Victorian Police Superintendent John Sadleir (arms folded), and Victorian Police Commissioner, Captain Frederick Charles Standish (far right)

(Courtesy of the Queensland Police Museum)

9

THE COVER-UP

The *cover-up* associated with the investigation into the Gatton murders, in fact, successfully concealed the wrongdoings of the Government and police force for 120 years. Discovery and decoding of historical documents, however, not only exposed the failure to secure and examine incriminating evidence, such as the bloodstained jumper belonging to Day, but also revealed how the authorities avoided arresting Day for the murders, involving authorities in another colony to keep Day and Burgess apart.

January 1, 1899 – Frank Burns was seen again, allegedly, in company of Burgess and Miller at Perseverance, Burgess making his way from there through the bush to the Bunya Mountains, north-east from Dalby.[1,2]

Chaston outlined in his statement dated February 8, 1899, which can be found at the end of the Introduction, that he was in Brisbane with Miller on this date.[3] It appears, however, that Chaston, then known by the surname of Cox, was working at the time with Day at Clarke's butchery.[4]

January 4, 1899 – Parry-Okeden sent the telegram from Gatton to Stuart, about the search for the whip used, in my opinion, to rape Norah and Ellen, also advising therein that Foxton was told that *Lewis*, who was Day, *cannot go strait*.[5]

The telegram confirms that on or before this date, the Government and police force in Queensland were protecting Day from arrest for the Gatton murders. This was suspected but not made known to Day, who alluded to that as being a fact in a suicide note he wrote the following year in Sydney.

Around daylight, a special train transporting a party consisting of Parry-Okeden, Warren-White, Von Lossberg and Doctor Charles James Hill-Wray, Government Medical Officer for the Brisbane district, arrived at Gatton.

Ensuring they did not excite curiosity, the party disembarked from the train on the outskirts of town and stealthily made their way to the cemetery whereupon Michael, Norah an Ellen's bodies were exhumed and examined.[6]

January 5, 1899 – in a written communication, as alluded to before, Parry-Okeden created a special district for the investigation into the Gatton murders, officially appointing Urquhart as the Officer in Charge.[7]

Frank Hillman went into Brown and Walsh's paddock at Oxley to collect gum for tanning purposes associated with his business at Indooroopilly.

Exploring the surroundings, Hillman's son found the carcass of a pony fully saddled and bridled, the saddlery being removed by Hillman who took it to the Indooroopilly police station where it was handed over to Constable Henry Bell.[8]

Thomas Day gave a week's notice to terminate his employment at Clarke's butchery.[9]

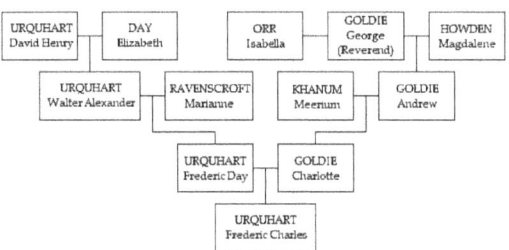

Day and Urquhart families

It might be coincidental, but in the above chart, it will be seen that Urquhart's great-great-grandmother on the paternal side of his family was formerly Elizabeth Day.

January 6, 1899 – the saddlery was identified by Frederick John (Fred) Hill, father of Alfred Stephen Hill, as being his property. Going with police to the paddock, Hill identified the carcass as being the piebald pony ridden by his son on December 10, 1898.[8]

Burgess allegedly made the statement to Constable Gillies at the Bunya Mountains that *the eldest Murphy girl,* who was Norah, *was a great flirt, and it was time she was put out of the road*, confirming that Norah was the intended victim.[2]

January 7, 1899 – upon Parry-Okeden's arrival at Gatton with Andrew Henry Barlow, who was the Acting Chief Secretary and member for Ipswich in the Legislative Assembly, Parry-Okeden requested Robert Hazlewood Lawson in the telegram, which can be found at the end of the Introduction, to examine the exhibits escorted by Arrell to the Police Depot.[10,11,12]

At the crime scene in Moran's paddock, Barlow hypocritically gave the assurance that no effort or expense would be spared by the Government to bring the offender or offenders to justice.[10]

Parry-Okeden, in effect, was given the authority to carry out a senseless and expensive operation outside of Gatton that *hoodwinked* some into believing everything was being done to bring those responsible for the murders to justice.

But for that shameful ruse, with their hands free to investigate, as should be expected, there is no doubt in my mind that Urquhart and Toomey would have arrested and successfully prosecuted Day for the Gatton murders.

This was confirmed 28 years later in an article published in *The Courier Mail* by Urquhart's good friend, Reginald Spencer Browne, who wrote:

> ... *if F. C. Urquhart had had his way, the story of the tragedy would have been made plain.*[13]

The body of Alfred Stephen Hill was found concealed under bushes, about 250 yards from where the carcass of the pony was discovered, confirming that Alfred had, in fact, been murdered.[14]

At the Royal Commission, during questioning of Christie about his suspicions concerning Day, "Why do you think this man," said Garvin to Christie, "was concerned in the Oxley murder?"

"Simply because I have learnt he arrived in Brisbane from New South Wales on the 6th of December, and the Oxley murder was committed on the 10th. Seeing he stopped a day in Brisbane, it would just leave him time to get into Oxley on the 10th, or the night of the

10th. He arrived at Gatton on the 14th and informed Mr Clarke, when he employed him on the road, that he was camped in the show-grounds."

"What would be his object in murdering this boy," said Garvin to Christie. "Did you come to any conclusion as to what his object was?"

"I did not say," clarified Christie, "he ever murdered the boy."

"How did you connect him with Oxley?"

"There is a swagman supposed to be passed by [Carus-Wilson] at Oxley on the 10th of December, and he was supposed to have handed him something. It was probably a revolver."

"You think [Carus-Wilson] handed the swagman something?"

"It might have been a revolver, as the cartridge corresponded both at Oxley and Gatton. Both cartridges corresponded with each other."[9]

Christie's evidence, which was accepted by those on the Royal Commission as being honest and reliable, identified that the same revolver was used in the Oxley and Gatton murders.

During questioning about a report Christie furnished, Noel said to Christie, "'You say you did not send that report in?"

Christie replied, "No, sir."

"Why?"

"I had my reasons for not sending it in."

"Did you show it to Inspector Urquhart?"

"No."

"Tell us your reasons," said Unmack to Christie, "for not sending it in?"

"On the 24th April last, me and Sergeant Arrell had a conversation with Detective Head. Head says, 'How is things now, Christie?' I said, 'In my opinion there is only one man in it, Clarke's man.' He said, 'What rot.' Sergeant Arrell says, 'Well, it looks very suspicious.' Next morning, I was sitting in the police office. Detective Head came in and said to Inspector Urquhart, 'I want to speak to you, sir.' Inspector Urquhart said, 'Very well,' and went out into the police yard with him. They had a conversation, and Head then went away. Inspector

The Cover-Up

Urquhart said to me, 'Where is Sergeant Arrell, Christie?' I said, 'He is inside, sir.' He said, 'Tell him I want him.' Sergeant Arrell came into the courthouse, and Inspector Urquhart said, 'You've got a lot to say about this man Day, Arrell. If I hear any more about this, out of this you go, out you go.' He said, 'The idea of you criticising the work of better men than yourself!' I had then just completed my report which I have just read, and I walked up the street, and a short while afterwards Inspector Urquhart followed me up the street. He said, 'Look here, Christie, I don't want you speaking about this man Day.' I said, 'I have simply made inquiries about him, sir. I spoke to Detective Head about him last night, and that is all I have been talking to about him. I do not see there is any harm in speaking to the detectives.' He said, 'Well, if I hear any more about this, Christie, I will make it hot for you if I get you talking about this man.' He said, 'You are a strange man. You have a lot of ideas in your head.' I said, 'Well, sir, I do not work on a one-man system. I work on several, and I consider that man is in it.' And I explained several points, which were in my report. He said, 'What rot, Christie, he is only a mere boy. He could not commit that crime. He is a beardless boy.' I said, 'If he is only a beardless boy, Bob King at Clarke's place told me he was thirty years old and weighed between 13 and 14 stone.' Inspector Urquhart said, 'Bob King is a damned liar if he told you such a thing.' I was afraid to send in my report through him threatening me."[9]

After dispatching Durham to Dalby to take charge of the case against Burgess, Parry-Okeden arranged for the headquarters to be relocated from the police barracks to the showgrounds where Urquhart was placed in overall command of the investigation.

Going along with what was said hypocritically by Barlow, about no effort or expense would be spared by the Government to bring the offender or offenders to justice, Parry-Okeden disgracefully deceived the public with an elaborate and expensive plan that included three sub-districts in the special district, appointing Galbraith to Tent Hill, Warren-White to Laidley, and Durham to Helidon. Sergeant Tom King with assistance of a constable and an Aboriginal tracker was given a roving commission.[10,15,16]

January 9, 1899 – Burgess was examined at the Dalby police station by Doctor Alexander Young-Fullerton, who found no scratches or bruises to connect Burgess with the Gatton murders.[15]

When Burgess appeared in the Dalby Police Court, Durham offered no evidence as the grounds for suspicion was based on the peculiar conduct of Burgess at the Bunya Mountains and what he said to Constable Gillies.[17]

Burgess was then taken into custody on a warrant for the theft of a saddle which, in effect, was a trumped-up charge, making it lawful for Burgess to be escorted to Toowoomba where he was confined in the lockup and kept apart from Day, which is exactly what was done several months later.[16]

Inspired by newspaper reports that Burgess had been arrested on a *trumped-up* charge, Austin McLaughlin of Pittsworth, south-west from Toowoomba, visited Gatton.

Convinced that Burgess was innocent, McLaughlin hired Joseph Vincent Herbert, a leading solicitor at Toowoomba, to defend the charge.[18]

January 9, 1899 – while the senseless and expensive operation was going on at Gatton, Carus-Wilson was arrested for *unnatural offences* committed on several boys at Ipswich when the steamer *Yarrawonga* arrived at Albany in Western Australia.[19,20]

If Carus-Wilson had escaped the Australian shores, it appears that the troublesome question of extradition between England and Australia would have prevented his return to Australia.[19,20]

January 10, 1899 – following an argument with Clarke at his butchery, Day and Chaston, alias Cox, left Gatton.[11]

Carus-Wilson appeared in court during the morning before the Resident Magistrate, John Arthur Wright, and was remanded in custody at Albany for seven days pending the arrival of police from Queensland.[19,20]

January 11, 1899 – the man seen at the sliprails being *Clarke's butcher*, as alluded to in the Introduction, was not included in a second statement taken from John Carroll.[21]

The Cover-Up

It will be remembered that Acting Sergeant Armitage, who was mentioned in Parry-Okeden's telegram dated April 13, 1899, which can be found at the end of the Introduction, obtained a warrant for the arrest of Claude on a charge of committing *buggery* with his father at Oxley on December 10, 1898.[22]

At the Royal Commission, "I would like to ask you a question with reference to [Carus-Wilson]," said Dickson to Parry-Okeden. "Is it a fact that [Carus-Wilson's] boy was arrested on a charge of sodomy at the time [Carus-Wilson] was arrested?"

"I believe it came out in evidence that he was arrested," replied Parry-Okeden, "but I do not know what for."

"Was he not arrested on a warrant?"

"I believe so."

"Who swore that information?"

"I could not tell you. I think it was Fahey, who gave the information. My instructions, of course, were that the boy was not to be arrested under any circumstances if possible."

"I understand this was a case of false swearing?"

"I do not know who laid the information."

"Do you know whether there were any grounds for laying it?"

"I have no idea, except the grounds that he was with the man, at the time he went away. Of course, when there was an information against [Carus-Wilson] for suspected murder, and he would have been in a position, possibly, to leave an important witness in another colony if there had been no means of bringing him back."

"But you do not justify laying a charge of that sort against him?"

"I do not know who laid the information."

"Would you approve of laying an information against a person," said Noel to Parry-Okeden, "about whom there could be no suspicion for the purpose, perhaps, of frightening him into making some confession or statement?"

When Parry-Okeden answered, "Certainly not," Dickson responded, "It is false swearing!"

"Do you not think it was an improper thing," said Noel to Parry-Okeden, "to lay an information against that crippled boy?"

"I do not know what the information was."

"Sodomy? Was that information laid against the boy?"

"Yes, so far as I understand the circumstances."

"The police evidently did that for the purpose of bringing him back, but I do not approve of it," declared Garvin. "They had power to bring him back without resorting to a charge of that sort. It was an improper thing to lay a charge of that kind against an unfortunate child."

"Besides he was only thirteen years of age, and the charge could not be legally laid against him," added Noel. "I do not know who the sapient magistrate was?"

"Some officer," queried Secretary James William Blair, "must have sworn the information?"

"It was tantamount," said Dickson, "to perjury!"

"I tried to get the information," declared Blair, "but I could not."

"I have no knowledge," protested Parry-Okeden, which prompted Garvin to respond, "Whoever the constable was who did it, did not know his duty as a constable."[23]

Parry-Okeden misled the Royal Commission as Armitage obtained the warrant on January 11, 1899, Parry-Okeden afterwards referring to Armitage in his telegram to Stuart dated April 13, 1899, which can be found at the end of the Introduction.

January 14, 1899 – Thomas Day obviously being found employment with Chaston in the Queensland Permanent Artillery, same as what Parry-Okeden asked Stuart to do later if Day could not get into work at the college, might have had something to do with Parry-Okeden's son, Lieutenant Uvedale Edward Parry-Okeden, taking two months' leave of absence from A Battery.[24]

Moreover, it appears the Government through Parry-Okeden might have considered that Chaston, who was born at Scone in New South Wales, was a better influence for Day when compared with the wayward Burgess.

The Cover-Up

January 18, 1899 – at 9.30 am, Burgess appeared in the Toowoomba Police Court before Frederick William Galloway, Clerk of Petty Sessions, and Archibald Munro, Justice of the Peace, for the alleged theft of a saddle.

When the case was called, Herbert rose and made application to speak on behalf of the prisoner, prompting Galloway to say to Herbert, "On what grounds?"

"I am engaged to defend him."

"Who instructed you to take charge of the case?"

"I think that it is impertinence on your part," responded Herbert, "to ask that question."

After advising that he was waiting on certain evidence before proceeding with the prosecution, Durham asked for a further adjournment, prompting Herbert to respond, "I would like the evidence read, which had been taken at the previous hearing of the case, and also the evidence of arrest."

Galloway replied, "We have none."

"What! No evidence even of arrest," queried Herbert, who added, "I am entitled to have the proceedings read at every adjournment of the case. I do not know whether the newspapers have frightened everybody in the country. It is a strange way of going on. Under the Justices Act, the whole of the previous depositions must be read at every adjournment. It is also usual to hand the papers to the Solicitor appearing. I ask your Worships to hand me down the depositions already taken."

"We have none!"

"No evidence of arrest?"

"Not yet!"

"Are you going to remand a man," queried Herbert, "who has not even been arrested on a charge of larceny?"[16]

The information was eventually produced by Durham to the effect that on or about December 22, 1898, Burgess did unlawfully steal one riding saddle, property of Frank McNamara of Toowoomba.

"You see what the charge is," said Galloway to Herbert. "Have you anything to say?"

"Only there must be some evidence to show for a remand," replied Herbert, who added, "If your Worship would only listen to law, perhaps you would act upon it. There must be some evidence to show that the man is charged before the Court with something."

"The accused is arrested under a warrant on sworn information," said Galloway. "That is sufficient."

"I ask for a further remand," interrupted Durham, "for eight days."

"We presume that you will make an effort," queried Galloway, "to bring him up in the meantime, if possible?"

"Certainly, if the case is ready."

"The application for a further remand for eight days is granted."

"May I ask you one favour, your Worship," queried Burgess. "I ask for a remand to Brisbane."

"The offence is alleged to have been committed at Toowoomba," said Galloway to Herbert, "so we cannot remand the prisoner."

Burgess was seen smiling as he was led from the courtroom to the lockup.[16]

The *alibi* subsequently provided by Burgess through his solicitor proved that he was not in Toowoomba at the time when the saddle was stolen. Durham, consequently, withdrew the charge and substituted it with the offence of vagrancy. Upon being found *guilty* on that charge, Burgess was sentenced to two months' imprisonment in Boggo Road Gaol.[25]

January 23, 1899 – Carus-Wilson was brought up on remand before Resident Magistrate Wright at Albany.

Acting Sergeant George Fay of Ipswich police produced a warrant signed by Acting Police Magistrate Augustus Henry Warner-Shand of Ipswich.

Upon Carus-Wilson being identified by Fay as the person named in the warrant, "You are now in charge of the Queensland police," said Wright to Carus-Wilson, "and are remanded to Queensland in their care," following which Carus-Wilson was removed from the courtroom to the lockup.

Claude was then brought before Wright behind closed doors in the Resident Magistrate's room. Upon evidence of arrest being given, Wright handed Claude over to the custody of Fay.[26]

January 24, 1899 – during questioning of Burgess at the Magisterial Inquiry, about what he did at Ipswich prior to making his way to Gatton, Urquhart said to Burgess, "Did you buy anything there – clothes, or anything like that?"

"No, nothing," replied Burgess, "no silk pocket handkerchiefs."[27]

This confirms that the *signature* of *Jack the Ripper* was a handkerchief, a fact known by Burgess, who, in my opinion, was one of Day's accomplices in England and Australia.

January 30, 1899 – assisted by Sergeant John Gaffney and Acting Sergeant Joseph Wyer, and with Claude in his care, Fay took custody of Carus-Wilson and boarded the steamer *Gabo* at Albany.

Disembarking eight days later from the *Gabo* at Melbourne, the party boarded the steamer *Peregrine*, travelling non-stop from there to Brisbane.[28,29]

February 13, 1899 – at 9 am, upon the arrival of the *Peregrine* at the Howard Smith and Son's wharf, Brisbane, Carus-Wilson was taken immediately to the lockup in the city whereas Claude was placed under house arrest.[28,30]

February 14, 1899 – during the afternoon, Carus-Wilson appeared before Police Magistrate Henry Taylor Macfarlane in the Ipswich Police Court.

After hearing evidence of his arrest and escort to Queensland, a remand of eight days to prepare a case for the prosecution was granted by Macfarlane.

A court was then arranged behind closed doors for Claude's appearance that resulted in Macfarlane discharging Claude to end what must be regarded as the most abhorrent abuse of powers in the history of law enforcement in Queensland.[31,32]

February 15, 1899 – Toomey advised in a report to Urquhart, as alluded to before, that Day had seen Burgess *in the Toowoomba lockup but failed to identify him*.³³

February 16, 1899 – Miller visited the Globe Restaurant and apparently was never seen again in Brisbane.³⁴

February 17, 1899 – an inquest into the death of Alfred Stephen Hill at Oxley on December 10, 1898, was opened in the South Brisbane Police Court before Justices of the Peace, William Harris and Thomas Austin. After hearing all available testimony, the inquiry was adjourned *sine die*.³⁵

February 22, 1899 – the hearing against Carus-Wilson for committing an *unnatural offence* with a boy, together with three additional charges of committing similar offences with other boys, commenced in the Ipswich Police Court before Macfarlane.³⁶

February 27, 1899 – Constable Thomas Collis advised in a report that inquiries failed to locate Miller, who was removed as a suspect for the Gatton murders.³⁷

March 22, 1899 – three days prior to the release of Burgess from Boggo Road Gaol where he served time on the vagrancy charge, Stuart sent the memorandum to various police stations.

Stuart instructed in the memorandum, as alluded to in the Introduction, that *all police will keep as close an eye as possible on his movements, wiring ahead in likely directions, and informing the Officer in Charge of the C. I. Branch at Brisbane*.³⁸

If this does not sheet it home to you, the extent and expense that the authorities went to, to keep apart the *psychopathic killer*, Day, and his accomplice, Burgess, there are other revelations that should leave you in no doubt.

While no record of this happening can be found in England, here in Australasia, irrefutable evidence is held by the Queensland State Archives and Archives New Zealand.

March 24, 1899 – after evidence was heard, Carus-Wilson was committed to stand trial in the Ipswich Circuit Court on April 18, 1899,

The Cover-Up

on three charges of committing and one for an attempt to commit *unnatural offences* with four boys at Ipswich.[36]

April 4, 1899 – upon receiving information that Burgess had passed through Munbilla, south-west from Ipswich, making his way towards Killarney or Warwick, Stuart sent the telegram to Durham. Stuart suggested, as alluded to in the Introduction, that if Durham picked *two smart constables and put them on him, they might succeed in getting a case against him, as he is a menace to the general public*.[39]

April 5, 1899 – at 9 am, Constable Thomas Auld of the Criminal Investigation Branch, Brisbane, visited Carus-Wilson at the Boggo Road Gaol and arrested him on a warrant for the wilful murder of Alfred Stephen Hill.[40]

April 12, 1899 – Durham furnished the report to Stuart about inquiries made into the movements of Burgess upon his release from prison. After advising Stuart *the Condamine side of the district* had been searched, as alluded to in the Introduction, Durham informed Stuart that *Sergeant McDonald of Stanthorpe has sent Constable Wilson to Lucky Valley in that district*, and that *Constables Haye and Kiely have now been instructed to go towards Dugandan and see if he is on the eastern side of the range*.

Durham also informed Stuart that Day, alias James Ellis, *is at Killarney, and as soon as I hear that Burgess has been located, I will give every assistance*.[41]

Acting on advice received from First Class Constable Robert Kilpatrick of Wallangarra, south-west from Killarney, that Burgess had gone over the border into New South Wales, Durham sent a telegram, to that effect, to Stuart.[42]

April 13, 1899 – acting on the information from Kilpatrick that Burgess had gone over the border into New South Wales, which, as alluded to in the Introduction, was found later to be incorrect, "Re James Ellis," queried Durham in his telegram to Stuart, "What instructions shall I give now Burgess has left colony?"[43]

On the same day, Parry-Okeden sent the telegram to Stuart, which, as alluded to in the Introduction, has been decoded with the code used in his telegram to Stuart on January 4, 1899, outlining that *if our man, who was Day, could not find work at the Gatton Agricultural College, Stuart was to find him employment elsewhere*.[44]

Come on, let's be serious for a moment!

After protecting him from arrest for the Gatton murders, later keeping him apart from Burgess, the police force found Day work to prevent others from being killed.

While police were keeping Day and Burgess apart, it is obvious Day was then absent without leave from the artillery, having in mind that Durham advised in his report the day before to Stuart that Day, alias James Ellis, had been sighted at Killarney.[41]

April 18, 1899 – the trial of Carus-Wilson for committing an *unnatural offence* with a 13-year-old boy at Ipswich on November 18, 1898, was heard in the Ipswich Circuit Court before Judge Charles Edward Chubb.

After considering the evidence, the jury found Carus-Wilson *guilty* of an *attempted offence*.[45]

"Are there," said Chubb to Crown Prosecutor John James Kingsbury, "any other charges?"

"There are," replied Kingsbury, "three others."

"Do you propose to go on with them?"

"We do not, your Honour."

"Are you filing the informations?"

"We will file them."

After that exchange, Kingsbury *presented two informations for an offence and one for an attempted offence, and with regard to the three, the Crown entered a nolle prosequi*, thereby ending any further action of the kind against Carus-Wilson.[45]

Before passing sentence, Chubb told Carus-Wilson that *the Jury had taken a merciful view of the offence*, but in his mind, there was no doubt that *the principal offence had been committed*.

Chubb then sentenced Carus-Wilson to seven years' penal servitude.[45]

The Cover-Up

April 19, 1899 – in a report, which can be found at the end of this Chapter, Kilpatrick outlined why he sent a report and not a wire to notify Durham that Burgess, as previously advised, had not gone over the border into New South Wales.

"The man is a fool," wrote Parry-Okeden in the margin of the report, culminating in Kilpatrick being transferred from Wallangarra to Warwick.[46,47]

April 22, 1899 – after referring to Kilpatrick as a *fool*, Parry-Okeden failed to advise Fosbery at Sydney that the man who went over the border into New South Wales was not Burgess.

Seeking clarification of the situation, Fosbery sent a telegram to Parry-Okeden, which, in effect, confirms that the police force in New South Wales was involved in the *shadowing* of Burgess to keep him apart from Day.[48]

It will be remembered also that Fosbery was responsible for calling off the search for an accomplice involved in the murders of Jack Phillips and Fanny Cavanagh at Carcoar.[49,50]

More to the point, those communications between Fosbery and Parry-Okeden confirm that there was cooperation between the colonies to protect Day from arrest for the murders he allegedly committed in Australia.

May 2, 1899 – it was reported in *The Queensland Times* that *Mr Parry Okeden will resign his position as Commissioner of Police, and that his place will be taken by a well-known and popular military officer.*[51]

The other referred to was obviously the Under Secretary for Justice, Major William Geoffrey Cahill, who did, in fact, six years later, replace Parry-Okeden as the Commissioner of Police.

May 4, 1899 – still without any advice from Queensland, Fosbery followed up his telegram and informed Parry-Okeden in a report, which can be found at the end of Chapter 3, that he did *not think the Queensland criminal Richard Burgess was at Lismore as stated.*[52]

May 5, 1899 – it was notified in *The Brisbane Courier* that Lieutenant Uvedale Edward Parry-Okeden had *resigned his position as lieutenant in the Queensland Permanent Artillery.*[53]

Seven days after that advice, it was reported in *The Week* that Lieutenant Parry-Okeden had been appointed *a lieutenant on the unattached list (Defence Force division) of the Queensland Defence Force (land)*.⁵⁴

One assumes that Lieutenant Parry-Okeden, who might have gained some insight about Day from his father, refused to serve with him in A Battery of the Queensland Permanent Artillery.

May 12, 1899 – Carus-Wilson was committed to stand trial for the wilful murder of Alfred Stephen Hill in the Southern Supreme Court at Brisbane.³²

Soon after, it was rumoured in legal circles that the Attorney-General would not file a bill in the case of *Regina v. Carus-Wilson* when an analysis of the evidence by Kingsbury, based on opinions from criminal lawyers, disclosed *grave discrepancies*, resulting in the belief that *the judge would not have allowed the case, in its present condition, to go before a jury*.⁵⁶

May 13, 1899 – the day after Lieutenant Parry-Okeden was placed *on the unattached list (Defence Force division) of the Queensland Defence Force (land)*, Day and Chaston were reported as deserters from A Battery of the Queensland Permanent Artillery.⁵⁷

It will be remembered that there is confirmation on page two of the report furnished by Toomey dated February 14, 1899, which can be found at the end of Chapter 6, that Day went to Toowoomba and *saw Burgess in the Toowoomba lockup but failed to identify him*.

At the Royal Commission, during questioning about Day, "You made no inquiries," said Noel to Urquhart, "to verify his statements about himself?"

"I told you," replied Urquhart, "what I did about it."

"You did nothing?"

"I did."

"You asked him if he was the murderer? He is not likely to say, 'I am the murderer'?"

"I put Acting Sergeant Toomey on to find out all he could get and report. He searched his hut, searched his clothes, had conversations

The Cover-Up

with him, and made every possible inquiry. He reported there was not the slightest hope of connecting him with the murder in any way, nothing to point to the fact that he could be in any way concerned in the matter. I had several conversations with Day, and he made a statement to me. They all tended the same way. The man is a young man and could not possibly have been a hardened criminal or anything of the kind. His behaviour all through was most satisfactory. He came down to me before he left Gatton and said, 'I have had a disagreement with Clarke, and I am leaving Gatton. Have you any objection?' I said, 'No. Where are you going?' He said, 'I am going to Toowoomba.' At that time Burgess was in custody in Toowoomba, and I said, 'If you are going through Toowoomba, go to the police station and have a look at this man they have got, and let me know if you have ever seen him. Inform the police if you have ever seen him about Gatton.' He went to Toowoomba and called at the police station and told them he had never seen him before. I do not know where exactly he went to from Toowoomba. He was absent for a little time. Then he passed down through Gatton again, which was duly reported to me. He came to Brisbane and went to the battery and joined the Permanent Artillery in his own name."

"Then he deserted? Is there not a warrant out for him now?"

"There is a warrant for him for desertion from the Permanent Force. We have not been able to find him."[11]

That statement by Urquhart was misleading as there is no mention in any Queensland Police Gazette until two years after Day's death that his arrest as a deserter was desirable.

May 16, 1899 – in a memorandum to the Under Secretary for Justice, Major Cahill, which was about the murder of Alfred Stephen Hill, Parry-Okeden wrote:

When I was sending escort to Western Australia to bring back E. L. C. Wilson, I supposed the boy, Claude, would be a witness, and in order that I might have power to bring him back also, I directed, as a precautionary measure only, that a warrant for his arrest should be procured, to be used if necessary, not otherwise. When I found he had been arrested needlessly, I felt annoyed. Please supply report and copy of proceedings, if any.[22]

With approval from the Chairman, in an addendum to the Commission's report, Dickson wrote:

Whether the charge was to be buggery or accessory to murder there was no evidence, in my opinion, to support either, and the action of the Commissioner in compelling, or being a party to what amounted to false swearing by a subordinate officer in laying an information of a charge in support of which he himself states he had no knowledge of any evidence, even if, as the Commissioner said, it was the only way of securing a witness, tends to set such a bad example to his subordinates that it should not be tolerated for a moment, and must operate as a warrant and excuse for the many rumours of false swearing to obtain convictions so generally hurled at the Police Force for some time past.[58]

If Dickson, then, had been aware of the decoded telegrams, one wonders what he would have said?

Moreover, what Dickson alluded to in his addendum was that the illegal and improper *ways* and *means* used by Parry-Okeden set a *bad example* for his subordinates.

That being so, it is fair to say that the administration of the police force was *rotten from the top*!

May 19, 1899 – acting on the advice of Kingsbury, Attorney-General Arthur Rutledge filed a *no true bill* against Carus-Wilson for the murder of Alfred Stephen Hill.[59]

Carus-Wilson was discharged when the wilful murder charge was abandoned, but he remained in prison and served out his time for the sentence imposed on him for the attempt to commit an *unnatural offence* on a boy at Ipswich.[60]

May 25, 1899 – Gunner Dalrymple Hughes deserted from the Permanent Artillery at Albany, Western Australia.

Four days later, acting on a request from Captain J. A. Campbell of the Chief Staff Office in Perth, Western Australia, that Gunner Hughes was to be arrested for desertion, Hughes was taken into custody by police when the steamer *Shannon* arrived at Adelaide in South Australia.[61]

That one instance highlights how extraordinary it was that Day was not hunted down and arrested for being a deserter from the Queensland Permanent Artillery. All that was done instead by the various police forces was to observe and report the *psychopathic killer's* whereabouts.

July 20, 1899 – the Governor of Queensland, Lord Lamington, appointed the Royal Commission, which is referred to throughout this forensic examination, to:

> *Inquire into the Constitution, Administration, and Working of the Criminal Investigation Branch of the Police Force of Queensland, as well as into the Relations subsisting between such Branch and the Police Force generally, and also into the general Organisation, Distribution, Control, and Enrolment of such Police Force, including such Branch, and also the Discipline and Efficiency thereof, and the System under which Promotions, Transfers, and Appointments are made therein.*[62]

It was instructed that the report was to reach the Chief Secretary, on or before October 31, 1899.[62]

August 1, 1899 – the Royal Commission inquiring into the Queensland police force was opened by Noel at the Office of the Commissioner of Police in the Treasury Building, George Street, Brisbane.[62]

September 29, 1899 – at the Royal Commission, when questioned by Garvin about Day's antecedents, Urquhart replied, "Day never was lost," which infers that others kept Urquhart informed as to Day's whereabouts.[62]

Five days after the Royal Commission was given that assurance, a report from the Office of the Commissioner of Police, Brisbane, with an "annexure" prepared by Urquhart, which can be found at the end of this Chapter, was sent to the Commissioner of Police at Wellington, New Zealand.[64]

In response to the request from Queensland, which supports the contention that others kept Urquhart informed, New Zealand police were instructed, as alluded to in the Introduction, to be on the lookout for the deserters, Day and Chaston, and that any inquiry made *should be of such a nature as not to alarm offenders*.[64]

Moreover, it will be remembered that after seeing pieces of liver laid out on a newspaper, the *young man* told the *respectable middle-aged woman* at Aldgate that it was given to him by a friend, who could have been Burgess, Miller or Chaston, on a New Zealand boat.[65]

The deserters possibly going to New Zealand after deserting in Queensland, enhances the suspicion that the young man at Aldgate was Day.

October 11, 1899 – rather than advise that a warrant had been taken out for the arrest of Day and Chaston, the South Australian Police Gazette, as alluded to in the Introduction, instructed that *special and very cautious inquiries are requested, with a view of locating offenders only, and the inquiry should be of such a nature as not to alarm them*.[66]

October 13, 1899 – same as the South Australian Police Gazette, as alluded to in the Introduction, it was requested in the Tasmanian Police Gazette *that special efforts be made to locate these offenders, and that inquiries be of such a nature as not to alarm them*.[67]

October 16, 1899 – John Bennett Tunbridge, formerly of the Metropolitan Police, London, who was then the Commissioner of Police at Wellington, New Zealand, sent a report to the Commissioner of Police, Brisbane, which can be found at the end of this Chapter, advising that special inquiries were being made to located Day and Chaston.[68]

Nine days later, the New Zealand Police Gazette instructed that *special inquiry is requested for these men in New Zealand, but it is not desirable that they should be apprised of such inquiry. If traced, information is to be sent by wire to the Commissioner of Police, Wellington*.[69]

Tunbridge's signature on the report for the above entry in the New Zealand Police Gazette, which can be found at the end of this Chapter, confirms his involvement in the search for Day and Chaston.

The Cover-Up

Whether police did or did not locate the deserters in South Australia, Tasmania or New Zealand will remain a mystery. What can be said, however, is that the request was extraordinary, to say the least, suggesting Parry-Okeden and Urquhart were extremely concerned that a *psychopathic killer* if spoken to by police might unleash and commit further murders.

How did Parry-Okeden, Stuart, Urquhart and the others who took part in this disgraceful *cover-up* live with themselves, knowing that they were protecting a *psychopathic killer*?

The answer to that question was provided in an interview with Parry-Okeden published in *The Argus* on April 12, 1899, wherein Parry-Okeden said, "Yes, I really believe that when I die, 'Gatton' will be found written on my heart."[70]

Such was the burden carried by Parry-Okeden that when he died, Urquhart wrote:

> Full was the load your constant spirit carried,
>   The heat, the burden of the days gone past;
> Long was the waiting for the rest that tarried,
>   Now it has come at last.
>
> Through many trials of life's uncertain dealing,
>   Though oft times worn, and torn, and tempest tossed;
> Thy kindly ways the gentle heart revealing,
>   Were kept and never lost.
>
> Goodbye; good friend and Chief of old respect,
>   Now you have reached the traveller's final Bourne;
> May you still know the monument erected,
>   In these our hearts who mourn.[71]

While it is not mentioned as such, the poignancy of the last two lines leaves one in no doubt that Parry-Okeden and Urquhart regretted their involvement in the *cover-up* that protected Thomas Day from arrest for the Gatton murders.

Police Department
Darling Downs. S Dist
Toowoomba.
19th April. 1899.

First Class Constable Robert Kilpatrick stationed at Wallangarra states that on Wednesday the 12th instant a young man named Charles Leis. storekeeper Wallangarra told me that the man Burgess had crossed the border that morning and was going to Williandra. I showed him the photograph of Burgess as per form and also in the Police Gazette. he looked at them. and he said. he could swear that was the man who crossed the border. I then took the photographs to the Royal Hotel and showed it to Mrs McCook. Miss Coombe. and Miss Murray they identified him as being the man. who they saw having breakfast at the hotel that morning. James Coombe also said he saw him at the hotel: I then sent a telegram to Sub Inspector Durham. the Telegram shown me is the one.

He sent a definite wire before this tho that the man was Burgess. WED [?]

On Thursday the 13th I followed the direction the man had taken and overtook him at Clifton Creek about twenty miles from Wallangarra I saw the man at the time I came up he was with another man. I spoke to him. He told me that he came from Wallangarra and had had breakfast at the Royal Hotel and bought some stores at Leis's. When I came up to him I saw he was not Burgess and I recognised him as a man that I saw get off the Mail Train from Brisbane on the evening of the

Kilpatrick's report dated April 19, 1899, page 1

(Courtesy of the Queensland Government (Queensland Police Service))

The Cover-Up

> Eleventh. I said you are the man that got off the train on Tuesday when did you come from. He said. I came from Stanthorpe and round about Warwick. I examined the man. and he was not Richard Burgess He gave me the name of James Thomas Wilkinson. I then returned to my station and was there before 6 p.m.. I did not send a telegram to the Sub Inspector contradicting my previous telegram because I thought a report in writing sent next morning would do as well. I had received a Circular Memorandum. dated the 6th April giving me instructions how to act.
> When I received the Sub Inspector's wire of the 13th. Asking if I had seen Burgess myself I did not reply by wire: but sent in written report.
>
> W. Kilpatrick
> Constable 352

Annotations in left margin: "The man is a fool" / "WBOO" / "a damn fl[ool]"

Kilpatrick's report dated April 19, 1899, page 2
(Courtesy of the Queensland Government (Queensland Police Service))

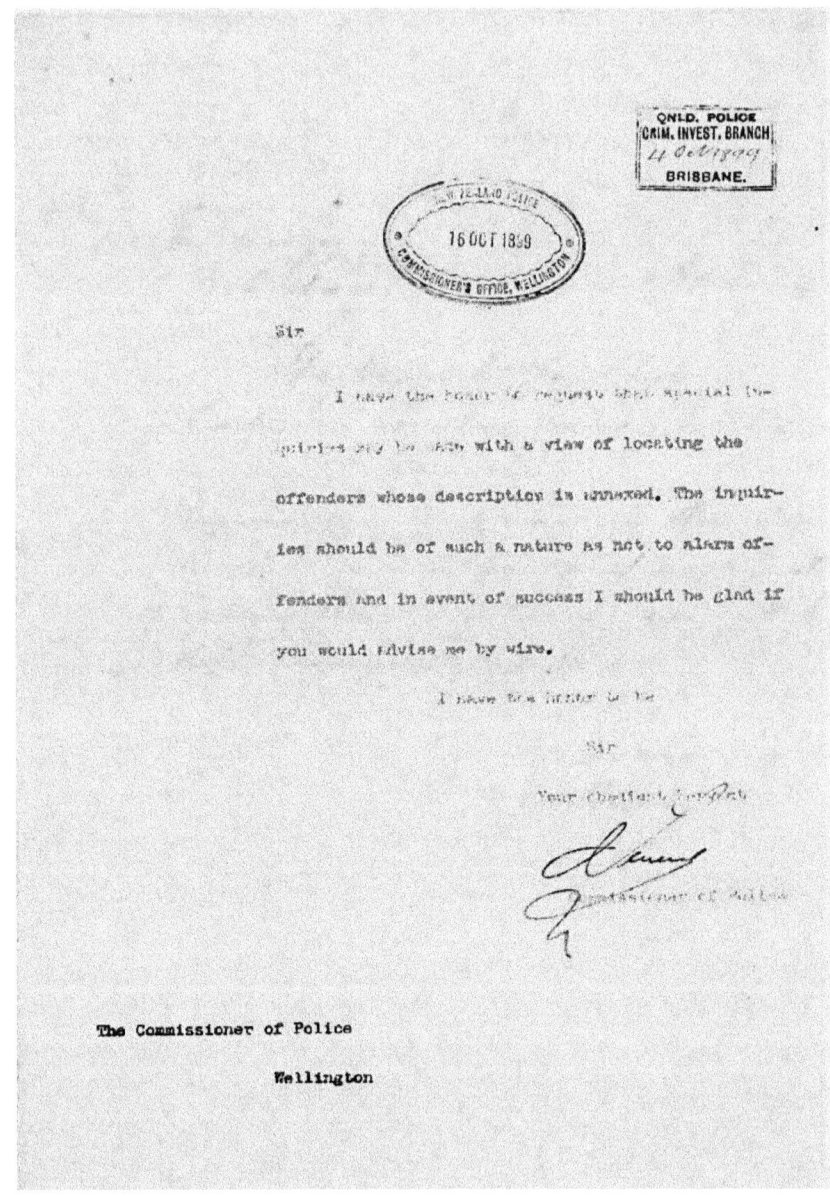

Parry-Okeden's report dated October 4, 1899
(Courtesy of Archives New Zealand The Department of Internal Affairs Te Tari Taiwhenua)

The Cover-Up

> Extract from Queensland Police Gazette of 27 May 1899
> page 252
>
> Departure from Her Majesty's service
>
> Deserted from "A" Battery Queensland Permanent Artillery at Lytton Fort on the 13th inst. Thomas Day gunner and William Charl Chasten gunner. Descriptions –1st, 22½ years of age 5 feet 8½ inches high medium build fresh complexion dark brown hair hazel eyes a labourer and native of Gunnamulla Queensland. Said to be known by Mr. Clark Went Hill Station. 2nd, 25½ years of age 5 feet 10½ inches high fresh complexion light brown hair blue eyes a blacksmith and native of Stone N.S.Wales. O.1038 30 May 1899
>
> *Urquhart*
> Inspector B/c

Urquhart's extract from the Qld Police Gazette of May 27, 1899
(Courtesy of Archives New Zealand The Department of Internal Affairs Te Tari Taiwhenua)

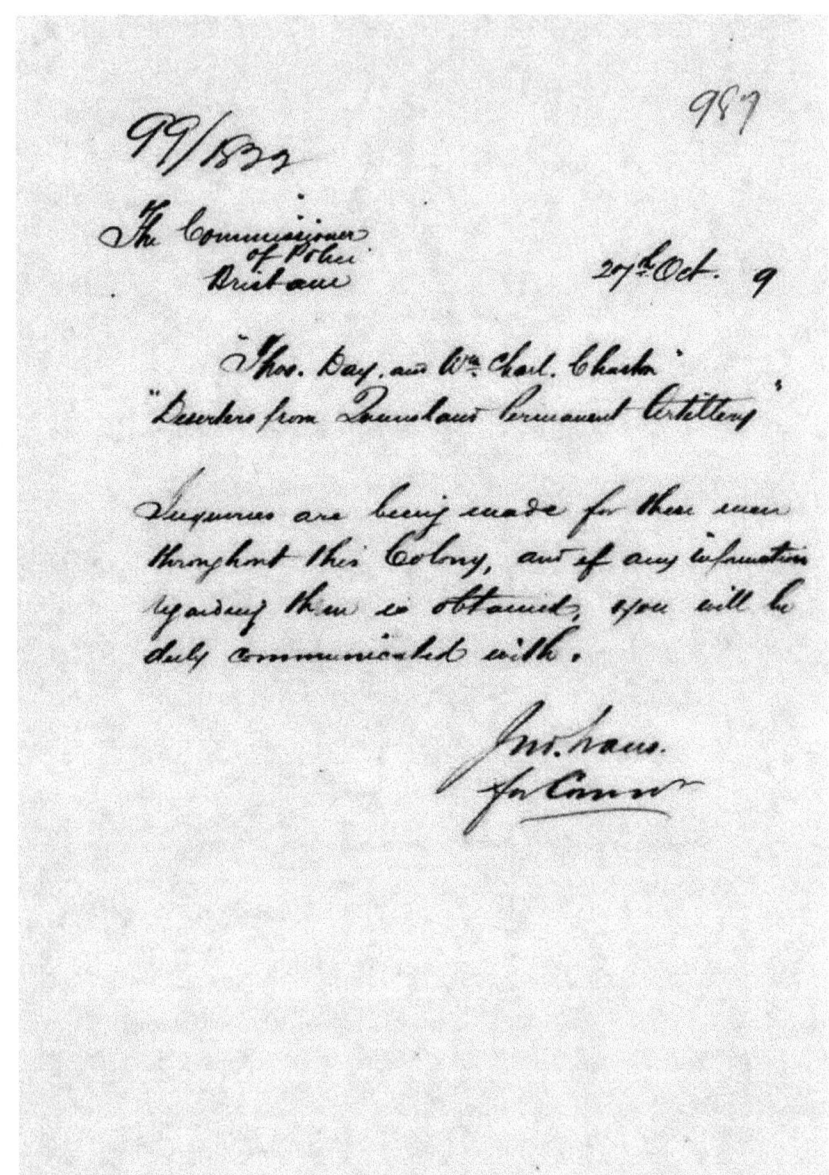

Tunbridge's report dated October 27, 1899
(Courtesy of Archives New Zealand The Department of Internal Affairs Te Tari Taiwhenua)

The Cover-Up

Entry in N.Z. Police Gazette dated October 25, 1899

(Tunbridge's signature marked by an arrow)

(Courtesy of Archives New Zealand The Department of Internal Affairs Te Tari Taiwhenua)

10

DAMNING EVIDENCE

James (Jim) Gibney was a highly-respected Crown Prosecutor and Judge of the District Court during my time as a Queensland police officer. Together with his brother, Desmond, in their book, *The Gatton Mystery*, the brothers wrote:

> *There is, we have no doubt, in the conduct of human affairs, a point of time at which apparent coincidence ceases to be mere coincidence and becomes a significant pattern of facts. We hold the view that, in regard to Thomas Day, that point of time was reached when his bloodstained jumper was seen by King on 28 December 1898. We hasten to add that we are far from saying that, at that or at any stage, there was sufficient or any proof that Day was the criminal agent in respect of any of the crimes committed. But what we do say is that, with the discovery of blood on his jumper, Day ought reasonably to have been the subject of lively suspicion, which warranted a minute examination of his antecedents and a very close checking of his movements, particularly during the week or so before his arrival at Gatton.*[1]

Before expanding on what was alluded to above, apart from him being *fond* of May Cook, John Lunny offered Toby Burke a share if he helped him claim the legacy outlined in the two letters found in Moran's paddock. Burke did help Lunny, but his efforts apparently were not successful.[2,3,4]

One does not believe that Toby Burke took part in the murders. It appears, however, that he was involved in some way with the "In Memoriam" notice and letters being found at the crime scene.

At the Royal Commission, "What about the rug," said Dickson to Thomas Wilson, who arrived in Moran's paddock shortly after Arrell and McNeil. "She was stretched out on the rug. Was the rug disarranged, or was it laid out carefully?"

"It was laid out carefully."

"Was Norah's head on the rug?"

"I think the top part of her head was over the rug, but her face was rather sunk into the ground."

"Would you at first sight come to the conclusion that there had been a struggle?"

"Naturally, you would think there had been a struggle, but there was no sign of any. The ground was not disturbed in any way. We looked very carefully to see if there had been a struggle."

"Was McNeil with you when you were looking at Norah?"

"Yes, all the party were there. We were all standing round."

"Did he say anything to you?"

"Not that I am aware of, nothing particular."

"Then you examined the other bodies?"

"We went across, and next looked at Ellen."

"Was there anything to indicate a struggle there?"

"Not the slightest."

"What was done? Did Sergeant Arrell do anything?"

"Nothing in particular."

"What steps were taken?"

"He looked to see how the murder was likely to have been done. He examined the head slightly and looked casually round the bodies, but there was no work done. The bodies were not touched in any way."

"Did you discuss what anybody was to do?"

"We thought it would be better not to touch the bodies at that time, and that there might be tracks about. I am not a professional tracker, and do not know much about tracks, and we wanted to keep the place clear. That was the first arrangement when we went there, not to disturb anything, so that if there were any tracks it might be easy to find them."

"Were orders given to keep the place clear?"

"Yes."

"By whom, and to whom?"

"I was left there with Mr Devitt, when the others went away, to look after the bodies, and not let anyone go near them."

"Did you two stay there then?"

"Yes."

"Did anybody come to look at the bodies?"

"I think there were two came, then McNeil and the mother of the girls came. I think they were about the second parties who came."

"Did you warn anybody coming near that they should keep clear?"

"Yes."

"Did they refuse to keep clear?"

"Some of them it was hard to keep away, but the parties generally did not interfere, they kept away."

"And you stayed there till the sergeant came back, did you?"

"I left [Robert Ballantyne] in charge, and as I was going into town, I met the sergeant at a short distance from the bodies."

"How long," said Garvin to Wilson, "have you known McNeil?"

"I never knew him before the day I saw him at Mr Gilbert's."

"Were you speaking to him on the ground?"

"Only just speaking. I did not ask him any questions."

"Have you had any conversation with him since?"

"No."

"Never since the day you went out with him?"

"Never, only just speaking to him, passing the time of day."

"Did you ever ask him if he had come to any conclusion about the murder?"

"No."

"Never heard of him expressing himself in that way?"

"He never did to me."

"Did you ever hear that he had done so to any other person?"

"Well, there is so much talk generally you can hardly say who made use of an expression of that kind."

"Did you," said Noel to Wilson, "know the man Day?"

"No, I did not."

"Did you come to the conclusion," said Dickson to Wilson, "that Michael Murphy and his sisters were killed on the spots where they were lying?"

"Yes, I think they were struck then. I came to the conclusion that they were struck at the places where they were lying because their faces were partly driven into the ground."[5]

One agrees with Wilson that the heads of Michael, Norah and Ellen were pulverised with the hardwood stick as they laid dead or dying on the ground.

Wilson also was not the only one to describe how the blows forced the heads into the soil.

"There was nothing to indicate," said Dickson to Wilson, "that they had been carried there or placed in those positions?"

"I do not think their faces would have sunk into the ground so much if the bodies had been carried there. Their faces were slightly pressed into the ground."

"That would apply to Michael, too?"

"Yes, though his face was hardly so much sunk in the ground as the others. Norah's was most in the ground, the side of her mouth seemed to be pretty well sunk in the ground."

"Did you see Michael's trousers, were they buttoned or unbuttoned?"

"I do not think his clothes were disarranged at all."

"Then his trousers were buttoned?"

"Yes."[5]

Michael was masturbated apparently while he was still alive as Von Lossberg discovered during the post-mortem examination that *there was a swelling of the prepuce.*

"From the position in which he was lying," said Dickson to Wilson, "do you think he had fallen down there, or that he had been placed there?"

"I came to the conclusion, after we knew that he had been shot, that he had been shot there and had then fallen to the ground."

"You came to the conclusion that he had been shot?"

"Yes, he looked as if he had lain down there, his hands were behind his back, and one person may have held him while another struck the blow. I was always of opinion that the blow was struck while he was on the ground."

"Do you say that at that time you thought he had been shot?"

"No, that since the bullet was found I came to the conclusion that he had been shot as he was standing there, and that he had fallen down and got the blow afterwards. Might I be allowed to make an explanation? I wish to say that there was not the crowd of people on the ground that has been represented. I think there were not very many more than twenty people on the ground altogether when I left, and that was near one o'clock. So that the ground was not so much rushed with people as the general public think it was."[5]

Lifting portion of the rug under Norah, Arrell *noticed dark stains on the underneath part, with dirt about the spot*.[6]

At the Royal Commission, "What sort of boots," said Dickson to Toomey, "did Day wear?"

"Bluchers," replied Toomey.[7]

Day's apparent accomplice, John Miller, according to Chaston, also wore *blucher boots*.[8]

It appears that an imprint of a *blucher boot* was found as much of the inquiry about Burgess focused on him buying a pair of the boots after terminating his employment with Mattingly at Killarney.[9]

At the Royal Commission, during questioning about the failure of Von Lossberg to complete the post-mortem examination on the body of Michael Murphy, "Is it improbable or unlikely," said Noel to Hill-Wray, who was involved in the exhumation and second post-mortem examinations, "that Doctor Von Lossberg desisted from the examination because he was blood-poisoned?"

"I do not know why he desisted," replied Hill-Wray, "and I will not give an opinion on that matter."

"Had there been a complete post-mortem examination," said Sadleir to Hill-Wray, "of Michael Murphy's head?"

"No."

"Had the scalp been removed?"

"No."

"Turned back, I mean?"

"I know what you mean."

"Had there been any severance of the skull by surgery?"

"There was a large wound about four inches long."

"I know, but there had not been any severing of the skull by cutting for examination?"

"No."

"Then Sub-Inspector Galbraith is wrong," said Noel to Hill-Wray, "when he said there were post-mortem appearances?"

"He is not wrong at all, because this wound was stitched up. I asked Doctor Von Lossberg why he stitched it up, and he said he did so on account of the people, who did not like to see the brain protruding."[10]

Having attended many post-mortems during my police career, one never encountered a situation like the one Von Lossberg found himself in at Gatton. That being so, much of what Von Lossberg did or did not do, in my opinion, was done to appease the crowd rather than to start a riot.

"That would account," said Noel to Hill-Wray, "for the post-mortem appearances to Sub-Inspector Galbraith?"

"It might."

"Can you say," said Garvin to Hill-Wray, "if a proper and careful examination had been made in the first instance, that the bullet would have been found?"

"Yes."[10]

Being permitted to ask questions during the evidence given by Hill-Wray, "It was not seen at the first," said Von Lossberg to Hill-Wray, "that the man was killed by a bullet?"

"You should have settled that at first," replied Hill-Wray. "If you could not settle it yourself, you should have asked for another man to help you."

"You are quite right," conceded Von Lossberg. "That is what ought to have been done?"

"It was clean, there was no trouble about it at all," declared Hill-Wray, who continued and said, "I don't care about exhumations at all."[11]

It will be remembered Von Lossberg gave evidence that too many were in the room when he arrived, and that during the post-mortems, people walked in and out of the room while he was conducting the examinations.

Von Lossberg stood alone in that allegation, but one assumes he was correct, having in mind the statement made about stitching up the wound to appease the concerns of the people.

"Were you able to form any opinion," said Sadleir to Hill-Wray, "as to the weapon by which they had met their death?"

"It was a heavy blunt instrument."

"Could you say that there were any projections on the instrument that had left a mark upon the scalps?"

"No. I say that about the same force was used in each of the three cases, and it was unnecessary force. I am of opinion, also, that it was an ambidextrous man who inflicted the blows, that is, if the position in which Michael Murphy was found, as described to me, was correct. A right-handed man could not have inflicted the wound on Michael Murphy."

"Would it not be possible if the man had been standing on the other side?"

"Of course, I am only going by the position described to me. I put the man in that position, and he could not have received the wound on the right side from a right-handed man. The girls were struck on the left side."

"Could he not have received it," said Garvin to Hill-Wray, "from a right-handed man delivering the blows from behind him?"

"No, not according to the position described."

"Did you inform any police officer," said Noel to Hill-Wray, "of that opinion of yours?"

"I think I gave that in evidence at Gatton."

"At the time you formed that opinion, did you tell any police officer?"

"Yes, I told Inspector Urquhart. I could not say positively that I did not also tell Mr [Warren-White]."

"The reason I ask, of course, is that they would then search for a man known to be left-handed as one of the probable murderers?"

"Yes, that was my opinion, that the man could use right and left hand as well. I gave that opinion in my evidence, and that the one weapon was used, by one man, in each of the three cases, with about the same force, and with unnecessary force."[10]

John Franklin Clarke, son of Arthur George Clarke, told the Gibney brothers that Day lifted him, then aged eight years, and his older brother, Arthur George Clarke, *onto his shoulder and carried them about the paddock near their father's butchery*.[12]

One assumes that Day lifted one boy after the other, placing one on each shoulder. If that is what he did, it appears that Day might have been ambidextrous.

Furthermore, the authorities in England also suspected that *Jack the Ripper* used both right and left hands.

"Would a man receiving that first blow," said Garvin to Hill-Wray, "be knocked down?"

"Yes, that one blow would kill him."

"In falling, would the person be apt to disturb the ground with his feet or hands?"

"It would depend what the ground would be."

"Light soil?"

"I was at the place."

"Well, on that ground, do you think there would be any marks caused by the man falling?"

"I do not think it would follow altogether that there would be marks."

"Do you think the persons struck were standing up when they were struck?"

"I do not think so. I think they were down."

"Sitting up or lying down?"

"Lying down."[10]

Hill-Wray's opinion corroborates the evidence of Wilson that the heads of Michael, Norah and Ellen were pulverised with the hardwood stick while they laid dead or dying on the ground.

"You disagree with Doctor Von Lossberg," said Noel to Hill-Wray. "He thinks Michael Murphy was in an erect attitude, sitting or standing up, when he received the bullet wound?"

"I do not say about the shooting. I say he was down when he got the bash on the head."

"Will you tell me if it is customary, or if you would expect to find an emission of semen in the case of a man killed by a bullet wound in the head?"

"No."

"Do you know of any cases of that kind?"

"No, I never heard of it. It is said to follow strangulation, hanging, but it does not always."

"You never heard of it in the case of death by a bullet wound?"

"No."

"You see, Doctor Orr proved semen on the trousers of Michael Murphy?"

"Yes."

"You would not expect that to be an emission, the result of a bullet wound?"

"No."

"Or that it would result from the other wound?"

"No."

"Would you expect to find it," said Dickson to Hill-Wray, "after a battering of the skull?"

"No, in my opinion, Michael Murphy did not require any blow on the head. It was evidently that the murderer wanted to make sure there was no life remaining, and he gave them all the same."[10]

At Carcoar, the witnesses left alive by Bertie Glasson testified against him afterwards, Bertie making the statement on the gallows that he was *dying for the sins of another* who, in my opinion, was Thomas Day, alias *Jack the Ripper*.

That being so, there is a correlation between the Carcoar and Gatton murders, having in mind what was alluded to by Hill-Wray about making sure that no one was left alive to testify later at Gatton.

Moreover, if a perpetrator did not ejaculate on Michael's trousers, having in mind what Von Lossberg said about the *swelling of the prepuce*, it appears that a perpetrator forcefully masturbated Michael, resulting in the semen being found on his trousers.

The Gatton murders were as vile and gruesome as the Whitechapel murders in England.

"Do you know," said Dickson to Hill-Wray, "is it possible to distinguish human blood from animal blood?"

"Well, tied down to a strict oath, I do not suppose you could."

"Is it not possible to discover from bloodstains whether the blood is that of a human being, or that of a sheep, a goat, or an elephant?"

"I think you could go pretty near it."

"I have seen the statement that on the question whether blood is that of a dog, a pig, a rabbit, a horse, or a human being, it would be a daring man who would give a decided opinion, but that it certainly is possible to come to a conclusion as to whether blood is that of a human being, a sheep, a goat, or an elephant, do you agree with that?"

"Yes."

"In your opinion," said Noel to Hill-Wray, "is it advisable that a police officer should have an analysis made of bloodstains found on the coat of a suspected man?"

"If there is nothing more than the bloodstains, I do not think it would be necessary."

"Why?"

"You see, if it was only a stain, there are so many ways of accounting for it. If it was a case where the thing could be accounted for, if there was broken skin about the body, or he had been in contact with anybody who had been bleeding, you must take many things into consideration."

"If the man," queried Sadleir, "was a butcher?"

"If he was a butcher, you would have something to bring against him."

"And if he was not suspected, you would never think of examining him?"

"No."[10]

In a memorandum dated January 16, 1899, which can be found at the end of Chapter 8, Parry-Okeden requested an examination by Doctor Orr to establish if there were any bloodstains on the clothing of Richard Burgess.[13]

If Thomas Day, who was seen by several witnesses with *spots* of blood on his jumper, had been on the same footing as Burgess, his clothing also would have been analysed, consequently, the evidence of Hill-Wray corroborates that the Government and police did, in fact, protected Day from arrest for the Gatton murders.

"Are there microscopists and sufficiently powerful microscopes," said Sadleir to Hill-Wray, "to find out these things?"

"Yes."

"There are three separate ways of finding the distinction," said Dickson to Hill-Wray, "by the stereoscope, by salts, and another means?"

"Yes, there are plenty of men quite capable of finding it out."

"In the case of the police interviewing a man for the purpose of questioning him as to certain marks upon his coat or jumper, and when a murder has been committed," said Garvin to Hill-Wray, "do you mean to say that there is no necessity to take possession of that coat or jumper?"

"A great deal would depend upon what explanation was given to the police."

"But will a guilty man admit his guilt?"

"If a man is accused, then you would take him in charge. If I am accused of committing a murder, then take me in charge and take possession of my clothes as a matter of course. But if I gave a satisfactory account of myself and my action, then you must leave something to the judgment of the police."[10]

John Carroll told Toomey five days after the murders that he believed the man at the sliprails was *Clarke's butcher*.[14]

That statement alone was enough, according to Hill-Wray, for Thomas Day to be suspected, but the *spots* of blood on Day's jumper together with Carroll's statement was more than ample reason, in my opinion, why Day should have been held on suspicion of being concerned in the Gatton murders.

"Supposing a man says, 'I have been killing sheep,' and there were bloodstains on his coat," said Noel to Hill-Wray, "do you not think it would be exceedingly desirable to have an analysis made?"

"I would have the statement of the man verified."

"By analysis?"

"No, by some person who could bear out the statement that he had been killing sheep."

"But supposing some person comes forward and says that the man at the sliprails was so-and-so, and a particular coat belonged to that man," said Garvin to Hill-Wray, "would you not then take possession of the coat?"

"Yes."

"And supposing someone said that man had not been killing sheep," said Dickson to Hill-Wray, "would you think it necessary then to take possession of his coat?"

"I do not know," replied Hill-Wray. "You have to put yourself in the position of the man who is conducting the case. There are many side issues you have to look at. You cannot be running in every man who has a spot of blood on his coat and have a professional or analytical examination of that. I am quite with you that if the man was accused of murder the examination should take place."

"There may be probable results from the analysis," said Noel to Hill-Wray. "The person making it may say, 'In my opinion this is human blood, but I will not swear to it'?"

"Exactly, that is all he could say."

"Do you not think therefore, it is an advisable thing to adopt that course if there is suspicion?"

"Yes, if there is suspicion."[10]

At the Royal Commission, "Do you remember," said Garvin to Bob King, who worked with Thomas Day at Gatton, "the day the bodies were found?"

"Yes."

"It was on the 27th December?"

"Yes."

"Did you see Day that morning?"

"Yes."

"What time in the morning?"

"About half-past six. I had a sheep to kill. I went out from the township to kill a sheep."

"Where did you see him?"

"About the yard."

"How was he dressed?"

"He had on a singlet, a white handkerchief round his neck, and dark trousers."[15]

Prior to the assault and robbery, Emma Elizabeth Smith was seen in Osborne Street at Whitechapel, England, *talking to a man dressed in dark clothes with a white neckerchief around his neck* which, in my opinion, was the *signature* of *Jack the Ripper*.

The morning after the Gatton murders, Thomas Day was wearing the *signature* around his neck, having the night before used a handkerchief to secure the hands of Norah and Ellen behind their backs.

The *signature* provides a correlation between the murders committed in England and Australia.

"When did you see him," said Garvin to King, "after you heard of the finding of the bodies?"

"After [Thomas Wilson] came up the street."

"What time?"

"After nine or about that. I did not take particular notice."

"Do you remember when you saw Day after that?"

"I saw him in the evening when I went out to kill a bullock."

"Was that the first time you saw him after hearing of the murders?"

"No, he was at the shop."

"What time?"

"About nine o'clock."

"Did you have any conversation with him?"

"He went pretty well straight away after he heard it. He did not say anything to me about it at the time."

"Who told him about the murders?"

"He was there when [Thomas Wilson] told me."

"Did he make any remark?"

"No."

"How was he dressed then?"

"The same as I told you when I saw him at the yard in the morning, dark pants, singlet, white handkerchief round his neck."

"Did you have any conversation with him that day about the murders?"[15]

After saying, "I would like to read some notes I have here," King read the notes, as follows:

> *Between the 16th and the 26th, the day of the Gatton murders, Day assisted me twice to kill, and I then noticed that he was a stronger man than myself in pulling a bullock into position for skinning. He had a blue jumper and a big slouch hat. When at work, I only saw him wear the jumper on one rainy evening. This was no killing day, and there were no bloodstains on it then. The next time I saw this jumper was in Day's room on the 28th December. I noticed that it had blood spots on it on the sleeves and the breast. On the 29th the police took him in about 11 pm that night to the courthouse. Next day I saw him at the slaughter-yard. We had a conversation about him being examined by the police. I asked him what they said about the blood on the jumper, and he made some reply and said he would wash the bloody thing.' I advised him not to wash it, but he said he must.*[15]

Despite several saying that Thomas Day did not do any killing, it is obvious from what King told the Royal Commission that Day had experience as a slaughterman and was, in fact, involved in the killing at Clarke's butchery, established clearly during further questioning of King.

"Could he have got that blood on his jumper," said Sadleir to King, "when killing with you?"

"No. He wore that jumper not on killing days."

"Did he wear it on the 28th?"

"No. I saw it in his room on the 28th."

"Describe the blood marks," said Garvin to King, "that you saw on the jumper on the 28th?"

"It was on the sleeves and over the breast, on both sleeves, from about the size of a two-shilling piece down."

"Were they all over the sleeves, big spots down to small ones, on the jumper?"

"Yes."

"Are you quite sure?"

"Certain."

"Did you examine it carefully?"

"I did. That was about the first man that entered my head after I heard about the murder on the 27th. I heard this boy Carroll mention this man, and I heard others also."

"Did those bloodstains appear to be fresh?"

"They were fairly fresh. I did not take particular notice to see if they were really fresh, but he had only come down on the 16th, and he wore it on one occasion that was a killing day."

"Did you take the jumper down and examine it when you saw it in his room?"

"I did. He was the first man I thought about."

"Do you think the stains," said Dickson to King, "might have been caused by simply carrying meat?"

"He never carried any meat."

"The detective [Toomey] said there was merely a smudge on the arm?"

"They were spots."

"Could any person be deceived," said Garvin to King, "with regard to those bloodstains, whether they were smudges, did they look like splashes, or what?"

"That is what I took them for to be, splashes or spots."

"Was Day in the room when you examined the jumper?"

"No."

"When did you speak to him?"

"On the 30th."

"Did you ask him whether there was blood on the shirt?"

"Yes, and he said, 'Wash the bloody things'."

"How many bloodstains were on the shirt?"

"Fifty or sixty."

"You never saw Toomey examine the coat?"

"No."

"Did you give any of this information," said Noel to King, "to the police?"

"Yes."

"At what time?"

"A short time after I got the information."

"Did you speak to Toomey about the bloodstains?"

"Yes, and Toomey told me to shut up, and that Day was innocent."[15]

Bob King was another badgered by Urquhart and Toomey into not saying anything about Thomas Day.

"On what day," said Garvin to King, "did Toomey say this?"

"I can't say."

"After Day," said Noel to King, "had gone away?"

"Yes. I can get a witness to this conversation with Toomey."

"Did you ever ask Day," said Garvin to King, "where he was on the 26th?"

"No."

"Who is the witness," said Dickson to King, "you refer to?"

"My wife."

"Is she here?"

"No."

Being permitted to ask questions, "Are you," said Toomey to King, "a good judge of character?"

"Yes."

"Well, don't you think, after looking at Day, that he was a quiet man?"

"Yes, but he had a bad look in his eyes."

"As far as you thought?"

"Yes."

"Do you remember me coming into your shop and asking whether Day wore a jumper?"

"Yes."

"What date would that be?"

"Sometime before Christmas."

"Do you know what Day was doing when he was wearing the jumper?"

"He was employed in my shop."

"Did he bring any meat into your shop?"

"No."

"Do you remember telling me that you were not sure that Day wore a jumper? Speak the truth like a man?"

"I don't remember that."

"What were Day's duties?"

"Just getting in wood and looking after the horses."[15]

One has no doubt that King exaggerated a bit, and that some of his evidence was not credible. Overall, however, what he told the Royal Commission was incriminating, particularly what he said about the *splashes* or *spots* of blood on the jumper apparently worn by Day during the murders.

The wood would have been collected from the Swamp Paddock adjoining Clarke's butchery.

It will be remembered that eight years after the Oxley and Gatton murders, a revolver was found secreted in a hollow tree felled for firewood in the Swamp Paddock.[16]

"Had he," said Toomey to King, "any experience in killing?"

"No," replied King, which, as alluded to before, was not entirely correct.

"He never handled the meat?"

"No, I did that myself."

"What did I ask you with regard to the blood on the jumper?"

"You only asked me if Day was wearing a blue jumper."

"Was that all?"

"Yes."

"Did I not refer to blood being on the jumper?"

"No."

"Are you quite sure about that?"

"Yes."

"Don't you remember me asking you if there was blood on the jumper?"

"No."

"Then, what was my object in coming to you?"

"I don't know. You were talking about the shot."

"You are one of the men who have been blowing this business up about Day?"

"Yes, because I had my suspicions about the man."

"Did you tell me that you suspected another man?"

"No."

"Was the jumper hidden when it was found?"

"No."

"Did you see," said Garvin to King, "any firearms in Day's possession?"

"No."

"Did he appear to be a sane man?"

"Yes."[15]

When questioned about the sanity of Thomas Day, "He is the only man," said Sadleir to Christie, "you wished to sheet the crime home to?"

"Yes. On the morning of the discovery, Day went into a shop kept by Annie Smith and asked for a razor. He took the razor and put it in his pocket without asking whether it was a good one, and he had a clean shave."

"What sort of a beard had he?"

"A stubbly beard."

"Why did he shave," queried Sadleir, who added, "To disguise himself?"

"Probably."

"What did he want the razor for?"

"To commit suicide if he was charged."

"That is your opinion?"

"Yes."[17]

The year after, in my opinion, it was Thomas Day, then known as Thomas Furner, who died in the Sydney Hospital from a self-inflicted gunshot wound to the head.

"Did Day," said Dickson during further questioning of King, "associate with anybody?"

"No."[15]

That answer by King was not correct as during questioning of Arrell, about his knowledge of strangers to the district, particularly those employed at Clarke's butchery, "Did you," said Dickson to Arrell, "know a man named Cox there?"

"No," replied Arrell.

"Did you find out at any time that a man named Cox was working at Clarke's?"

"I heard after I came back from Brisbane that a man had gone there three days after the murder, and when Day cleared out, he cleared out too, or shortly afterwards."[18]

It was alluded to before that the man named Cox appears to have been Chaston, who might have been granted or was absent without leave from A Battery of the Queensland Permanent Artillery over the Christmas/New Year holidays.

During other questioning of King about Day, "What were," said Dickson to King, "his habits at night?"

"I never saw him much after six o'clock, six o'clock would be the latest I saw him at night."

"You suspected this man," said Garvin to King, "from the start?"

"I did, according to those who saw him on the road. That is what I went by. He answered to the description."

"What motive do you think he would have for committing an offence of this kind?"

"That is a question I cannot answer," replied King, who added, "What motive would anyone have?"

"You heard," said Dickson to King, "he had been seen on the road?"

"I did."

"When did you hear it first?"

"Sometime after."

"About how long, have you any idea? A month or a week?"

"About a fortnight or so."

"Who told you this?"

"I heard of it from [John Carroll] and [William Burnett]."

"Young Carroll?"

"Yes, Johnny Carroll."

"Before you heard that," said Garvin to King, "had you formed any opinion yourself?"

"Not before I heard that. As soon as I heard from a number, who saw the man on the road that night, I did. After that I got it really into me that he was the man."

"That is very interesting," said Sadleir to King. "You know the girl Florence Lowe?"

"Yes."

"Was she there the same time as Day was at Clarke's?"

"No."

"Do you think she ever saw him there?"

"I do not think she did."

"Mr Clarke said she was at his place while he was there?"

"She was there on the morning he left. He left Clarke's on the 10th of January."

"What time?"

"Sometime in the morning. He was in Gatton a little after ten o'clock, and she went to work that day."

"Did she see him before the murders?"

"Not to my knowledge. She may have been there at the shop, but I cannot say.[15]

Lowe did, in fact, see Day before he left Gatton, but not before then, not even after in a line-up, which is how Lowe incorrectly identified Burgess as being the man at the sliprails.

One assumes that the man at the sliprails seen by Lowe was the accomplice, John Miller, who was shorter than Day and wore darker clothing.

Lowe obviously did not recognise Day as the man who accosted her at the sliprails or something, to that effect, would have been made known.

At the Royal Commission, during questioning about Day, "Did you form any opinion of the man," said Noel to Clarke, "while he was with you?"

"I cannot say I formed a very bad opinion of him."

"With regard to this bloodstained jumper, you have heard what Christie has said?"

"I did not hear all he said. I heard my name mentioned."

"Well, he said you objected to Day washing his jumper, and in defiance of or contrary to your wishes, he not only washed the jumper but boiled it?"

"Yes, I warned him. I cautioned him against washing his clothes. I told him to leave the stain in, that he should not wash anything of that kind, because they might be of some service. I thought the blood would have been analysed. In face of that he washed them, although I could not say he boiled them, and he used a scrubbing brush, soda, and water."

"Contrary to your wishes, and contrary to your advice?"

"Yes."[19]

Clarke was one of many who believed that police should have had Day's jumper analysed to determine if the *spots* of blood were from an animal or human.

"Did you," said Noel to Clarke, "see the stains?"

"Oh, yes."

"What were they like?"

"It is very hard for me to say, because I am not a professional at that sort of thing."

"Were they spots or smudges?"

"It is hardly likely, with the work that man did for me, that he would get such bloodstains on him, not the way they were placed."

"How were they placed?"

"On his sleeve and on his breast."

"Were they smudges or spots?"

"They were both. There was a clot of blood and spots. There was no real smear. If he had been carrying beef, he would have got a smear."

"You say there was no smear?"

"Not to my idea," which corroborated King's evidence and contradicted what was claimed by Toomey.

"But you did notice the other?"

"I did."

"And did you inform any member of the police force of what you had noticed?"

"I had a conversation with Detective Toomey, but that was afterwards."

"How long after?"

"I cannot say. I suppose it must have been three weeks after."

"But not before that?"

"No, not before."

"Then all the washing and scrubbing had taken place?"

"Oh, yes, all the stains had been taken off."

"Can you say whether any member of the police force saw this jumper before it was washed?"

"None except Toomey. He was the man who brought the jumper to me and asked me if I recognised it."

"Then you contradict Toomey when he says there was only one smear on the jumper?"

"I said there was no smear."

"Then he is not correct when he says that was the only mark?"

"It might have been there, but I did not detect it."

"He says that was the only mark. You are certain there were spots of blood on the breast?"

"Yes, on the left sleeve and on the breast, there was a fair amount, more than he usually had."

Garvin said to Clarke, "About how many spots?"

"I should say there were near a dozen."

"What would be the size of them?"

"Some of them would be the size of a shilling, and others not larger than No. 3 shot."[19]

Clarke's evidence is more credible than King's and exposes that blood splashed onto the jumper when Day, with the hardwood stick held in his left hand, as alluded to by Hill-Wray, struck Michael's head on the ground.

"When did you," said Garvin to Clarke, "first notice these spots on the jumper?"

"It was Detective Toomey who brought the jumper to me and asked me if I knew the man had such a jumper."

"Can you remember the date?"

"I cannot."

"You remember the day of the murders, the 26th December, the day of the races. Do you know if Day had the jumper on, on that day?"

"That was the Monday."

"Yes?"

"No, we had not killed on that day."

"When was the last date you saw the jumper on him prior to seeing the blood?"

"The only day that I can remember seeing the jumper on that man was on the previous Saturday, that would be the 24th."

"What time of the day was it when you saw him?"

"In the morning, about ten o'clock."

"If these blood spots had been on the jumper then would you have noticed them?"

"I think so."

"But you never saw any blood spots on the jumper until Detective Toomey showed it to you?"

"No, because I never saw the blood spots before Toomey brought the jumper to me."

"Were the blood spots fresh?"

"They certainly were not old."

"As they got old they would become black?"

"They were not very black, they were inclined to be shiny."

"And you know from experience that blood, as it gets older, gets black. Did you notice if the blood was quite old?"

"It was blackish."

"What conclusion did you come to," said Noel to Clarke, "as to the age of the blood? Did you come to any conclusion?"

"That is more than I can say."

"You did not come to any conclusion?"

"I did not come to any conclusion."

"I understood you to say that the nature of Day's employment would not produce any blood spots at all?"

"The work that he did for me was carrying. He merely had to lift pieces of beef."

"He had to lift pieces of beef only?"

"Yes, and carcasses of sheep. He did no killing. He was no butcher."[19]

Clarke made it clear at the beginning that he did not wish to give evidence at the Royal Commission. Then, he contradicted what King said about Day helping him with the killing of sheep and bullocks, leaving one in no doubt that Clarke did his best to conceal what he knew about Day.

"The lifting of those," said Noel to Clarke, "would not have put spots of blood on his jumper?"

"It is possible."

"Did you ever see him," said Garvin to Clarke, "lifting beef with his jumper on him?"

"No."

"What was his usual practice in lifting beef, had he his jumper on or off?"

"He only lifted small joints, and he would put them on his shoulder."

"Would he lift them with his jumper on, or in his shirt sleeves?"

"Usually in his shirt sleeves."

"Do you think, from your examination of that jumper, that the lifting of beef or sheep could have caused those spots in the way they appeared on the jumper?"

"It is possible."

"When Day went to bed every night," said Dickson to Clarke, "did he keep his boots on?"

"I cannot say that he did."

"Did you tell Christie so at any time?"

"I have gone down at three o'clock in the morning to call the man, and I have found him lying on the bed dressed, but that was only occasionally."

"Had he his boots on?"

"Yes."[19]

Not only did Day sleep fully-dressed with his boots on, but Burgess did the same when he worked for McGrory at Esk, confirming that both were always ready to affect an escape should they be sprung unexpectedly by police.

"Did you give a display of fireworks," said Noel to Clarke, "on Boxing Night?"

"I did."

"At what time?"

"Between eight and nine o'clock. I know that, because I looked at the clock at ten minutes to nine, and called the children in."

"Was Day there?"

"No."

"Do you know where he was then?"

"No, I do not."

"Had you seen him before that?"

"Yes, having his tea."

"About what time?"

"I cannot say exactly, but it was about half-past six."

"Were all the others connected with the house at the fireworks?"

"Yes."

"Was Day the only one who was not there?"

"Yes, that is all."

"How long," said Garvin to Clarke, "was Day in your employment?"

"A little over a fortnight."

"What was his general conduct during that time?"

"Very fair, I had nothing to complain of."

"Was he at all eccentric in his behaviour?"

"Well, he was a quiet, reserved kind of man, that is the only thing. He would talk about nothing at all."

"Did you notice any peculiarity about him?"

"I cannot say, except that he was very reserved."

"Did Day," said Dickson to Clarke, "deliver meat to the Murphys at any time?"

"No."

"While Day was there, did the Murphys come to your shop?"

"I cannot answer that question. It is possible they did."

"Were they in the habit of calling at your shop?"

"No, because the meat was delivered at their place, but they did occasionally call at the shop for meat."

"Do you know whether either of the girls called at your shop that week?"

"No."

"Do you know the Murphy family very well?"

"Very well, indeed."

"Did you know the girls very well?"

"Very well, indeed."

"Did you know with whom they associated?"

"Yes."

"Do you know whether Norah or Ellen Murphy had sweethearts about Gatton?"

"I do not know that they had."

"Do you remember," said Garvin to Clarke, "the morning of the discovery of the bodies?"

"Yes."

"Did you see Day that morning?"

"Oh, yes."

"Did you have any conversation with him in reference to the murders?"

"That morning he took sheep in, and he was the man who came and told me about the murder."

"What did he say, as nearly as you can remember?"

"He asked me if I had heard of the dreadful accident."

"Tell us what he said in his own words?"

"He asked me if I had heard of the dreadful accident. I said, 'What accident?' He said, 'I hear that one of the Murphys is killed.' I asked him how it happened, and he said, 'The horse bolted.' I asked, 'Where?' He said, 'In Moran's paddock.' I said, 'I would not believe it, because Murphy's horse is quiet.' That is all I know about it."

"Did you ask him who told him?"

"No, I did not."

"What time," said Noel to Clarke, "was that?"

I cannot remember what time it was."

"Well, about what time?"

"I cannot remember, though I have been trying to remember ever since."

"He only spoke of it as an accident, then," said Garvin to Clarke. "When did you hear it was a murder?"

"I should say about ten o'clock."

"Did you have any conversation with Day after you heard of the murders?"

"No."

"Why?"

"Because it was a thing he would never talk about."

"How do you mean," said Noel to Clarke, "he would never talk about it?"

"If you mentioned the thing to him he would not answer you back. He would not discuss the matter at all."

After saying, "You say, he told you that he had heard of an accident," Garvin asked Clarke, "When you heard that it was not an accident, but a murder, did you go to him and say, 'Those three people have been murdered'?"

"No, I do not think I did, because there were lots afterwards came to the shop, and I do not think I spoke to Day of it afterwards."

"Do you remember any other person having a conversation with Day?"

"No."

"How, then, did you come to the conclusion that Day would not talk about the matter?"

"Because I mentioned the subject to him, and he would only say, 'Well,' or something like that, and turn away. He would not enter into a discussion at all."

"Did you notice, when you were speaking to him about the murder, any peculiarity in his manner?"

"Only a perfect state of indifference. He did not seem to interest himself in the matter at all."

"Was that his general demeanour?"

"I think so."

"Even prior to that?"

"He was very reserved. He would say, 'Yes' or 'No,' and that was all. I never saw him enter into a conversation with any person. My man says the same thing of him now."

Noel said to Clarke, "What man?"

"King."

"Did King ever tell you," said Garvin to Clarke, "that he had had a conversation with Day about the murders?"

"No, he says what I say, that Day would never enter into a conversation, or say anything."

"You saw him pretty early on the morning of the 27th, that is the morning of the discovery of the bodies?"

"I know I sent sheep into town that morning, and it must have been pretty early, but I cannot say what time it was."

"Did he go about his work that morning in the usual way?"

"Yes."

"Do you know," said Noel to Clarke, "what clothing he was dressed in that morning?"

"If I remember rightly, he had only his shirt and trousers on. I am pretty well certain he had no jumper on that morning."

"Do you know," said Garvin to Clarke, "where he kept his clothes?"

"As far as I know, he kept them in his bunk."

"Had you ever occasion to go into his room?"

"No, I never went inside his room until Toomey came to me."

"What date was that?"

"I cannot tell you. I suppose it must have been the day the murder was discovered."

"Did you look at the jumper that day?"

"That was the day Toomey brought it up, I think. I cannot remember the dates now, it is so long ago."

"Had you," said Dickson to Clarke, "formed a bad impression of Day?"

"No, I cannot say I formed a bad impression of him."

"Had you ever any reason for removing him from the work at the coppers? Used he to work at the coppers before this?"

"No, he never worked at the coppers."

"You did not remove him from that work, then?"

"His work was simply driving the cart about."

"He simply did," said Noel to Clarke, "labourer's work?"

"That is all."

"We were told," said Sadleir to Clarke, "that you said you removed him from the boilers, fearing that he would throw you into the boilers?"

"That I was afraid he would throw me into the boiler?"

"Yes?"

"That gets into rather an outside subject altogether. I would rather not go into that."

"Is it a fact that you said so?"

"Well, I suppose you want to know the rights inside and out of that too. This is a matter I don't care about talking about. If you wish to know I will tell you. When the wife was alive she advised me to have nothing at all to do with this man. She had a very bad opinion of him, and told me to be careful, that it was quite likely he might knock me on the head. He is a very powerful man, and a big man, too."

Noel said to Clarke, "He is?"

"Yes. That is how that originated that yarn about the coppers."

"Your wife had expressed distrust of this man to you?"

"Yes. You see that is how that originated."[19]

Clarke's late wife, formerly Ada Caroline Robinson, was living at Tent Hill when they married.

One assumes that Ada knew Thomas Day when he worked for Clarke at Tent Hill, confirmed as being a fact in a later Queensland Police Gazette.

"Was this," said Sadleir to Clarke, "before or after the murder?"

"After, most decidedly."

"I want you to go back to the 24th, the day, Day wore the jumper that Toomey showed you?"

"Yes, that would be the 24th."

"What work was Day doing on the 24th?"

"He took a lot of bones and offal down to the yard, and that morning it was raining, a slight shower. He went down and made up the fires and came back. That, I think, is about the extent of his work that day. Of course, he cleaned up the shop, you know."

"Would he get his jumper soiled by any work he had to do that day?"

"No, he had no killing to do that day."

"But he had some meat to carry?"

"No, I don't think so. To the best of my belief, he had no meat to carry that day."

"Detective Toomey saw the jumper before it was washed?"

"Yes, before it was washed."

"Was Florence Lowe employed by you while Day was with you?"

"No."

"When, before or after?"

"After."

"Do you know whether she knew Day?"

"I think not. I am not certain, but I think not. Possibly she saw him, but I am certain she was not there at the time Day was employed."

"You cannot say whether she knew him or not. Did she have any opportunities of seeing Day while he was in your employment?"

"Yes, because she passed the place."

"Was she ever at your place while Day was there?"

"I am not sure of that."

"You have spoken to her since, have you not?"

"Yes."

"Did she say anything at all as to whether she knew Day while he was at your place?"

"Well, she said she saw him."

"At your place?"

"Yes."[19]

This is proof, as alluded to before, that Lowe saw Day before he left Gatton.

"Did she say anything to you about the man she had met at the sliprails," said Sadleir to Clarke. "Did she ever speak to you about that?"

"No."

"Did you never hear it?"

"Of course, I knew very well the girl had to go to Toowoomba, and that sort of thing," conceded Clarke, "but so far as any conversation about the man at the sliprails, I don't know."

"You did not know she had seen a man at the sliprails?"

"Yes, I knew that."

"How long have you known it, a considerable time?"

"I really cannot tell you how long."

"Did you know she had seen a man at the sliprails while she was in your employment?"

"Yes."

"Did she ever describe him to you?"

"No."

"Did she ever connect Day with him in any way?"

"Not to my knowledge."

"Did she say anything about knowing this man she saw at the sliprails?"

"She never said anything to me. It is only what I saw in the papers. She never spoke to me about it."

"Were Day and yourself on very good terms while he was working for you?"

"Well, up to the day he gave me a week's notice."

"Did he ever while in your employment," said Noel to Clarke, "express dissatisfaction with the nature of his work?"

"No."

"He gave you notice, then, for no apparent reason?"

"He complained of the food, not of the work."

"That was his reason for going, the kind of food?"

"Yes."

Dickson said Clarke, "Had Day a beard?"

"No."

"Used he to shave while at your place?"

"All except his moustache."

"Had he a razor at your place?"

"I cannot say. I believe he had, because he shaved."[19]

It will be remembered that Christie told the Royal Commission that he believed Day bought the razor to commit suicide rather than to be taken into custody by police.

One assumes that it was a straight razor, often referred to as a cut-throat razor.

"Did he," said Dickson to Clarke, "shave before the murders?"

"Yes, he came to my place shaved."

"You do not know whether he had a razor at your place before the murders?"

"I am not sure."

"Had he any firearms?"

"Not that I know of."

"Had you any firearms about your place?"

"Yes."

"What firearms?"

"A revolver and a gun."

"What sort of a revolver?"

"A six-chambered revolver. I think they call it a 'Tranter'."

"What bore?"

"450."

"Had you any rifle at all?"

"No."

"Were there any other guns about there that you knew of?"

"Not in my place."

"How did you kill your cattle?"

"By 'pithing'."

"Were none ever shot?"

Damning Evidence

"No."[19]

An outlined of the concluding comments at the Magisterial Inquiry into the deaths of Michael, Norah and Ellen Murphy by Acting Police Magistrate Warner-Shand was reported in *The Queenslander* on April 1, 1899, as follows:

> Mr Shand said he could not allow the proceedings to close without remarking on the extreme apathy shown throughout by the blood-relations of the victims of the tragedy. With the exception of Dan, they appeared to have taken no steps in the matter at all, nor had they offered to assist in the search in any way, even by the loan of horses of which they appeared to have plenty. They had given their evidence, too, in a reluctant and contradictory manner, excepting Mrs McNeil, whose evidence had been given with readiness, contrasting well with the other members of her family. The family appeared to accept it all as kismet and had desired to bury the whole matter. Such conduct he considered beyond all comprehension and precedent. He had himself been accused by one of them of pressing the family because he called them to give evidence and assist in the work of unearthing the murderers. In conclusion, he desired to congratulate the Police Department on having such an officer as Inspector Urquhart, who had conducted this protracted and anxious inquiry in such a patient and assiduous manner.[20]

Before that article, a *startling theory of the Gatton tragedy* appeared in a Victorian newspaper, *The Bendigo Independent*, on March 25, 1899, as follows:

> A most startling theory accounting for the Gatton tragedy and pointing towards the perpetrator has filtered through from Gatton to Bendigo and probably to other parts of Australia. It has, I believe, travelled by that very customary route for stories and theories to travel in Australia, namely by the stock routes. When I first heard of it, it seemed to be so fiendishly outrageous as to be altogether out of the question an utterly impossible solution of the crime. But when I came to recall this and that piece of evidence, and here and there, the want of evidence, it began to flash on me that after all there might therein be

an explanation of this un-surpassingly horrible tragedy. If so, it was a crime of which, even yet, the public have only grasped about a third part of its terrible and atrocious origin and the circumstances of its execution. I cannot for one moment depart from generalities. Someday, however, there may be astounding revelations. Someone may drop a few words, or someone may find the burden of the concealment of such a crime to be insupportable. It may be slowly driving them mad, and then in order to secure a few hours of sanity, certain words may be said. Then, according to the sensational theory that has come along via the back blocks, from Queensland, as such items could not travel in the newspaper post bags, there will all at once burst on the public a story of human passion and revenge which will transcend anything that they have yet read in history or fiction, in books or newspapers or seen enacted on the stage in the most blood-curdling and creepy built-up tragedies. When the denouement comes, that is, if it does not come in our time, there will for a day or two be blank astonishment and unbelief that the perpetration of such a crime was possible in civilised Australia. But in a day or two, it will begin to be plain enough, and also reasonable enough, why in the face of a series of complex and circumstances with which no police force was ever before confronted, the Queensland police have been apparently quite helpless yet. I do not believe that the Queensland police are as helpless in the matter as is generally supposed. Very much of the evidence that was taken by the Coroner at Gatton during the last fortnight was seemingly relevant of nothing whatever. It was apparently a case of calling up one person after another and questioning him or her merely for the sake of asking questions. But I can now see that there was a hard and stern object in it all. The evidence taken does not appear to have led up to the point at which the inquest could have been terminated with an arrest. This arrest would have undoubtedly been the most sensational yet made in Australia. But you may be perfectly satisfied that the authorities will never give up the search for the solution of the mysterious crime, but that in rotation each and every one of the Queensland detectives who fancies himself a little will be trying his hand on it, until, as I said before, in very desperation of fear and remorse, somebody utters the few words that are wanting.[21]

Damning Evidence

Surviving two decades of the corruption in the Queensland police force known as the *Joke*, it was evident at the beginning of my research that a *cover-up* was associated with the investigation into the Gatton murders.[22]

Who exactly was involved is the question one could not answer clearly when *Oxley-Gatton Murders: Exposing the Conspiracy* was published.

With the discovery of telegrams and correspondence relating to the *shadowing* of Richard Burgess, it was revealed that the conspiracy to pervert the course of justice went as high as Home Secretary Foxton in the Queensland Government.

That being so, Burgess making the statement after his release from prison that *it was Jack the Ripper and someone else who committed the deed* made it abundantly clear that the *cover-up* went beyond the shores of Australia.[23]

There is no doubt in my mind that Thomas Day was the notorious serial killer known as *Jack the Ripper*, and that the *cover-up* went as high as the Royal family in England, which would explain the reason why, as alluded to in *The Bendigo Independent*, no one *dropped a few words*, to that effect, until now.

Scandalous, some might say, but all the *dots* connect, leaving no mystery as to why *Jack the Ripper* was not arrested for the Gatton murders as well as for others committed in England, Australia and possibly America.

11

THE CONSPIRATORS?

Section 132 of the Criminal Code Act 1899, which provides that *any person who conspires with another to obstruct, prevent, pervert, or defeat the course of justice is guilty of a crime*, came into force in Queensland on January 1, 1901.[1,2] On the same day, Australia became an independent nation *when the British Parliament passed legislation allowing the six Australian colonies to govern in their own right as part of the Commonwealth of Australia.*[3]

One believes that a conspiracy to pervert the course of justice involving Foxton, Parry-Okeden, Stuart, Urquhart and Toomey has been clearly established. For the crime to be concealed, others of a higher status in Australia and England must have been involved, so let us examine who they might have been.

November 25, 1899 – there is no doubt in my mind that the reason for Premier James Robert Dickson tendering the resignation of his Government to the newly-appointed Lieutenant-Governor, Sir Samuel Walker Griffith, had something to do with the soon-to-be-released report of the Royal Commission.[4,5]

November 29, 1899 – the Royal Commission *met for the last time and signed their report*, handing it immediately to the Under Secretary, Henry Stephen Dutton.[6]

December 1, 1899 – after tabling the Royal Commission's report, Dickson handed over to Andrew (Anderson) Dawson, who was requested by Lord Lamington to form a Government.[5,6,7]

December 7, 1899 – upon Dawson advising Lord Lamington that he could not govern without the factional support of Edward Barrow Forrest, Robert Philp became the Premier of Queensland.[5,7] Dickson was not relegated to the back benches, being appointed by Phillip as the Chief Secretary.[8]

During the upheavals, not much was done about the criticisms and recommendations outlined in the report of the Royal Commission, the

The Conspirators?

opportunity to overhaul and reorganise the police force becoming buried deep in the political quagmire.

February 22, 1900 – a warrant was issued at Melbourne for the arrest of Thomas Day, alias William McKay, described as *a labourer, 31 years of age, 5 feet 9 to 10 inches high, medium build, fair complexion, fair moustache only, thin face, long nose, wore a dark coat and vest, white moles, and black soft-felt hat,* for the offence of *driving without lights*.[9]

It will be remembered that just over four months earlier, Parry-Okeden requested that inquiries made by police to locate the deserters, Day and Chaston, in South Australia, Tasmania and New Zealand *should be of such a nature as not to alarm offenders, and in the event of success, I should be glad if you would advise me by wire.*

The same did not happen in Victoria as the notification in the Victorian Police Gazette of February 11, 1899, was the same as the one in the Queensland Police Gazette.[10]

That being so, one assumes that Day was also well-known to police in Victoria.

June 10, 1900 – adding weight to the supposition that it was Day wanted on the warrant abovementioned, four months later, Burgess was arrested by Constable Henry Toole at Trentham, Victoria, for using obscene language, and for being a rogue and vagabond.

On the way to the lockup, Burgess allegedly said to Toole, "I am Dick Burgess, the Gatton murderer. I have shot a Queensland policeman, and would shoot others."[11,12,13]

Turning up at different locations in Victoria, one assumes that the Victorian police kept Day and Burgess apart, same as what happened earlier in Queensland and New South Wales.

June 11, 1900 – Burgess appeared in court at Trentham before Police Magistrate William Ross Anderson and Benjamin Trewhella, Justice of the Peace.

Burgess conceded that he had been arrested by the Queensland police on suspicion of being concerned in the Gatton murders, and that drink was the cause of the trouble he got himself into at Gatton and subsequently at Trentham. He also admitted that he told Constable

Toole that he was Dick Burgess but denied saying he was the Gatton murderer. The constable, however, was adamant that Burgess had uttered those words.[11,12,13]

Found *not guilty* of being a rogue and vagabond, Burgess, however, was found *guilty* for using obscene language and was fined £5 in default of one month's imprisonment.[11]

On the same day, Burgess was remanded in custody at the Castlemaine Gaol on a charge of raping Elizabeth Parsons, living by herself at the time in Trentham.[11,14]

During this appearance, Burgess, who was positively identified from photographs sent to Trentham by Queensland police, told the authorities in Victoria that he was 34 years of age, a native of Ballarat, Victoria, and that he had spent most of his life in New South Wales and Queensland.[12,15]

One assumes that Burgess might have been born about 1866 at Ballarat, and that he might have been brought up in Ireland, if not in England by his alleged grandmother.

June 18, 1900 – after hearing evidence from witnesses, Burgess was committed to stand trial at the next sittings of the Castlemaine Supreme Court for the rape of Elizabeth Parsons.[14]

July 19, 1900 – Burgess appeared on the charge of rape before Justice Edward Dundas Holroyd.[16]

Upon the jury returning a verdict of *guilty* for the offence of attempted rape, Burgess was sentenced to seven years' imprisonment with hard labour in the Castlemaine Gaol.[13,16]

October 23, 1900 – a young man using the surname of Burns, synonymous with Frank Burns seen in company of Burgess after the Gatton murders, booked into a lodging house located at 174 Castlereagh Street, Sydney, about 317 yards from the premises of Farmer & Co in Pitt Street.[17,18]

October 24, 1900 – Burns was found lying in a pool of blood on the bed in his room with a gunshot wound in the right ear, a five-chambered revolver, one chamber discharged, being found on the bedcovers beside him.[18,19]

The Conspirators?

It will be remembered that Michael Murphy was shot behind the right ear, providing a correlation with the Gatton murders.

Constable William Sloper Cox from No. 1 police station, Sydney, attended and arranged for Burns to be conveyed to the Sydney Hospital where he was admitted by Doctor Henry Charles Morisset Delohery.[18,19]

At the hospital, Burns told Doctor Hugh Busby and Constable Cox that his correct name was Thomas Furner, synonymous with the name of Bertie Glasson's manager of the butcher's shop at Carcoar, he was 26 years of age, and that his family lived somewhere on either the Paterson or Manning rivers in New South Wales.[18,20]

Burns, Furner and Day were obviously one and the same person, so, from hereon, Burns and Thomas Furner will be referred to as Thomas Day.

Busby deposed at the inquest that the *deceased appeared to be a man of 28 or 30 years of age,* corroborating what Bob King told Christie that Thomas Day was 30 years of age.[21]

Thomas Day being *28 or 30 years* was an opinion expressed by a doctor, confirming that Day would have been about 19 years at the time of the first Whitechapel murders and around 30 years when he was at Gatton.

Moreover, when the warrant was taken out in Victoria for the arrest of Thomas Day, alias William McKay, who was around the age provided by Busby, one assumes that a *wire* would have been sent to Queensland for Parry-Okeden to be advised.

October 25, 1900 – Thomas Day died under the name of Thomas Furner in the Sydney Hospital.[22]

October 26, 1900 – City Coroner Woore held an inquest into the death of Thomas Day. A suicide note found in a pocket of Day's coat, excluding a statement relating to several people within the Gatton district, which was omitted on instructions from Woore, was published in *The Evening News*, as follows:

Just a few words, wishing to inform the public about the Gatton murders, which I suppose, or hope, will be found out when I am no more. I am going to my long rest, but still before I leave this world, I wish to state which I know for a certain fact – a statement thereafter about several people within the Gatton district was omitted on instructions from Woore, then the note continued – *How I know, the public may wonder, but I do not wonder, as <u>I am quite sure that the case was to be kept quiet among the police, which I think is about time they were shown up</u>. All the police seem good for is to run the unfortunate woman from one end of Sydney to the other. I am a man of the world, and in my travels, I have seen some cruel doings of the police, and "forties," "pimps," "spielers," or whatever you call them. A man can be a police and a man, but one out of 50 is not. So, hoping the Gatton affair will go ahead, I will conclude. I wish all on this earth goodbye, and I hope all my friends will forgive me for this action, as I feel that I cannot live any longer. I was always misfortunate, and it's no use saying one thing and meaning another. I had one good friend, of which I got the photo in my pocket, but she is dead, and I feel my life a burden without her. So, farewell to all.*[18]

A photograph of a young woman with the words, "She was my guide. She was faithful and true. God bless her and forgive me, too, I know I shall be happy," written on the back thereof, was also found on Thomas Day.[18]

The suicide note, which, unfortunately, could not be found in official records, was written by pencil in a notebook.[18]

A Railway Department lead pencil, which has a bearing on letters written in England and New South Wales, was found in Moran's paddock, providing a correlation between the murders committed in England and Australia, and the suicide in Sydney.[23]

One assumes the young woman pursued from *one end of Sydney to the other* was May Cook, that May ran away with Day when he worked for Clarke at Tent Hill, and that May was subsequently returned to her mother at Lower Tent Hill where she died afterwards from possibly an illegal abortion.[18,24]

October 27, 1900 – Day was buried under the name of Thomas Furner in the Church of England section (Zone C, Section MMMM, Allotment 1529) of the Rookwood Cemetery at Sydney.[25]

The Conspirators?

"Well," you might ask, "if he was Church of England, why did the Catholic priest, Father Daniel Walsh, allow him to confess his sins at Gatton?"

All will be revealed in due course.

It was highly unusual then for a suicide to be buried in *consecrated ground* at the Rookwood Cemetery. This was made abundantly clear two years before Day's death during the burial of Martin Cusack, published in the *Newcastle Morning Herald and Miners' Advocate*, as follows:

> *The remains of Martin Cusack were interred in the Rookwood Cemetery at 11 o'clock today. The cemetery authorities refused to allow the corpse to be buried in consecrated ground, or during the hour of the ordinary burial services. The spot where Cusack was buried is a stretch of ground alongside the main suburban railway line, and between that and the mortuary. The upper portion is used for burying paupers, and all the ground below a certain line of trees is reserved for the burial of murderers and suicides. On the hearse arriving from the Parramatta Morgue, a little string of a dozen friends formed behind the vehicle and proceeded to the cemetery. Mrs Cusack was not present – neither were any of the deceased's relatives. There was no service, the coffin being simply taken from the hearse and placed in the grave.*[26]

Moreover, with the burial of James Hanwin, who died in the Sydney Hospital on November 21, 1900, which was the month after Day's death, it was determined by the authorities that even a *pauper* must be buried in accordance with their religion.[27]

It can be assumed, therefore, that Thomas Day was extended privileges not afforded to others who died at their own hands in Sydney, and that someone with influence, immediately after the inquest, had Day buried as a Church of England in *consecrated ground* at the Rookwood Cemetery.

Late at night of the day that Thomas Day was admitted, *a man called at the hospital to see him, and said he had been working at the Kent Brewery for* Finlay Elgin Munro, a Master Builder of Sydney, and *a life fellow of the London Institute of Builders*.[28,29]

Jack the Ripper

Of the belief that it is not going to be easy to convince everyone that Thomas Day was *Jack the Ripper*, the following chart is provided for others to gain an understanding of what one says about Thomas Day being protected from arrest for the murders he committed in England and Australia.

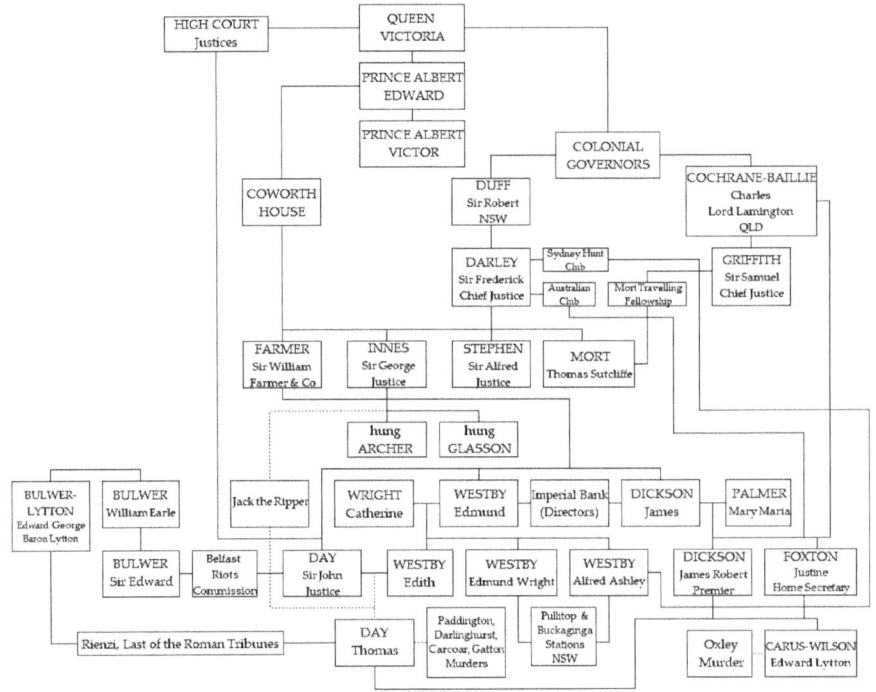

Persons of Interest

While working for Munro at the Kent Brewery, Day was known as Robert Furner, changing his name to Thomas Furner at the Sydney Hospital.[28]

The Kent Brewery was part-owned by Robert Lucas Tooth, a former identity of Darling Point, Sydney, which is where Sir William Farmer once lived, and a member of the Legislative Assembly in New South Wales, whose family was from Kent, England, and who so happened to be resident in London at the time of Day's death.[30,31]

One assumes that Sir William Farmer's business partner, John Pope, who was a Mason and Vice President of the Sydney Hospital,

The Conspirators?

made the arrangements for the burial on behalf of the maternal side of Day's family.[32]

Soon after Day's demise, reporting upon the progress of the investigation into the Gatton murders ceased when a rumour circulated in the newspapers, one being *The Queanbeyan Age* on August 31, 1901, that *the perpetrator of the triple murder is a lunatic*.[33]

Another article published eight days later in *The Sunday Times*, outlined that *the only excuse for the rumour is the insanity of a man with a similar name to one who was associated with the tragedy*.[34]

Others can go on believing that Thomas Day did not die in the Sydney Hospital on October 25, 1900, but I do not. If his body was to be exhumed, deoxyribonucleic acid (DNA) testing might reveal exactly who he was?

After the murder of Alice McKenzie on July 17, 1889, apparently the last of the *Jack the Ripper* murders in England, the serial killer was hidden at Hatfield House, allegedly, by Prime Minister Robert Arthur Talbot Gascoyne-Cecil.

When a rumour circulated that *Jack* was connected to the House of Lords, it appears that Home Secretary Henry Matthews instructed Chief Commissioner James Monro to discontinue all further inquiries into the atrocities.[35]

No record, to that effect, apparently exists in England, but there are records, as alluded to in the Introduction and provided throughout the book, which proves, *beyond reasonable doubt*, that Day was protected from arrest in Australasia.

Once again, in his report to the Commissioner of Police in New Zealand on October 4, 1899, which was after Day and Chaston deserted from the Queensland Permanent Artillery, Parry-Okeden requested that *inquiries should be of such a nature as not to alarm offenders, and in the event of success, I should be glad if you would advise me by wire*.

More to the point, Urquhart was involved in that one instance of Day being protected as Parry-Okeden's report, which can be found at the end of Chapter 10, was processed through the Criminal Investigation Branch, Brisbane.[36]

Jack the Ripper

Sir Robert William Duff, who was a Mason, was a Privy Councillor to Queen Victoria before taking up his appointment as Governor of New South Wales from May 29, 1893, to March 15, 1895.[37,38]

Just over three months before Jack Phillips and Fanny Cavanagh were murdered at Carcoar, Bertie Glasson and his wife, formerly Annie May Summerbelle, attended the first reception hosted by Lady Duff at Government House.[39,40]

When Emma Harrison was murdered at Darlinghurst, which was two months before Duff took up his appointment, Sir Frederick Darley was the Acting Governor of New South Wales, Darley being supported at the swearing-in ceremony by Sir Alfred Stephen, who encouraged Darley to migrate from Ireland to Australia.[41,42,43]

Much could be written about Darley, but his wife, formerly Lucy Forest Brown or Browne, is of more interest. She was the daughter of the notorious Captain Sylvester John Brown, her brother being Thomas Alexander Brown or Browne, who, under the pseudonym of Rolf Boldrewood, wrote the novel *Robbery Under Arms*.[42,44]

Among the schoolfellows with Thomas Brown at the Sydney College was Alfred Stephen, who was knighted later by Queen Victoria, and who, as alluded to before, supported Darley when he became the Acting Governor of New South Wales.[45]

Captain Brown was a very volatile person, and to get away from the continuous turmoil he found himself in at Sydney, Brown and his family migrated in 1840 from New South Wales to Victoria.[46,47]

The domestic violence becoming unbearable, Brown moved into Melbourne, his wife and children remaining in the house on the estate known as *Hartlands* at Heidelberg until it was allegedly burnt down by Brown.

Brown's family then moved in with Thomas, who had changed his surname from Brown to Browne, and who by that time was living on the run known as *Squattlesea Mere*, near Port Fairy.[48,49]

When *Hartlands* was sold, a portion of the estate was purchased by James Robert Dickson's relative, James Jackson, who built *Toorak House*, which, for many years, was the Governor's residence in Victoria.[50]

The Conspirators?

Dickson, who also named his Queensland residence *Toorak*, became seriously ill at the Australian Club, Sydney, where he was a lodger just prior to his death on January 10, 1901.[51]

Serving on the committee, Darley was probably with Dickson at the club, so follow the chart closely, and you will see how those relationships in England and Australia are interwoven.[42]

When the foundation stone of a new building for the drapery business of Farmer & Co was laid in Pitt Street, Sydney, the chairman of the ceremony was Sir William Farmer's good friend, Sir Alfred Stephen.[45]

Farmer and Stephen were involved in the early beginnings of the Anglican Diocesan Synod of Sydney.[52,53]

Of note, Sir Alfred Stephen was a cousin to Sir James Stephen, grandfather of James Kenneth Stephen, who, allegedly, was one of Prince Albert Victor's tutors.[54,55]

Another of Farmer's good friends, Thomas Sutcliffe Mort, who established the Mort Travelling Fellowship, had the honour of laying the foundation stone for the new building of Farmer & Co in Pitt Street.[45]

Samuel Walker Griffith was the first recipient for high honours achieved at the University of Sydney.

When the Acting Chancellor, Professor Morris Birbeck Pell, presented Griffith with the award, Sir Alfred Stephen was among the guests.[56,57]

Griffith, who was born at Merthyr Tydfil, Wales, was referred to as a *favourite son* during his visits to the country of his birth at the time when Prince Albert Edward, later Edward VII, King of the United Kingdom and the British Dominions and Emperor of India, was the Prince of Wales.[58]

It will be remembered that Justice George Innes, a Mason, hung Archer for the murder of Farmer's employee, Emma Harrison, and that Innes, who was *related by marriage* to the accused, hung Bertie Glasson, for the Carcoar murders.[59]

Prior to migrating back to England, Farmer served with Innes as the churchwardens for the incumbent and parishioners of St Mark's Anglican Church at Darling Point, Sydney.[60]

The mother of Sir Robert Duff was formerly Elizabeth Innes, possibly a relative of Justice Innes.[38]

One assumes, as alluded to before, that Day was the illegitimate son of Sir John Charles Frederick Sigismund Day, son of Captain John Day of the 49th Regiment of Foot and Emilie Hartsinck, who was referred to in the *Somerset and West of England Advertiser* as being a *Dutch lady of a Catholic family*.[61,62]

A Roman Catholic, Sir John Day first married Henrietta Rosa Maria Brown, who died in 1893. Seven years after her death, Day married Edith Westby, daughter of Edmund Westby and Catherine Wright, who was Church of England, and who was 23 years younger than Day.[61,62]

It was a simple wedding with no reception, suggesting that the event was a formality to solemnise something that happened in the past.[63]

Prior to the union, Edith, who became known as Lady Day, was living off her own means with her widowed mother at 50 Rutland Gate in Westminster, London.[64]

According to Samuel Henry Day in *Family Papers*, there was no child to his father's second marriage.[61]

One assumes, however, there was a son, Thomas Day, who was born out of wedlock, and whose birth was not registered, something that was not uncommon in those days. For instance, the birth in 1875 of an unrelated Thomas Day was not registered in New South Wales until 42 years later.[65]

Prior to serving as a judge of the High Court of Justice, Sir John Day made his fortune from writing a book, *The Common Law Procedure Act*, and as a merchant with a limited company.[61]

That was at a time when Edith's father, Edmund Westby, and James Dickson, father of the Premier of Queensland, were merchants and directors of the Imperil Bank Limited, London.[66]

The Conspirators?

James Dickson, same as Sir William Farmer in England and Australia, was a drapery merchant.[67]

With his father-in-law, John Waldron Wright, Edmund Westby was a timber merchant in England before migrating to Australia where he was a timber merchant, trade assignee, insurance broker, and financial agent at Melbourne. When he returned to England, Westby was a director of financial and insurance institutions.[68,69,70,71]

Sir John Day served from 1882 to 1901 as a judge of Her Majesty's High Court of Justice in England and Wales.[72]

On his retirement, Sir John Day was granted an annuity of £3,500, and the following year, which was two years after the death of Thomas Day, he was appointed as a Privy Councillor by Queen Victoria.[61]

December 28, 1900 – on the retirement of Chief Inspector John Stuart, who was severely criticised by the Royal Commission, it was recommended that a position should be created for a Deputy to assist Commissioner Parry-Okeden.[73]

Instead of carrying out the recommendation, acting on advice provided by Home Secretary Foxton, the Executive Council promoted Inspector Alexander Douglas-Douglas to Chief Inspector.[74,75]

In his article *A Journalist's Memories* published by *The Brisbane Courier*, Reginald Spencer Browne linked Douglas-Douglas with the conspiracy when he stated that *at Gatton, we saw Douglas-Douglas, too, at times, but Galbraith was right-hand man to Urquhart*.[76]

April 6, 1901 – acting on advice of the Executive Council, Lord Lamington assigned Douglas-Douglas to all the police districts in Queensland, giving him jurisdiction over the entire force. Prior to that arrangement, the authority of the Chief Inspector did not extend beyond the boundaries of the Brisbane District.[77]

Of interest here and elsewhere in the book, Griffith of the Irish Constitution and Dickson and Foxton of the English Constitution, were active Masons, for instance, apologies from the three were read out in the North Australian Lodge No. 796 on May 21, 1896.[78]

September 21, 1901 – an amendment in the Queensland Police Gazette described Thomas Day as *a labourer, 5 feet 8½ inches high, 34 to*

38 inches chest measurement, sallow complexion, dark-brown hair, hazel-green eyes, oblique parallel lines tattooed on the left forearm, and a Roman Catholic.[79]

This revelation that Day was a Roman Catholic, which came after he was dead and buried, corroborates the rumour that Day confessed to Father Daniel Walsh at Gatton.

Moreover, the *sallow complexion* connects Day with the *dark man* at Carcoar, and the suspect in England described as being of *dark complexion*.

It also confirms the statement of William Burnett at the Royal Commission that Day was of *dark complexion*.

December 19, 1901 – the term of Lord Lamington as Governor of Queensland came to an end.[80]

June 18, 1902 – at the invitation of the Sir Arthur Rutledge, Attorney-General for Queensland, a party consisting of:
- Sir Samuel Walker Griffith (Lieutenant-Governor and Chief Justice of Queensland);
- Justice Patrick Real (Supreme Court of Queensland);
- Justin Fox Greenlaw Foxton (Home Secretary, Queensland Government);
- Captain Alexander Ramsay Harman (Aide-de-Camp to the new Governor of Queensland, Lieutenant-General Sir Herbert Charles Chermside);
- John James Kingsbury (Crown Prosecutor);
- Arthur Feez, Edwyn Mitford Lilley, Duncan John Reay Watson, and John Laskey Woolcook (all leading members of the Bar in Queensland);
- Chief Inspector Alexander Douglas-Douglas (Queensland Police Force);
- William Geoffrey Cahill (Under Secretary, Department of Justice, Queensland);
- Sir Edward Austin Stewart-Richardson (Aide-de-Camp to the former Governor of Queensland, Lord Lamington), and
- J. P. O'Sullivan

The Conspirators?

had a meeting with Sir Frederick Darley onboard the steamer *Moana* at the Pinkenba Wharf in the Brisbane River.[81,82,83]

It was Rutledge who filed a *no true bill* to abort the trial of Carus-Wilson. His decision was made after an analysis of the evidence by Kingsbury and criminal lawyers, obviously those invited to the meeting with Darley.[84]

Justice Patrick Real from Limerick, Ireland, was possibly more than just an acquaintance.[85]

The J. P. O'Sullivan might have been Patrick (Paddy) O'Sullivan, a former soldier, who was from Kerry, Ireland.

During the coronation of Queen Victoria, O'Sullivan allegedly assaulted another with a bayonet. He was found *guilty* and was sentenced to 15 years' transportation, arriving in 1838 at Sydney on the ship *Bengal Merchant*.[86]

Seizing the opportunity when provided with a ticket-of-leave, Paddy O'Sullivan became a successful businessman and politician at Ipswich. When granted a conditional pardon, he married Mary Real, Justice Real's sister.[86]

What convinced me that Darley was involved in Day being protected from arrest for the murders committed in Australia was a statement he made that it was Rutledge, who recommended him to be admitted to the Bar in Queensland.[81]

It is a fact that Darley, Griffith and Rutledge were very good friends, Darley admitting Griffith to the Bar of New South Wales in 1891.[87]

Ten years later, which was before the meeting onboard the steamer *Moana* at the Pinkenba Wharf, Griffith together with Rutledge were invited guests at a Dinner Party hosted by Darley at the Union Club in Sydney.[88]

It did not come as a surprise to see Chief Inspector Douglas-Douglas and William Geoffrey Cahill, Department of Justice, in the party because therein was the nucleus of those in authority who, in my opinion, protected Day from arrest for the Gatton murders, and aborted the trial of Carus-Wilson.

Sir Frederick Darley's father, Henry Darley, of Wicklow, Ireland, was a barrister and Clerk in Chancery, the title changing to Master of Chancery on his departure.[89]

After Henry Darley's time in the Chancery, Carus-Wilson's grandfather, the Right Honourable Edward Litton, served as the Member for Coleraine in the House of Commons and Master of Chancery in Ireland.[90]

Between 1881 and 1883, Sir Frederick Darley served with Sir George Innes and Sir William Charles Windeyer in the Parkes-Robertson Ministry as Vice-President of the Executive Council and Representative of the Government in the Upper House of New South Wales.[91] And, yes, it was the same Windeyer, who was appointed by Griffith as a temporary judge in Queensland.[92]

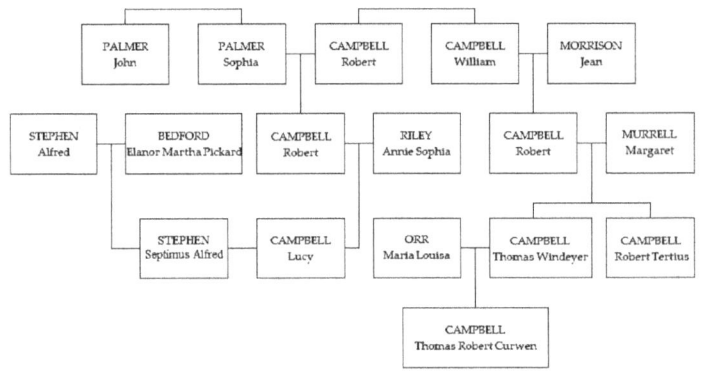

Campbell, Palmer and Stephen families

In the above chart, it will be found that the father of Reverend Thomas Robert Curwen Campbell, who married James Robert Dickson and Mary MacKinlay in St Paul's Church of England at Carcoar, was Thomas Windeyer Campbell, and that father and son were related to Sir Alfred Stephen.[93]

Furthermore, it might have been the case that Dickson's mother, formerly Mary Maria Palmer, was related to Sophia Palmer, a sister of John Palmer, who arrived in New South Wales with the *First Fleet* as the purser of Governor Arthur Phillip's flagship *Sirius*.[94,95]

While in the presence of the Royal family as the Sheriff of London, Sir William Farmer received a snuffbox from the Emperor of Germany

The Conspirators?

as a memento of his Imperial Majesty being entertained by the City of London Corporation in 1891.[96,97]

One instance that stands out from the others to connect Farmer and Darley was the marriage of Constance Campbell, daughter of Farmer's good friend, Alexander Campbell, to Darley's brother, Cecil West Darley.[98,99]

One of the recommendations of the Royal Commission was for Urquhart to be replaced as head of the Criminal Investigation Branch at Brisbane. Acting on that recommendation, the Government sent a cable to Sir Horace Tozer, Agent-General of London, requesting him to find a suitable replacement from Scotland Yard.[100]

The request was withdrawn when Tozer advised *it was impossible to get a man who would in any way be able to take up the position, unless he engaged one of those who had retired from the force on a pension, whereas a younger officer was required.*

Home Secretary Foxton, who believed that Urquhart had *gained such experience as makes him at present much more suitable for the post than any other officer available,* decided that Urquhart should remain as head of the Criminal Investigation Branch in Queensland.[101]

September 30, 1902 – farcically, after Thomas Day's death, the Criminal Investigation Branch, Brisbane, advised in the Queensland Police Gazette that a warrant had been issued for Day's arrest.

One assumes this was done by Urquhart to end the investigation into the Gatton murders, Day being seen, allegedly, with a female in a train at Landsborough, north from Brisbane, metaphorically riding off into the sunset with his sweetheart, never to be heard of again.[102]

March 22, 1904 – after serving less than five years of the seven years' sentence for attempting to commit an *unnatural offence* with a boy at Ipswich, Carus-Wilson was released from St Helena Island and transported to Brisbane in the steamer *Otter*.[103]

Reverend Hugh Thomas Molesworth of St Peter's Church of England at Wynnum, east of Brisbane, was with Carus-Wilson during the journey from St Helena to Brisbane.[104,105]

March 25, 1904 – accompanied by a clergyman, quite possibly Molesworth, Carus-Wilson slipped quietly out of Australia on the steamer *Marathon* bound for England, his name being found afterwards in the manifest.[105]

Between 1904 and 1917 – Carus-Wilson was in and out of prison in England for false pretences, gross indecency and indecent assault on a male.[106]

April 3, 1904 – baffled that every step taken to discover the perpetrator of his son's murder had met with negative results, some of the comments made by Fred Hill to a reporter were published in the *Truth*, as follows:

> *It has been freely stated that Wilson was related to some mighty magnate in the land, but of this Mr Hill cannot get definite information, although he has repeatedly endeavoured to do so. He is most anxious to satisfy himself on this point, as it would help to clear up much of the mystery which exists on account of the police having failed to effect an arrest all these long years.*[107]

One assumes that what Fred Hill alluded to might have had something to do with Thomas Day, allegedly, being hidden by Lord Salisbury at Hatfield House after the murder of Alice McKenzie on July 17, 1889.[35]

Before the letters allegedly written by Charles Stewart Parnell were found to be forgeries, which was prior to the murder of Alice McKenzie, Salisbury and Lord Randolph Henry Spencer Churchill, father of the later great-statesman, Sir Winston Churchill, were expected to be called to give evidence at the Parnell Commission, one of the judges being Sir John Day.[61,108,109]

When confronted in the hut on Clarke's butchery, Day was reading *Rienzi, Last of the Roman Tribunes* by Edward George Earle Bulwer-Lytton, uncle of General Sir Edward Earle Gascoyne Bulwer, who served with Sir John Day on the Belfast Riots Commission.[66,110]

One also feels obliged to mention that John Stanley Angus Frewen whose father, John Frewen, was a wholesale draper in England, worked as a draper for Farmer & Co at Sydney, and another relative,

The Conspirators?

Hugh Morten Frewen, was renowned for his lecturing on *Bimetallism* throughout Australia.[111,112,113]

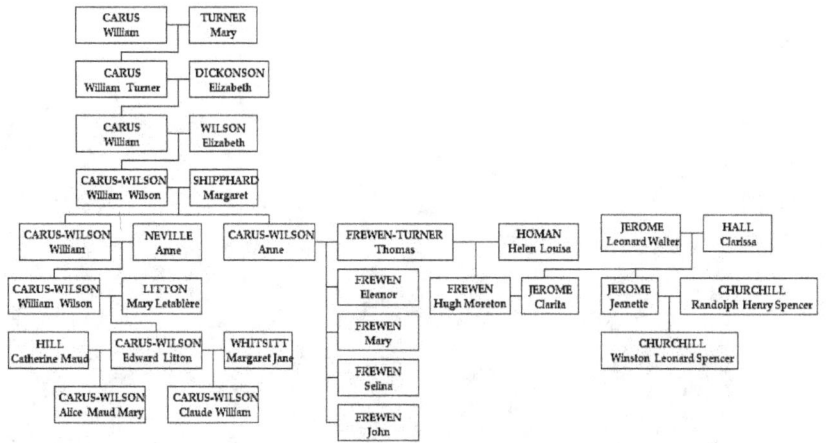

Carus-Wilson and Churchill families

It will be seen in the above chart for the Carus-Wilson and Churchill families that Carus-Wilson was *related by marriage* to Lord Randolph Churchill.

June 13, 1908 – Sir John Day passed away, the worth of his estate being proven at £102,886, whereas the estate of Sir William Farmer, who died in the same year, was proved at £41,683.[114,115]

Sir William Farmer was a *mighty magnate*, but Sir John Day was more *powerful* and *influential*.

Lady Darley and Sir Frederick Darley with their son, Captain Darley

(Courtesy of the National Library of Australia)

The Conspirators?

Senior Officers of the Queensland Police Force

Back Row (L-R) Sub-Inspector Henry Ross, Sub-Inspector Charles Savage, Sub-Inspector James Geraghty and Sub-Inspector Hugh Malone

Front Row (L-R) Inspector John Warren-White, Chief Inspector Alexander Douglas-Douglas, Commissioner William Edward Parry-Okeden, Inspector Frederic Charles Urquhart and Inspector James Nethercote

(Courtesy of the Queensland Police Museum)

CONCLUSION

During the 1860s, William Henry Day, brother of Sir John Day whom one suspects was Thomas Day's father, selected the land on which the town of Dayboro, north-west from Brisbane, now stands.[1] With that fact in mind, going back to Noel saying to Urquhart that Day gave a false birthplace when he joined the Queensland Permanent Artillery, "I am aware of that," replied Urquhart. "I am not sure it is false."

"You are not?"

"No, I know he said his birthplace was Cunnamulla."[2]

If not at Kent, England, one assumes that Thomas Day was born somewhere in Queensland with the full knowledge of William Henry Day, who in 1859 joined the Civil Service of Queensland as a clerk in the Colonial Secretary's office. Twenty-four years later, he was appointed the Water Police Magistrate for Brisbane, and the year after, the second Police Magistrate for Brisbane. When he retired in 1890, he was the Police Magistrate for South Brisbane.[3]

At the end of this Conclusion, apart from advising me that the investigation into the Gatton murders is still a *cold case*, there is permission from the Queensland Government for any image found at the Queensland State Archives to be published in this book.[4]

On June 26, 2018, the Homicide Investigation Unit, Queensland Police Service, advised that there was a need to balance *the priorities of this office whilst having regard to the available police resources and the specific details of each unsolved homicide.*[5]

In effect, the investigation into the Gatton murders will not be reopened with a view to closing the *cold case*.

That being so, if the Government had not given improper and unlawful instructions to the police force, it is my considered opinion that Edward Litton Carus-Wilson and Thomas Day would have been hung for the Oxley and Gatton murders.

More to the point, this was the beginning of nine decades of corruption within the Government and police force of Queensland that

Conclusion

was interrupted in the 1980s but not completely eradicated by the Fitzgerald Inquiry.[6]

Another who suffered under the tyranny of Parry-Okeden was Inspector James Nethercote, who can be found in the photograph of senior police officers at the end of Chapter 11.[7]

It was expected, as recommended by the Royal Commission (1899), that when Urquhart was moved to a position in the Civil Service of equal pay and status to his then office in the police force, Nethercote would take over as head of the Criminal Investigation Branch, Brisbane, neither of which happened.[8]

Instead, Nethercote was re-assigned from Roma Street to Ipswich in 1900, transferred back to Roma Street in 1903, and was sent out west to Charleville in 1905.[9]

Highly regarded as an investigator and prosecutor, Nethercote had never lived outside a city. Unable to ride a horse to inspect the stations in his district, Nethercote was provided with a buggy and horse to perform that duty. When the inland climate played havoc with his fair English complexion, Nethercote's request for a re-assignment back to the coast was denied, resulting in him developing a skin condition that led to depression and eventually to Nethercote's retirement in 1908 due to ill health.[10]

Same as Arrell, Christie and Nethercote, my advancement in the police force was *blocked* by the corruption known as the *Joke*. This was identified by the Fitzgerald Inquiry, and after passing a specially-arranged course, my promotion to the rank of Inspector took effect on October 16, 1989.[6,11]

My career as a Commissioned Officer, however, was short-lived, as a report furnished by me on November 6, 1990, which can be found at the end of this Chapter, was altered without my knowledge and permission.[12]

If you look at the letter 'g' in the fourth line of the last paragraph on page one, and fourth line of the first paragraph on page two, you will see that the two-page report was prepared by different manual typewriters.[12]

In effect, after retyping the first page, removing my acknowledgement in the first paragraph that the owner of the vehicle was my wife's employer, the page was re-attached to the second page on which there was my signature.[12]

Then, a completely different minute was provided in the left margin of the first page, which is easily identifiable, simply by looking at the numeral "4" in the date of the minute, and the "4" on the first line of the report.[12]

The report was subsequently called into question, resulting in my demotion to Senior Sergeant on February 11, 1992, for failing to acknowledge therein that the person issued with the notice was my wife's employer.[13]

Much could be said about what happened, but that will be left for my future book, *Surviving the Joke: Honesty Does Not Always Pay*.

Conclusion

Office of the
Minister for Police and
Minister for Corrective Services

Ref No: 2018/7145 & 7939 JF

1 6 APR 2018

1 William Street Brisbane
PO Box 15195 City East
Queensland 4002 Australia
Telephone +61 7 3035 8300
Facsimile +61 7 3221 0794
Email police@ministerial.qld.gov.au
ABN 65 959 415 158

Mr Neil Bradford

Dear Mr Bradford

I refer to representations made on your behalf by the Honourable Annastacia Palaszczuk MP, Premier and Minister for Trade, about the unsolved 1898 Gatton murders and approval to publish images of historical documents from the Queensland State Archives for your forthcoming book.

A copy of your correspondence was forwarded to the office of the Honourable Mark Ryan MP, Minister for Police and Minister for Corrective Services, and I have been asked to respond to you on behalf of the Minister on this occasion.

The Minister appreciates your concerns and referred this matter to the Queensland Police Service (QPS) so that our office can be better informed about the issues you have raised.

In relation to your request for permission to publish images of historical documents, all images relating to Series ID 9189 from the Queensland State Archives, where the QPS has been identified as the copyright owner, has approval to be published in your book titled *"Jack the Ripper: His Australian Murders"*.

Please give attribution to the QPS by including the following statement under or beside each relevant image:

Courtesy of the Queensland Government (Queensland Police Service)

Further, the QPS Homicide Investigation Unit advised that the Gatton Murders remain a cold case investigation.

I trust this information is of assistance. Should you wish to discuss this matter further, please contact Detective Senior Sergeant Tara Kentwell, State Crime Command on telephone 3364 4150.

Thank you for contacting the Minister.

Yours sincerely

Ellen McIntyre
Chief of Staff

Letter from the Minister for Police dated April 16, 2018
(Courtesy of the Queensland Government)

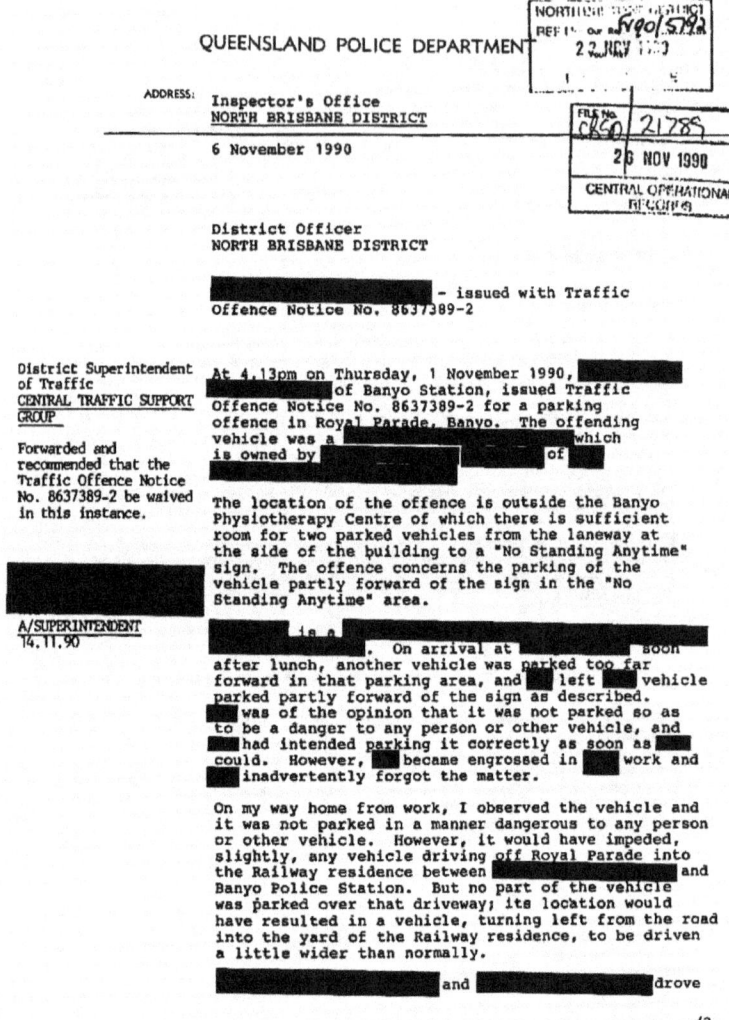

Author's altered report dated November 6, 1990, page 1
(Courtesy of the Crime and Corruption Commission)

Conclusion

- Page 2 -

into the yard of the Railway residence, prior to the time of the offence, and the Constables felt that the parked vehicle impeded their turn off the road, and in ▮▮▮▮▮▮▮▮▮▮▮▮▮▮▮▮ words to me on the night of 2 November 1990, "it was just about obstructing the driveway there", but under no circumstances was it parked dangerously.

▮▮▮▮▮ was dismayed by being issued with a notice, but ▮▮▮▮ intended paying the fine. However, as I have told ▮▮▮▮▮▮▮▮▮ I consider that as the vehicle has been parked there correctly for the past five months, a fact of ownership which should have been known by the Constables, it would have been sound public relations to request that it be parked correctly rather than to issue a ticket in the first instance.

I have advised the Constables and ▮▮▮▮▮▮▮▮▮▮ Officer in Charge, Banyo, that I would furnish a report requesting that the notice be waived, in the interest of improving public relations, and I respectfully request that favourable consideration be given to my request.

[signature]
N.R. BRADFORD
INSPECTOR

Author's altered report dated November 6, 1990, page 2

(Courtesy of the Crime and Corruption Commission)

ABBREVIATIONS USED IN ENDNOTES

ADB	Australian Dictionary of Biography.
ANZ	Archives New Zealand.
BDM	Births, Deaths and Marriages.
BNR	Bradford, Neil Raymond. *Oxley-Gatton Murders: Exposing the Conspiracy*, 2015, BookPal, Brisbane, Australia.
BR	Burgess, Richard. *Life of Richard Burgess: The Notorious Highwayman and Murderer*, 1914, Ward and Reeves, New Zealand.
DSH	Day, Samuel Henry. *Family Papers* (Classic Reprint Series), 2016, Forgotten Books, United States.
GG	Government Gazette.
NSWPG	New South Wales Police Gazette.
NSWSAR	New South Wales State Archives and Records.
NZPG	New Zealand Police Gazette.
QPG	Queensland Police Gazette.
QSA	Queensland State Archives.
RRC	Report of the Royal Commission on Police Inquiry (1899), *Queensland Parliamentary Service*, <http://www.parliament.qld.gov.au/documents/tableOffice/TabledPapers/1899/1399T145.pdf>.
SAPG	South Australian Police Gazette.
SKES	Skinner, Keith and Evans, Stewart. *The Ultimate Jack the Ripper Sourcebook: An Illustrated Encyclopedia*, 2001, Robinson, London, United Kingdom.
TNA	The National Archives, United Kingdom.
TPG	Tasmanian Police Gazette.
VPG	Victorian Police Gazette.
WG	Webster, Gerald. *I Walked at Dawn*, 1949, Allan Wingate Limited, London.

ENDNOTES

BACKGROUND

1. Inquiry Opened, *The Telegraph*, January 24, 1899, page 5.
2. Gatton Tragedy, *The Telegraph*, March 25, 1899, page 2.
3. The Oxley Murder, *The Brisbane Courier*, February 18, 1899, page 4.
4. RRC.

INTRODUCTION

1. BNR – pages 2, 3, 64, 68, 69, 72, 83, 84, 86, 121, 131, 152, 154, 167, 194, 202, 205, 211, 212, 215-217.
2. RRC – pages 447-449.
3. RRC – pages 442, 454.
4. QSA – Statement of John Carroll, December 31, 1898, Series ID 9189/Item ID 294456.
5. RRC – pages 442, 443, 488.
6. QSA – Telegram from Commissioner W. E. Parry-Okeden, January 4, 1899, Series ID 9189/Item ID 294453.
7. Queensland, *The Weekly Times*, July 6, 1912, page 26.
8. Criminal Code Act 1899, *Office of the Queensland Parliamentary Counsel*, viewed online, August 25, 2018.
9. RRC – page 432.
10. The Gatton Murders, 26 December 1898, *Queensland Police Media*, posted online, October 15, 2013.
11. QSA – Telegram from Commissioner W. E. Parry-Okeden, January 7, 1899, Series ID 9189/Item ID 294453.
12. RRC – pages LXII, LXIV, 400, 405, 411, 439, 442, 443, 446, 450-454, 488.
13. QSA – Statement of John Carroll, January 11, 1899, Series ID 9189/Item ID 294456.
14. BNR – pages 140-159.
15. QSA – Memorandum from Chief Inspector Stuart, March 22, 1899, Series ID 9189/Item ID 294495.

16. QSA – Telegram from Chief Inspector Stuart, April 4, 1899, Series ID 9189/Item ID 294495.
17. QSA – Report from Sub-Inspector H. R. P. Durham, April 12, 1899, Series ID 9189/Item ID 294495.
18. QSA – Telegram from Sub-Inspector H. R. P. Durham, April 13, 1899, Series ID 9189/Item ID 294495.
19. QSA – Telegram from Commissioner W. E. Parry-Okeden, April 13, 1899, Series ID 9189/Item ID 294495.
20. RRC – page 444.
21. QSA – Statement of Duncan Robert McGregor, January 11, 1899, Series ID 9189/Item ID 294488.
22. RRC – pages 678-681.
23. RRC – page 643.
24. RRC – pages 452, 655.
25. A Gatton Discovery, *The Brisbane Courier*, December 26, 1906, page 4.
26. QPG – Deserters from Her Majesty's Service, May 27, 1899, Volume XXXVI, Number 33, Thomas Day and William Charles Chaston, page 252.
27. SAPG – Deserter from H.M. Service, October 11, 1899, Thomas Day and William Charles Chaston, page 167.
28. TPG – Deserter from H.M. Service, October 13, 1899, Thomas Day and William Charles Chaston, page 164.
29. NZPG – Deserters from Her Majesty's Service, October 25, 1899, Thomas Day and William Charles Chaston, page 232.
30. A Downs Scare, *The Darling Downs Gazette*, June 28, 1899, page 2.
31. QSA – Circular Memorandum from Inspector Urquhart, February 8, 1899, Series ID 9189/Item ID 294493.
32. QSA – Statement of William Chaston, February 8, 1899, Series ID 9189/Item ID 294493.
33. Latest Details, *The Bristol Mercury*, November 10, 1888, page 8.
34. The Queensland Horrors, *The Blayney Advocate and Carcoar Herald*, January 21, 1899, page 2.
35. QSA – Letter from James Tracey, January 29, 1899, Series ID 9189/Item ID 294453.

Endnotes

1. WHITECHAPEL MURDERS

1. TNA – Special Report of Detective Inspector George Payne, October 14, 1896, Reference Number MEPO3-142 pt2 (211) Ripper Letters.
2. BDM – Death of Annie Dickson, Queensland, Reference Number 1880/C628.
3. Brisbane, *The Maryborough Chronicle*, January 20, 1880, page 2.
4. Brisbane, *The Maryborough Chronicle*, February 3, 1880, page 3.
5. No Title, *The Brisbane Courier*, October 16, 1878, pages 2, 3.
6. ADB – Sir James Robert Dickson (1832–1901).
7. Marriages, *The Sydney Morning Herald*, January 7, 1882, page 1.
8. BDM – Marriage of Edward Litton Carew Wilson and Margaret Jane Whitsitt, New Zealand, Reference Number 1882002370.
9. NSWPG – No. 2, January 11, 1899, Edward Liton Carns Wilson wanted for questioning, page 1.
10. Wilson's Career at Broken Hill, *The Advertiser*, January 11, 1899, page 5.
11. NSWSAR – Unassisted Immigrant Passenger Lists, 1885, stowaway Thomas Day on the steamer *Bombay*.
12. Arrival of the Bombay with immigrants, *The Sydney Morning Herald*, June 6, 1885, page 8.
13. BDM – Death of Margaret Wilson, England, Reference Number DYD 750137.
14. BDM – Birth of Claude William Carus Wilson, England, Reference Number BXCD 525994.
15. Wilson in Adelaide, *The South Australian Register*, January 11, 1899, page 5.
16. Shocking Murder in Whitechapel, *The Western Times*, April 10, 1888, page 7.
17. SKES – pages 3-7.
18. The Whitechapel Murders, *The Bendigo Advertiser*, November 3, 1888, page 6.
19. SKES – pages 8-22.
20. SKES – pages 23-54.
21. SKES – pages 55-120.

22. Jack the Ripper, *The Inquirer and Commercial News*, June 15, 1892, page 5.
23. SKES – pages 134-198.
24. SKES – pages 199-266.
25. A Strange Story, *The Western Daily Press*, October 9, 1888, page 8.
26. Latest Details, *The Bristol Mercury*, November 10, 1888, page 8.
27. SKES – pages 396-398.
28. The Whitechapel Tragedies, *Launceston Examiner*, November 30, 1888, page 2.
29. SKES – pages 371-387.
30. SKES – pages 418, 419.
31. Camp, Anthony John. *Royal Mistresses and Bastards: Fact and Fiction, 1714–1936*, viewed August 25, 2018.
32. Camp, A. *Mary Jane Kelly*, email, May 15, 2017.
33. Ridley, Jane. *Bertie: A Life of Edward VII*, 2012, Chatto & Windus, London, United Kingdom, pages 54-63.
34. Middlemas, Keith. *The Life and Times of Edward VII*, 1972, Weidenfeld & Nicolson, London, United Kingdom, page 31.
35. The Prince and The Chorus Girl, *The New Zealand Herald*, Volume XXVIII, Issue 8724, November 14, 1891, page 2.
36. The Suicide of Lydia Manton, *The West Australian*, November 27, 1891, page 6.
37. Marriott, Trevor. *Jack the Ripper: The 21st Century Investigation*, 2005, John Blake, London, United Kingdom, pages 267-269.
38. Adventures of A Gaiety Girl, *The Auckland Star*, Volume XXXI, Issue 83, April 7, 1900, page 13.
39. SKES – pages 469-488.
40. Marriage of Edward Lytton Carus-Wilson and Catherine Maud Hill, Parish Register for Westbourne Park St Luke, Borough of Westminster, England, 1889, page 85, Entry No. 169.
41. SKES – pages 495-530, 593.
42. DSH – Section III, (482).
43. The Imperial Bank (Limited), *The Evening Standard*, April 26, 1864, page 1.

Endnotes

2. JACK'S AUSTRALIAN MURDERS?

1. TNA – Jack the Ripper letter, October 14, 1896, Reference Number MEPO3-142 pt2 (234,236) and MEPO3-142 pt2 (235-236v).
2. GG – Hanging of George Martin Walter Archer, New South Wales, 1893, page 5468.
3. GG – Hanging of Edwin Hubert Glasson, New South Wales, 1894, page 1201.
4. The Treatment of Burgess, *The Capricornian*, February 18, 1899, page 19.
5. Sunningdale, *Reading Mercury, Oxford Gazette, Newbury Herald, and Berks Country Paper*, January 18, 1890, page 6.
6. ADB – Sir William Farmer (1832–1908).
7. NSWSAR – Unassisted Immigrant Passenger Lists, 1890, T. W. Day on the steamer Coromandel.
8. The R.M.S. Coromandel, *The Sydney Morning Herald*, March 25, 1890, page 8.
9. The Whitechapel Murders, *Supplement to The Horsham Times*, December 23, 1890, page 1.
10. Knowing the Aussie accent, *Australian Geographic*, viewed August 25, 2018.
11. Mysterious Death of a Woman, *The Sydney Morning Herald*, December 30, 1892, page 3.
12. Mysterious Death of a Woman, *The Sydney Morning Herald*, December 31, 1892, page 11.
13. Mysterious Death of a Woman, *The Daily Telegraph*, December 30, 1892, page 5.
14. Strange Death of a Woman, *The Australian Star*, December 31, 1892, page 6.
15. The Whitechapel Murders, *The Bendigo Advertiser*, November 3, 1888, page 6.
16. SKES – pages 3-7.
17. No Title, *Wagga Wagga Express*, January 5, 1893, page 3.
18. Hollis, R. *Court records*, email, January 31, 2018.
19. BDM – Birth of Edith Westby, Victoria, Reference Number 16525/1849.

20. 1881 England Census for Edith Westby.
21. Obituary, *The Daily Advertiser*, March 8, 1911, page 3.
22. BDM – Birth of Alfred Ashley Westby, Victoria, Reference Number 15201/1847.
23. Personal, *The Argus*, January 28, 1929, page 8.
24. In Riverina, *Town and Country Journal*, August 28, 1880, page 19.
25. RRC – page 438.
26. Sydney Hunt Club, *The Sydney Morning Herald*, April 17, 1893, page 3.
27. Horrible Tragedy, *The Evening News*, March 26, 1893, page 4.
28. The Bourke-Street Murder, *The Australian Star*, May 6, 1895, page 5.
29. SKES – pages 371-387.
30. The Burton-Street Murder, *Wagga Wagga Express*, April 18, 1893, page 4.
31. The Burton-street Murder, *The Evening News*, April 8, 1893, page 6.
32. The Burton-street Murder, *The Evening News*, April 14, 1893, page 5.
33. The Inquest, *The Sydney Morning Herald*, March 28, 1893, page 5.
34. The Burton-street Tragedy, *The Sydney Mail*, April 22, 1893, page 816.
35. SKES – pages 55-120.
36. The Sydney Murder Case, *The Advertiser*, April 15, 1893, page 5.
37. The Whitechapel Tragedies, *Launceston Examiner*, November 30, 1888, page 2.
38. The Murder of Emma Harrison, *The Australasian*, April 22, 1893, page 26.
39. The Darlinghurst Tragedy, *The Singleton Argus*, June 14, 1893, page 1.
40. The Burton-street Murder, *The Evening News*, April 7, 1893, page 4.
41. The Murder of Emma Harrison, *The Australasian*, April 8, 1893, page 24.
42. Bourke-Street Murder, *The Australian Star*, April 11, 1893, page 5.

Endnotes

43. The Burton-street Tragedy, *The Evening News*, June 9, 1893, page 4.
44. The Murder of Emma Harrison, *The Australasian*, April 15, 1893, page 25.
45. The Sydney Murder Case, *The Express and Telegraph*, April 11, 1893, page 3.
46. Woman Strangled, *The Week*, March 30, 1893, page 23.
47. NSWSAR – Gaol Description and Entrance Books, April 19, 1893, George Martin Walter Archer.
48. The Burton-street Tragedy, *The Sydney Morning Herald*, April 12, 1893, page 4.
49. The Woolloomooloo Tragedy, *The West Australian*, April 13, 1893, page 6.
50. Central Criminal Court, *The Sydney Morning Herald*, June 12, 1893, page 8.
51. Law Report, *The Sydney Morning Herald*, June 17, 1893, page 13.
52. The Execution, *The Australian Star*, July 11, 1893, page 6.
53. Execution of Archer, *The Katoomba Times and Blue Mountaineer*, July 14, 1893, page 2.
54. VPG – Prisoner discharged from Castlemaine Gaol, Supplement to Edition No. 18, May 2, 1894, Richard James Burgess.

3. SINS OF ANOTHER

1. Burton, Kelly. *Reform of the Double Jeopardy Rule on the Basis of Fresh and Compelling Evidence in New South Wales and Queensland*, 2004, James Cook University Law Review 84, viewed August 25, 2018.
2. The Carcoar Tragedy, *The Molong Express*, September 30, 1893, pages 3-5.
3. The Description of the Premises, *The Bathurst Daily Free Press & Mining Journal*, September 25, 1893, page 2.
4. The Slaying of The Twain, *The Broadford Courier*, December 1, 1893, page 4.
5. The Evidence, *The Bathurst Daily Free Press & Mining Journal*, September 26, 1893, pages 2, 3.
6. Bertie Glasson's Previous Career, *The Bathurst Daily Free Press & Mining Journal*, September 27, 1893, page 2.

7. An Appalling Tragedy, *Australian Town and Country Journal*, September 30, 1893, pages 13, 14.
8. The Inquest Continued, *The Bathurst Daily Free Press & Mining Journal*, September 27, 1893, page 2.
9. RRC – page 455.
10. Glasson's "Dream," *The Western Star*, October 28, 1893, page 4.
11. Hollis, R. *Court records*, email, January 31, 2018.
12. Cain's Blood-Red Hand, *The National Advocate*, September 27, 1893, page 2.
13. RRC – page 477.
14. RRC – pages 443, 451.
15. VPG – Richard James Burgess, 1894, conviction for unlawful assault.
16. QSA – Statement of Frederick Ross, January 11, 1899, Series ID 9189/Item ID 294488.
17. The Carcoar Murders, *The Burrowa News*, October 13, 1893, pages 2, 3.
18. BNR – pages 4-26.
19. An Accomplice Suggested, *The Age*, September 28, 1893, page 5.
20. The Inquest Resumed, *The Sydney Morning Herald*, September 27, 1893, pages 7, 8.
21. The Carcoar Tragedy, *The Daily Telegraph*, September 29, 1893, page 5.
22. Carcoar Murders, *The Telegraph*, September 26, 1893, page 5.
23. The Carcoar Murders, *The Maitland Mercury and Hunter River General Advertiser*, September 28, 1893, page 5.
24. The Carcoar Tragedy, *The Bathurst Daily Free Press & Mining Journal*, September 26, 1893, page 2.
25. Execution of Glasson, *Goulburn Evening Penny Post*, November 30, 1893, page 2.
26. QSA – Letter from James Tracey, January 29, 1899, Series ID 9189/Item ID 294453.
27. The Carcoar Tragedy, *The Goulburn Herald*, September 29, 1893, page 2.
28. The Carcoar Tragedy, *The Age*, September 28, 1893, page 5.
29. The Victims, *The Advocate*, September 30, 1893, page 7.

Endnotes

30. Cain's Blood-Red Hand, *The National Advocate*, September 30, 1893, page 2.
31. The Carcoar Tragedy, *The Australian Star*, October 20, 1893, page 5.
32. Wilful Murder against Edwin Hubert Glasson, *The Molong Express*, September 30, 1893, page 5.
33. The Carcoar Tragedy Trial, *Newcastle Morning Herald and Miners' Advocate*, October 23, 1893, page 5.
34. The Carcoar Tragedy, *Goulburn Evening Penny Post*, October 24, 1893, page 4.
35. The Carcoar Murder, *The National Advocate*, October 21, 1893, page 2.
36. The Carcoar Murders, *The Riverine Grazier*, December 1, 1893, page 2.
37. Local and General News, *Wagga Wagga Express*, June 5, 1894, page 2.
38. Obituary, *The Daily Advertiser*, March 8, 1911, page 3.
39. No Title, *Wagga Wagga Express*, September 17, 1895, page 2.
40. Law Report, *The Sydney Morning Herald*, June 17, 1893, page 13.
41. No Title, *The Evening Telegraph and Star*, June 12, 1894, page 4.
42. Laying of the Foundation Stone of New Masonic Hall, Toowoomba, *The Queensland Figaro*, April 3, 1886, page 5.
43. ADB – Sir William Farmer (1832–1908).
44. Miscellaneous, *The Sydney Mail*, June 1, 1889, page 1158.
45. Arrival of Sir William Farmer at Adelaide, *The Sydney Morning Herald*, October 31, 1894, page 5.
46. Victoria House Employees, *The Sydney Mail*, November 24, 1894, page 1061.
47. Sir William Farmer Interviewed, *The Clarence and Richmond Examiner*, November 27, 1894, page 3.
48. DSH – Section V, (483).
49. Return of Sir William Farmer, *Reading Mercury, Oxford Gazette, Newbury Herald, and Berks County Paper*, March 30, 1895, page 4.

4. OLD JACK COMES "HOME" AGAIN

1. Jack the Ripper, *The Inquirer and Commercial News*, June 15, 1892, page 5.
2. Deeming's Career, *The Sydney Morning Herald*, May 24, 1892, page 6.
3. Queensland Governors, *Queensland Government*, viewed June 16, 2017.
4. Lady Lamington, *Table Talk*, July 2, 1903, page 24.
5. SKES – pages 719-723.
6. TNA – Jack the Ripper letter, October 14, 1896, Reference Number MEPO3-142 pt2 (234,236) and MEPO3-142 pt2 (235-236v).
7. TNA – Special Report of Detective Inspector George Payne, October 14, 1896, Reference Number MEPO3-142 pt2 211.
8. NSWSAR – Unassisted Immigrant Passenger Lists, 1890, T. W. Day on the steamer Coromandel.
9. The R.M.S. Coromandel, *The Sydney Morning Herald*, March 25, 1890, page 8.
10. BDM – Death of Edith May Cook, Queensland, Reference 1896/C3324.
11. QSA – List of Exhibits, Series ID 9189/Item ID 294453.
12. RRC – page 446.
13. QSA – Report of First Class Constable Michael Carew, January 25, 1899, Series ID 9189/ID 294453.
14. QSA – The facts against Richard Burgess up to-date, January 15, 1899, Series ID 9189/Item ID 294488.
15. BR – pages 3-6.
16. A Suicide's Letter, *The Evening News*, October 27, 1900, page 5.
17. QSA – Statement of Tobias Burke, February 8, 1899, Series ID 9189/Item ID 294493.
18. QSA – Report of Constable Charles Bell, February 4, 1899, Series ID 9189/Item ID 294453.
19. QSA – Report of Acting Sergeant Rob McNeill, February 7, 1899, Series ID 9189/Item ID 294453.
20. QSA – Report of Constable Charles Bell, February 7, 1899, Series ID 9189/Item ID 294453.

Endnotes

21. The Oxley Tragedy, *The Brisbane Courier*, April 7, 1899, page 7.
22. RRC – page 443.
23. The Gatton Tragedy, *The Brisbane Courier*, February 3, 1899, page 6.
24. District Court, *The Warwick Examiner and Times*, June 5, 1897, page 2.
25. Charge of Corrupting Youth, *The Brisbane Courier*, January 9, 1899, page 6.
26. QSA – Statement of Duncan Robert McGregor, January 11, 1899, Series ID 9189/Item ID 294488.
27. The Leyburn Case, *Warwick Argus*, May 28, 1898, page 7.
28. The alleged Leyburn outrage, *The Warwick Examiner and Times*, May 21, 1898, page 7.
29. The Triple Murder, *The Kalgoorlie Miner*, January 10, 1899, page 5.
30. QSA – Statement of Robert McGrory, January 28, 1899, Series ID 9189/ID 294453.
31. Latest Details, *The Bristol Mercury*, November 10, 1888, page 8.
32. Jack the Ripper, *The Age*, September 16, 1898, page 5.
33. Street Disturbance, *The Argus*, September 16, 1898, page 6.
34. QSA – Statement of William Chaston, February 2, 1899, Series ID 9189/ID 294493.
35. The Leyburn Case, *Warwick Argus*, May 24, 1898, page 3.
36. District Court, *The Warwick Examiner and Times*, June 4, 1898, page 2.
37. Robert Grosvenor, 1st Marquess of Westminster, *Wikipedia*, viewed August 25, 2018.
38. New Zealand Murders, *The Mercury*, July 24, 1866, page 2.
39. BR – page 22.
40. QPG – Supplement, January 28, 1899, Volume XXXVI, No. 9, description of Frank Burns, page 85.

5. OXLEY MURDER

1. St Helena Prison, *The Gympie Times*, May 17, 1898, page 3.
2. The Gatton Tragedy, *The Brisbane Courier*, February 3, 1899, page 6.

3. QSA – Statement of Frederick Ross, January 11, 1899, Series ID 9189/Item ID 294488.
4. The Gatton Tragedy, *The Brisbane Courier*, February 3, 1899, page 6.
5. QSA – Statement of William Chaston, February 2, 1899, Series ID 9189/ID 294493.
6. QSA – Report of Constable Martin Hayes, January 4, 1899, Series ID 9189/Item ID 294493.
7. QSA – Memorandum from Inspector Urquhart, February 8, 1899, Series ID 9189/Item ID 294493.
8. Social Gossip, *The Brisbane Courier*, December 2, 1898, page 7.
9. The Gatton Horror, *The Albury Banner and Wodonga Express*, October 6, 1899, page 19.
10. RRC – page 442.
11. QSA – Statement of Duncan Robert McGregor, January 11, 1899, Series ID 9189/Item ID 294488.
12. QSA – Report of Constable John Cassidy, January 11, 1899, Series ID 9189/Item ID 294493.
13. RRC – page 398.
14. The Oxley murder, *The Evening News*, February 18, 1899, page 6.
15. Statement by Mr Hill, *The Worker*, January 14, 1899, page 10.
16. The Oxley Tragedy, *The Brisbane Courier*, April 7, 1899, page 7.
17. The Oxley Murder, *The Brisbane Courier*, April 26, 1899, page 7.
18. The Oxley Murder, *The Brisbane Courier*, April 14, 1899, page 7.
19. Murder at Oxley, *The Brisbane Courier*, January 9, 1899, pages 4, 5.
20. The Oxley Tragedy, *The Queensland Times*, January 28, 1899, page 6.
21. WG – pages 58-64.
22. BNR – pages 61-63.
23. The Oxley Murder, *The Queenslander*, February 25, 1899, page 370.
24. SKES – pages 134-198.
25. QSA – List of Exhibits, Series ID 9189/Item ID 294453.
26. QSA – Identification of Richard Burgess by William Heavingham Cushing, January 24, 1899, Series ID 9189/Item ID 294488.
27. Later Particulars, *The Queensland Times*, January 10, 1899, page 2.

Endnotes

28. The Gatton Tragedy, *The Warwick Argus*, February 4, 1899, page 2.
29. The Gatton Tragedy, *The Warwick Argus*, January 28, 1899, page 2.
30. Charge of Corrupting Youth, *The Brisbane Courier*, January 9, 1899, page 6.
31. Police Commission, *The Brisbane Courier*, September 26, 1899, page 7.
32. RRC – page 655.

6. BURGESS' ALIBI

1. RRC – page 450.
2. RRC – page 436.
3. RRC – pages 453, 454.
4. QPG – Deserters from Queensland Regiment, Royal Australian Artillery, September 21, 1901, Vol. XXXVIII, No. 57, Thomas Day and William Charles Chaston.
5. QSA – Report of Constable Martin Hayes, January 4, 1899, Series ID 9189/Item ID 294493.
6. QSA – Memorandum from Inspector Urquhart, February 8, 1899, Series ID 9189/Item ID 294493.
7. The Gatton Tragedy, *The Warwick Argus*, January 28, 1899, page 2.
8. Important Testimony from Clifton and Killarney, *The Queensland Times*, January 28, 1899, page 5.
9. QSA – Report of Constables Martin Hayes and John Cassidy, March 3, 1899, Series ID 9189/Item ID 294493.
10. QSA – Circular Memorandum of Inspector Urquhart, February 8, 1899, Series ID 9189/Item ID 294493.
11. QSA – Report of Constable James Holohan, February 3, 1899, Series ID 9189/Item ID 294493.
12. The Gatton Tragedy, *The Maitland Weekly Mercury*, February 4, 1899, page 7.
13. The Gatton Tragedy, *The Brisbane Courier*, December 30, 1898, page 4.
14. The Gatton Murders, *The Queensland Times*, February 14, 1899, page 6.
15. The Gatton Murders, *The Chronicle*, March 18, 1899, pages 27, 28.

16. The Gatton Murders, *The Queensland Times*, January 14, 1899, page 5.
17. Burgess's Statement, *The Week*, February 3, 1899, page 21.
18. The Gatton Tragedy, *The Darling Downs Gazette*, February 4, 1899, pages 2, 7.
19. The Gatton Tragedy, *The Brisbane Courier*, February 6, 1899, page 6.
20. The Gatton Tragedy, *The Northern Star*, February 11, 1899, page 5.
21. QSA – Statement of Beatrice Hallas, January 14, 1899, Series ID 9189/Item ID 294488.
22. QSA – Statement of Frank Hallas, January 14, 1899, Series ID 9189/Item ID 294488.
23. QSA – Report of Acting Sergeant Toomey, February 14, 1899, Series ID 9189/Item ID 294488.
24. QSA – Identification of Richard Burgess by Beatrice Hallas, January 24, 1899, Series ID 9189/Item ID 294488.
25. QSA – Identification of Richard Burgess by Frank Hallas, January 24, 1899, Series ID 9189/Item ID 294488.
26. QSA – Statement of Sidney Henry Hallas, January 14, 1899, Series ID 9189/Item ID 294488.
27. QSA – The Facts Against Richard Burgess Up-To-Date, January 15, 1899, Series ID 9189/Item ID 294488.
28. Startling Discovery told by Mrs Berg, *The Muswellbrook Chronicle*, January 18, 1899, page 3.
29. An Extraordinary Occurrence, *The Darling Downs Gazette*, February 4, 1899, page 7.
30. Proposed Dance at Gatton, *The Queensland Times*, March 18, 1899, page 6.
31. RRC – pages 405, 406.
32. The Gatton Tragedy, *The Sydney Morning Herald*, January 25, 1899, pages 7, 8.
33. Statement by The Brother-In-Law, McNeil, *The Riverine Herald*, January 6, 1899, page 2.
34. The Gatton Murders, *The Queensland Times*, March 11, 1899, page 2.

Endnotes

35. QSA – Statement of John Carroll, December 31, 1898, Series ID 9189/Item ID 294456.
36. The Gatton Murders, *The Queensland Times*, March 21, 1899, page 5.
37. Gatton Tragedy, *The Queenslander*, March 25, 1899, pages 524, 525.
38. QSA – Statement of Patrick Murphy, January 22, 1899, Series ID 9189/Item ID 294456.
39. The Gatton Murders, *The Albury Banner and Wodonga Express*, January 27, 1899, page 37.
40. The Search by A Brother-in-Law, *The Bathurst Daily Free Press & Mining Journal*, January 5, 1899, page 2.
41. QSA – Description of Lost Whip, January 11, 1899, Series ID 9189/Item ID 294453.
42. QSA – Statement of Walter Cook, February 21, 1899, Series ID 9189/Item ID 294451.
43. QSA – Statement of John Carroll, January 11, 1899, Series ID 9189/Item ID 294456.
44. RRC – pages 443, 444.
45. RRC – pages 435, 446.
46. Gatton Tragedy, *The Week*, March 17, 1899, page 12.
47. Gatton Tragedy, *The Brisbane Courier*, March 16, 1899, page 7.
48. QSA – Statement of Michael Donohue, December 31, 1898, Series ID 9189/Item ID 294453.
49. Gatton Tragedy, *The Brisbane Courier*, March 15, 1899, page 9.
50. The Gatton Tragedy, *The Brisbane Courier*, December 30, 1898, page 4.
51. QSA – List of Exhibits, Series ID 9189/Item ID 294453.

7. GATTON MURDERS

1. The Gatton Murders, 26 December 1898, *Queensland Police Media*, posted October 15, 2013.
2. The Gatton Tragedy, *The Sydney Morning Herald*, January 25, 1899, pages 7, 8.
3. Gatton Tragedy, *The Brisbane Courier*, March 16, 1899, page 7.
4. QSA – Statement of Louisa Theaurkuaf, Series ID 9189/Item ID 294456.

5. Gatton Tragedy, *The Telegraph*, January 10, 1899, page 5.
6. The Gatton Murders, *The Evening News*, March 15, 1899, page 6.
7. The Man at the Sliprails, *The Darling Downs Gazette*, March 15, 1899, page 3.
8. QSA – Statement of Catherine Byrne, Series ID 9189/Item ID 294456.
9. QSA – Report of Acting Sergeant Toomey, March 31, 1899, Series ID 9189/Item ID 294453.
10. The Gatton Murders, *The Chronicle*, March 18, 1899, pages 27, 28.
11. The Gatton Murders, *The Queensland Times*, January 14, 1899, page 5.
12. The Gatton Murders, *The Queensland Times*, March 11, 1899, page 2.
13. RRC – pages 447-449.
14. RRC – pages 406-412.
15. QSA – Acting Sergeant Toomey's report, January 19, 1899, Series ID 9189/Item ID 294453.
16. QSA – Identification of Richard Burgess by Lizzie Labinsky, January 24, 1899, Series ID 9189/Item ID 294488.
17. An Extraordinary Occurrence, *The Darling Downs Gazette*, February 4, 1899, page 7.
18. QSA – Statement of Thomas Bailey, December 31, 1898, Series ID 9189/Item ID 294456.
19. QSA – Statement of William Miller, December 31, 1898, Series ID 9189/Item ID 294456.
20. RRC – pages 429-431.
21. Father of Gatton Tragedy Victims Dies, *Smith's Weekly*, June 11, 1927, page 9.
22. RRC – pages 464-470.
23. QSA – List and Description of Exhibits, Series ID 9189/Item ID 294453.
24. RRC – pages 418-420.
25. QSA – Report of Doctor A. W. Orr, March 1, 1899, Series ID 9189/Item ID 294453.
26. RRC – page 534.

Endnotes

8. DON'T ARREST JACK!

1. RRC – pages 429-431.
2. The Queensland Horror, *The Evening News*, December 29, 1898, page 6.
3. The Gatton Tragedy, *The Brisbane Courier*, December 29, 1898, page 5.
4. Father of Gatton Tragedy Victims Dies, *Smith's Weekly*, June 11, 1927, page 9.
5. Farewell Banquet and Presentation, *The Queensland Times*, November 22, 1902, page 4.
6. Welcome Home, *The Queensland Times*, March 12, 1904, page 12.
7. QSA – Circular Memorandum of Inspector Urquhart, February 8, 1899, Series ID 9189/Item ID 294493.
8. RRC – pages 548-550.
9. The Queensland Horrors, *The Bathurst Daily Free Press & Mining Journal*, January 13, 1899, page 2.
10. RRC – pages 442, 454.
11. QSA – Statement of John Carroll, December 31, 1898, Series ID 9189/Item ID 294456.
12. QSA – Circular Memorandum from Inspector Urquhart, February 2, 1899, Series ID 9189/Item ID 294493.
13. RRC – pages 420-422.
14. RRC – page 478.
15. RRC – page 463.
16. RRC – page 405.
17. RRC – pages 438, 439.
18. QSA – Commissioner Parry-Okeden's memorandum dated January 16, 1899, Series ID 9189/Item ID 294453.
19. Mr W. S. King, *The Brisbane Courier*, September 3, 1931, page 16.

9. THE COVER-UP

1. QSA – Circular Memorandum from Inspector Urquhart, February 2, 1899, Series ID 9189/Item ID 294493.
2. The Gatton Tragedy, *The Maitland Weekly Mercury*, January 14, 1899, page 6.

3. QSA – Statement of William Chaston, February 2, 1899, Series ID 9189/ID 294493.
4. RRC – pages 411, 412.
5. QSA – Telegram from Commissioner W. E. Parry-Okeden, January 4, 1899, Series ID 9189/Item ID 294453.
6. The Gatton Tragedy, *The Brisbane Courier*, January 5, 1899, page 5.
7. RRC – page 432.
8. *The Brisbane Courier*, April 7, 1899, page 7.
9. RRC – pages 450-453.
10. The Oxley Tragedy, *The Brisbane Courier*, January 9, 1899, page 5.
11. RRC – pages 434, 435.
12. QSA – Telegram from Commissioner W. E. Parry-Okeden, January 7, 1899, Series ID 9189/Item ID 294453.
13. Death of Martin Donohoe, *The Brisbane Courier*, January 29, 1927, page 20.
14. RRC – pages 350-354.
15. The Gatton Tragedy, *The Brisbane Courier*, January 10, 1899, page 5.
16. Reports at Gatton, *Wagga Wagga Express*, January 12, 1899, page 2.
17. The Dalby Arrest, *The Queensland Times*, January 10, 1899, page 5.
18. The Gatton Tragedy, *The Warwick Argus*, February 4, 1899, page 2.
19. Wilson Arrested at Albany, *The Chronicle*, January 14, 1899, page 13.
20. Arrest of Wilson, *The Bathurst Daily Free Press & Mining Journal*, January 11, 1899, page 2.
21. QSA – Statement of John Carroll, January 11, 1899, Series ID 9189/Item ID 294456.
22. RRC – pages 681.
23. RRC – pages 676, 677.
24. No Title, *The Brisbane Courier*, January 23, 1899, page 4.
25. The Treatment of Burgess, *The Capricornian*, February 18, 1899, page 19.
26. A Serious Charge, *The Inquirer and Commercial News*, January 27, 1899, page 14.

Endnotes

27. Gatton Tragedy, *The Telegraph*, January 25, 1899, page 6.
28. E. L. C. Wilson, *The Queensland Times*, February 14, 1899, page 5.
29. Ipswich Sensation, *The Warwick Examiner and Times*, February 11, 1899, page 7.
30. Wilson's arrival at Brisbane, *The Evening News*, February 13, 1899, page 5.
31. Wilson Before the Court, *The Brisbane Courier*, February 15, 1899, page 5.
32. The Oxley Murder, *The Brisbane Courier*, May 13, 1899, page 4.
33. QSA – Report of Acting Sergeant Toomey, February 15, 1899, Series ID 9189/Item ID 294488.
34. QSA – Report of Constables Martin Hayes and J. Cassidy, March 4, 1899, Series ID 9189/ID 294493.
35. The Oxley Murder, *The Northern Star*, February 22, 1899, page 5.
36. The Wilson Case, *The Queensland Times*, March 25, 1899, page 4.
37. QSA – Report of Constable Thomas Collis, February 27, 1899, Series ID 9189/Item ID 294493.
38. QSA – Memorandum from Chief Inspector Stuart, March 22, 1899, Series ID 9189/Item ID 294495.
39. QSA – Telegram from Chief Inspector Stuart, April 4, 1899, Series ID 9189/Item ID 294495.
40. The Oxley Tragedy, *The Brisbane Courier*, April 6, 1899, page 5.
41. QSA – Report from Sub-Inspector H. R. P. Durham, April 12, 1899, Series ID 9189/Item ID 294495.
42. QSA – Report of Sub-Inspector H. R. P. Durham, April 19, 1899, Series ID 9189/Item ID 294495.
43. QSA – Telegram from Sub-Inspector H. R. P. Durham, April 13, 1899, Series ID 9189/Item ID 294495.
44. QSA – Telegram from Commissioner W. E. Parry-Okeden, April 13, 1899, Series ID 9189/Item ID 294495.
45. Ipswich Circuit Court, *The Brisbane Courier*, April 19, 1899, page 6.
46. QSA – Report of First Class Constable Robert Kilpatrick, April 19, 1899, Series ID 9189/Item ID 294495.
47. QSA – Papers relating to offender R. Burgess since his release from prison, Series ID 9189/Item ID 294495.

48. QSA – Telegram from Inspector-General Fosbery, April 22, 1899, Series ID 9189/Item ID 294495.
49. Identification of Glasson, *The Evening News*, September 26, 1893, page 4.
50. The Victims, *The Advocate*, September 30, 1893, page 7.
51. Our Brisbane Letter, *The Queensland Times*, May 2, 1899, page 2.
52. QSA – Report of Inspector-General Fosbery, May 4, 1899, Series ID 9189/Item ID 294495.
53. No Title, *The Brisbane Courier*, May 5, 1899, page 4.
54. Official Notifications, *The Week*, May 12, 1899, page 23.
55. The Oxley Murder, *The Western Champion*, May 16, 1899, page 6.
56. General News, *The Manaro Mercury*, May 22, 1899, page 3.
57. QPG – Deserters from Her Majesty's Service, May 27, 1899, Volume XXXVI, Number 33, Thomas Day and William Charles Chaston, page 252.
58. RRC – page XXXVII.
59. The Oxley Murder, *The Western Star*, May 20, 1899, page 2.
60. Oxley Murder, *The Toowoomba Chronicle*, May 20, 1899, page 3.
61. A Deserter from West Australia, *The Express and Telegraph*, May 30, 1899, page 2.
62. RRC – cover page.
63. RRC – page 434.
64. ANZ – Report of Commissioner of Police, Brisbane, and attached "annexure" from Inspector Urquhart, October 4, 1899, Reference Number R24473458.
65. Jack the Ripper, *The Inquirer and Commercial News*, June 15, 1892, page 5.
66. SAPG – Deserters from Her Majesty's service, October 11, 1899, Thomas Day and William Charles Chaston, page 167.
67. TPG, Deserter from H.M. Service, October 13, 1899, Vol. XXXVIII, Thomas Day and William Charles Chaston, page 164.
68. ANZ – Report of Commissioner of Police, Wellington, October 16, 1899, Item ID R24473458.
69. NZPG – Deserters from Her Majesty's Service, October 25, 1899, Thomas Day and William Charles Chaston, page 232.
70. The Gatton Murders, *The Argus*, April 12, 1899, page 11.

71. Perry, Harry C. *A son of Australia: memories of W.E. Parry-Okeden, I.S.O., 1840-1926*, 1928, Watson, Ferguson & Co. Ltd., Brisbane, Australia, page 337.

10. DAMNING EVIDENCE

1. Gibney, James and Desmond. *The Gatton Mystery*, 1977, Angus and Robertson, Australia, page 191.
2. QSA – Statement of Michael John O'Grady, February 13, 1899, Series ID 9189/Item ID 294453.
3. QSA – Statement of Tobias Burke, February 8, 1899, Series ID 9189/Item ID 294493.
4. QSA – Report of First Class Constable Michael Carew, January 25, 1899, Series ID 9189/ID 294453.
5. RRC – pages 473, 474.
6. Gatton Tragedy, *The Brisbane Courier*, March 16, 1899, page 7.
7. RRC – page 446.
8. QSA – Statement of William Chaston, February 8, 1899, Series ID 9189/Item ID 294493.
9. Burgess' Boots, *The Daily Telegraph*, January 16, 1899, page 5.
10. RRC – pages 530-532.
11. RRC – page 535.
12. Gibney, James and Desmond. *The Gatton Mystery*, 1977, Angus and Robertson, Australia, page 203.
13. QSA – Letter from Commissioner Parry-Okeden, January 16, 1899, Series ID 9189/ID 294453.
14. QSA – Statement of John Carroll, December 31, 1898, Series ID 9189/Item ID 294456.
15. RRC – pages 475-477.
16. A Gatton Discovery, *The Brisbane Courier*, December 26, 1906, page 4.
17. RRC – pages 451, 452.
18. RRC – page 412.
19. RRC – pages 453-456.
20. Gatton Tragedy, *The Queenslander*, April 1, 1899, page 584.
21. A Startling Theory of the Gatton tragedy, *The Bendigo Independent*, March 25, 1899, page 3.

22. The Fitzgerald Inquiry, *Crime and Corruption Commission, Queensland*, viewed online, August 27, 2018.
23. A Downs Scare, *The Darling Downs Gazette*, June 28, 1899, page 2.

11. THE CONSPIRATORS?

1. Criminal Code Act 1899, *Office of the Queensland Parliamentary Counsel*, viewed online, August 25, 2018.
2. Alleged Killing of a Peacock, *The Telegraph*, January 24, 1901, page 2.
3. Federation, *Australian Government*, viewed online, August 25, 2018.
4. The Political Crisis, *The Warwick Argus*, November 28, 1899, page 2.
5. Queensland Premiers, *Queensland Government*, viewed online, August 25, 2018.
6. Police Commission, *The Week*, December 1, 1899, page 22.
7. Political Crisis in Queensland, *The Kalgoorlie Miner*, November 28, 1899, page 5.
8. BNR – page 216.
9. VPG – February 28, 1900, Thomas Day wanted on a warrant of commitment, page 86.
10. VPG – Deserters from H.M. Service, October 11, 1899, Thomas Day and William Charl Chaston, page 327.
11. Burgess, The Gatton Suspect, *The Evening News*, June 16, 1900, page 5.
12. Gatton Burgess, *The Australasian*, June 16, 1900, page 37.
13. Charge of Assault, *The Kalgoorlie Miner*, June 13, 1900, page 5.
14. The Charge against Burgess, *The Warwick Examiner and Times*, July 4, 1900, page 3.
15. Burgess Receives Seven Years, *The Warwick Argus*, July 28, 1900, page 5.
16. The Trentham Outrage, *The Bendigo Advertiser*, July 20, 1900, page 2.
17. A Suicides Letter, *The Clarence River Advocate*, November 6, 1900, page 4.
18. A Suicide's Letter, *The Evening News*, October 27, 1900, page 5.

Endnotes

19. A Man Shot, *The Sydney Morning Herald*, October 25, 1900, page 7.
20. Suicide in The City, *The Sydney Morning Herald*, October 27, 1900, page 11.
21. Castlereagh-Street Suicide, *The Daily Telegraph*, October 27, 1900, page 14.
22. BDM – Death of Thomas Furner, New South Wales, Reference 11234/1900.
23. QSA – List of Exhibits, Series ID 9189/Item ID 294453.
24. BDM – Death of Edith May Cook, Queensland, Reference Number 1896/C3324.
25. Badovinac, M. *Burial of Thomas Furner*, email, November 24, 2017.
26. Cusack's Funeral, *Newcastle Morning Herald and Miners' Advocate*, March 18, 1898, page 5.
27. A Pauper's Burial, *Truth*, December 9, 1900, page 7.
28. Attempted Suicide, *The Daily Telegraph*, October 25, 1900, page 7.
29. Mr Finlay Munro, *The Cumberland Argus and Fruitgrowers' Advocate*, January 18, 1939, page 8.
30. Celebration at Messrs Tooth and Co's, *The Sydney Morning Herald*, March 20, 1900, page 4.
31. ADB – Sir Robert Lucas Tooth (1844–1915).
32. Sydney Hospital, *The Sydney Morning Herald*, April 5, 1900, page 8.
33. The Gatton Mystery cleared, *The Queanbeyan Age*, August 31, 1901, page 2.
34. The Gatton Mystery, *The Sunday Times*, September 8, 1901, page 7.
35. SKES – page 397.
36. Report of Commissioner of Police, Brisbane, *Archives of New Zealand The Department of Internal Affairs Te Tari Taiwhenua*, October 4, 1899, Reference ACIS 17627 273 1899/1822.
37. A List of Governors of New South Wales, *Parliament of New South Wales*, viewed online, August 25, 2018.
38. ADB – Sir Robert William Duff (1835–1895).
39. The Slaying of the Twain, *The Broadford Courier and Reedy Creek Times*, December 1, 1893, page 4.
40. Lady Duff's Reception, *Australian Star*, June 14, 1893, page 6.

41. Personal Portraits, *Illustrated Sydney News*, May 13, 1893, page 12.
42. ADB – Sir Frederick Matthew Darley (1830–1910).
43. The Acting Governor, *The Sydney Morning Herald*, March 3, 1893, page 3.
44. ADB – Thomas Alexander Browne (1826–1915).
45. The New Premises of Messrs Farmer and Company, *The Evening News*, September 22, 1873, page 3.
46. Mr T Alexander Browne, *Table Talk*, March 7, 1890, page 5.
47. The Late Mrs Cockshott, *The Sydney Morning Herald*, August 26, 1919, page 8.
48. Incendiarism, *The Australasian*, April 15, 1865, page 6.
49. Heidelberg Memories, *The Age*, September 5, 1936, page 21.
50. The Stately Homes of Toorak, *The Argus*, October 13, 1953, page 19.
51. Sir James Dickson, *The Evening News*, January 10, 1901, page 5.
52. ADB – Sir Alfred Stephen (1802-1894).
53. ADB – Sir William Farmer (1832-1908).
54. ADB – Sir James Stephen (1789-1859).
55. Prince Albert Victor, Duke of Clarence and Avondale, *Wikipedia*, viewed online, August 25, 2018.
56. ADB – Sir Samuel Walker Griffith (1845–1920).
57. The University of Sydney, *The Sydney Morning Herald*, April 10, 1865, page 5.
58. Sir Samuel Griffith in South Wales, *South Wales Daily News*, April 15, 1887, page 3.
59. BNR – pages 4-26.
60. Churchwardens, *The Sydney Morning Herald*, April 18, 1873, page 3.
61. DSH – Section V, (483).
62. Death of Sir John Day, *Somerset and West of England Advertiser*, June 18, 1908, page 8.
63. Wedding, *The Bath Chronicle*, May 24, 1900, page 2.
64. 1891 England Census for Edith Westby.
65. BDM – Birth of Thomas Day, New South Wales, Reference Number 1917/13613.

Endnotes

66. The Imperial Bank (Limited), *The Evening Standard*, April 26, 1864, page 1.
67. Dickson and Elsmore, *The Staffordshire Advertiser*, March 11, 1848, page 1.
68. At Garraway's Coffeehouse, Cornhill, *The Public Ledger*, January 2, 1840, page 1.
69. Deaths, *The Daily Express*, December 16, 1858, page 4.
70. Victoria, *Colonial Times and Tasmanian*, October 17, 1855, page 2.
71. 1871 England Census for Edmund Westby.
72. Death of Sir John Day, *The Mercury*, June 19, 1908, page 2.
73. Police Commission, *The Brisbane Courier*, December 2, 1899, pages 10, 11.
74. Police Appointments, *The Brisbane Courier*, December 29, 1900, page 11.
75. Police Changes, *The Telegraph*, April 18, 1900, page 2.
76. A Journalist's Memories, *The Brisbane Courier*, August 23, 1924, page 18.
77. Chief Inspector Douglas, *The Telegraph*, April 8, 1901, page 2.
78. Masonic Installation, *The Brisbane Courier*, May 23, 1896, page 9.
79. QPG – Deserter from Queensland Regiment, September 21, 1901, Volume XXXVIII, No. 57, amended description of deserter Thomas Day, page 442.
80. Queensland Governors, *Queensland Government*, viewed online, June 16, 2017.
81. Sir F. Darley, *The Telegraph*, June 18, 1902, page 2.
82. Sir Frederic Darley, *The Telegraph*, June 18, 1902, page 4.
83. Sir E. Stewart Richardson, *The West Australian*, April 21, 1899, page 5.
84. BNR – pages 173, 174.
85. ADB – Patrick Real (1846–1928).
86. ADB – Patrick O'Sullivan (1818–1904).
87. Sir Samuel W. Griffith, *The Australian Star*, March 4, 1891, page 5.
88. No Title, *The Sydney Morning Herald*, January 5, 1901, page 8.
89. Bench and Bar, *Truth*, May 2, 1897, page 5.
90. BNR – page 52.

91. Sir Frederick Darley, Chief Justice, *Dubbo Dispatch*, September 22, 1899, page 4.
92. ADB – Sir William Charles Windeyer (1834–1897).
93. Marriages, *The Sydney Morning Herald*, January 7, 1882, page 1.
94. ADB – Sir James Robert Dickson (1832–1901).
95. ADB – John Palmer (1760–1833).
96. The German Emperor in London, *The Western Daily Press*, July 11, 1891, page 8.
97. Victoria House Employees, *The Sydney Morning Herald*, November 19, 1894, page 3.
98. Personal Portraits, *The Illustrated Sydney News*, November 25, 1893, page 4.
99. ADB – Alexander Campbell (1812–1891).
100. The C.I. Branch, *The Brisbane Courier*, July 13, 1900, page 3.
101. The Criminal Investigation Branch, *The Brisbane Courier*, February 7, 1901, page 4.
102. QPG – Warrants Issued, October 4, 1902, Volume XXXIX, Number 71, Thomas Day, deserter from A Battery of Queensland Permanent Artillery at Lytton Fort, page 451.
103. Prisoner Wilson Released, *Darling Downs Gazette*, March 25, 1904, page 2.
104. Wicked Wilson, *Truth*, March 27, 1904, page 5.
105. "Wilson" Released, *The Queensland Times*, March 26, 1904, page 8.
106. Court Records, *County of London*, 1912, Item Number 15, offences committed by Edward Lytton Carus-Wilson, page 6.
107. The Oxley Murder, *Truth*, April 3, 1904, page 5.
108. No Title, *The Shields Daily Gazette and Shipping Telegraph*, March 15, 1889, page 3.
109. The Parnell Commission, *The Penny Illustrated Paper*, March 9, 1889, page 154.
110. The Belfast Riots, *The Belfast News-Letter*, September 29, 1886, page 5.
111. Funerals, *The Sydney Morning Herald*, February 9, 1894, page 8.
112. 1861 England Census for John S Frewin.
113. Mr Moreton Frewen at Broken Hill, *The Sydney Mail*, June 1, 1895, page 1138.

Endnotes

114. England & Wales, National Probate Calendar, 1908, John Charles Frederic Sigismund Day.
115. Sir William Farmer's Estate, *The Evening News*, August 11, 1908, page 4.

CONCLUSION

1. Dayboro Township, *The Telegraph*, June 7, 1917, page 5.
2. RRC – page 436.
3. Compulsory Retirement of Pensioners, *The Queenslander*, April 19, 1890, page 753.
4. Letter from the Minister for Police, *Queensland Government*, April 16, 2018.
5. Knight, C. *Cold case - unsolved 1898 Gatton murders*, email, June 26, 2018.
6. The Fitzgerald Inquiry, *Crime and Corruption Commission, Queensland*, viewed online, August 27, 2018.
7. BNR – pages 34, 47, 227-232.
8. Police Commission, *The Brisbane Courier*, December 2, 1899, pages 10, 11, at http://nla.gov.au/nla.news-article3706524.
9. Details of Service for James Nethercote, *Queensland Police Museum*, Service Number 351.
10. Creedy, B. *Oxley-Gatton Murders: Exposing the Conspiracy*, email, April 8, 2016.
11. Promotion of Neil Raymond Bradford to the rank of Inspector, *Queensland Government Gazette*, October 21, 1989.
12. Report of Inspector N. R. Bradford, *Queensland Police Department*, November 6, 1990.
13. Report of Assistant Commissioner W. Aldrich, *Queensland Police Service*, February 25, 1992.

BIBLIOGRAPHY

BOOKS

Bradford, Neil Raymond. *Oxley-Gatton Murders: Exposing the Conspiracy*, 2015, BookPal, Brisbane, Australia.

Burgess, Richard. *Life of Richard Burgess: The Notorious Highwayman and Murderer*, 1914, Ward and Reeves, New Zealand.

Day, Samuel Henry. *Family Papers*, 2016, Forgotten Books, United States.

Gibney, James and Desmond. *The Gatton Mystery*, 1977, Angus and Robertson, Australia.

Marriott, Trevor. *Jack the Ripper: The 21st Century Investigation*, 2005, John Blake, London, United Kingdom.

Middlemas, Keith. *The Life and Times of Edward VII*, 1972, Weidenfeld & Nicolson, London, United Kingdom.

Perry, Harry C. *A son of Australia: memories of W.E. Parry-Okeden, I.S.O., 1840-1926*, 1928, Watson, Ferguson & Co. Ltd., Brisbane, Australia.

Ridley, Jane. Bertie: *A Life of Edward VII*, 2012, Chatto & Windus, London, United Kingdom.

Skinner, Keith and Evans, Stewart. *The Ultimate Jack the Ripper Sourcebook: An Illustrated Encyclopedia*, 2001, Robinson, London, United Kingdom.

Webster, Gerald. *I Walked at Dawn*, 1949, Allan Wingate Limited, London, United Kingdom.

NEWSPAPERS

Australian

Australian Star
Australian Town and Country Journal
Colonial Times and Tasmanian
Cornhill, The Public Ledger
Darling Downs Gazette
Dubbo Dispatch
Goulburn Evening Penny Post

Bibliography

Illustrated Sydney News
Launceston Examiner
Newcastle Morning Herald and Miners' Advocate
Smith's Weekly
South Wales Daily News
Supplement to The Horsham Times
Table Talk
The Advertiser
The Advocate
The Age
The Albury Banner and Wodonga Express
The Argus
The Australasian
The Australian Star
The Bathurst Daily Free Press & Mining Journal
The Bendigo Advertiser
The Bendigo Independent
The Blayney Advocate and Carcoar Herald
The Brisbane Courier
The Broadford Courier
The Broadford Courier and Reedy Creek Times
The Burrowa News
The Capricornian
The Chronicle
The Clarence and Richmond Examiner
The Clarence River Advocate
The Cumberland Argus and Fruitgrowers' Advocate
The Daily Advertiser
The Daily Telegraph
The Darling Downs Gazette
The Evening News
The Express and Telegraph
The Goulburn Herald
The Gympie Times
The Inquirer and Commercial News
The Kalgoorlie Miner

The Katoomba Times and Blue Mountaineer
The Maitland Mercury and Hunter River General Advertiser
The Maitland Weekly Mercury
The Manaro Mercury
The Maryborough Chronicle
The Molong Express
The Muswellbrook Chronicle
The National Advocate
The Northern Star
The Queanbeyan Age
The Queensland Figaro
The Queensland Times
The Queenslander
The Riverine Grazier
The Riverine Herald
The Singleton Argus
The South Australian Register
The Sunday Times
The Sydney Mail
The Sydney Morning Herald
The Telegraph
The Toowoomba Chronicle
The Warwick Argus
The Warwick Examiner and Times
The Week
The Weekly Times
The West Australian
The Western Champion
The Western Star
The Worker
Town and Country Journal
Truth
Wagga Wagga Express
Warwick Argus

Bibliography

British

Reading Mercury, Oxford Gazette, Newbury Herald, and Berks Country Paper
Somerset and West of England Advertiser
The Bath Chronicle
The Belfast News-Letter
The Bristol Mercury
The Daily Express
The Evening Standard
The Evening Telegraph and Star
The Mercury
The Penny Illustrated Paper
The Shields Daily Gazette and Shipping Telegraph
The Staffordshire Advertiser
The Western Daily Press
The Western Times

New Zealand

The Auckland Star
The New Zealand Herald

ONLINE PUBLICATIONS

A List of Governors of New South Wales, *Parliament of New South Wales*, <https://www.parliament.nsw.gov.au/about/Pages/A-List-of-Governors-of-New-South-Wales.aspx>.

Browne, Reginald Spencer (1856–1943). *Australian Dictionary of Biography*, <http://adb.anu.edu.au/biography/browne-reginald-spencer-5394>.

Browne, Thomas Alexander (1826–1915). *Australian Dictionary of Biography*, <http://adb.anu.edu.au/biography/browne-thomas-alexander-3085>.

Burton, Kelly. *Reform of the Double Jeopardy Rule on the Basis of Fresh and Compelling Evidence in New South Wales and Queensland*, 2004, James Cook University Law Review 84, <http://www.austlii.edu.au/au/journals/JCULawRw/2004/5.html>.

Camp, Anthony John. *Royal Mistresses and Bastards: Fact and Fiction, 1714–1936*, <http://anthonyjcamp.com/page9.htm>.
Campbell, Alexander (1812–1891). *Australian Dictionary of Biography*, <http://adb.anu.edu.au/biography/campbell-alexander-3152>.
Criminal Code Act 1899, *Office of the Queensland Parliamentary Counsel*, <https://www.legislation.qld.gov.au>.
Darley, Sir Frederick Matthew (1830–1910). *Australian Dictionary of Biography*, <http://adb.anu.edu.au/biography/darley-sir-frederick-matthew-3366>.
Dickson, Sir James Robert (1832–1901). *Australian Dictionary of Biography*, <http://adb.anu.edu.au/biography/dickson-sir-james-robert-5979>.
Duff, Sir Robert William (1835–1895). *Australian Dictionary of Biography*, <http://adb.anu.edu.au/biography/duff-sir-robert-william-6026>.
Farmer, Sir William (1832–1908). *Australian Dictionary of Biography*, <http://adb.anu.edu.au/biography/farmer-sir-william-3498>.
Federation, *Australian Government*, <https://www.australia.gov.au/about-government/how-government-works/federation>.
Griffith, Sir Samuel Walker (1845–1920). *Australian Dictionary of Biography*, <http://adb.anu.edu.au/biography/griffith-sir-samuel-walker-445>.
Knowing the Aussie accent, *Australian Geographic*, <http://www.australiangeographic.com.au/topics/history-culture/2014/07/knowing-the-aussie-accent>.
O'Sullivan, Patrick (1818–1904). *Australian Dictionary of Biography*, <http://adb.anu.edu.au/biography/osullivan-patrick-4349>.
Palmer, John (1760–1833). *Australian Dictionary of Biography*, <http://adb.anu.edu.au/biography/palmer-john-2533>.
Prince Albert Victor, Duke of Clarence and Avondale, *Wikipedia*, <https://en.wikipedia.org/wiki/Prince_Albert_Victor,_Duke_of_Clarence_and_Avondale>
Queensland Governors, *Queensland Government*, <https://www.qld.gov.au/about/about-queensland/history/governors>.

Bibliography

Real, Patrick (1846–1928). *Australian Dictionary of Biography*, <http://adb.anu.edu.au/biography/real-patrick-8169>.

Report of the Royal Commission on Police Inquiry (1899), *Queensland Parliamentary Service*, <http://www.parliament.qld.gov.au/documents/tableOffice/TabledPapers/1899/1399T145.pdf>.

Robert Grosvenor, 1st Marquess of Westminster, *Wikipedia*, <https://en.wikipedia.org/wiki/Robert_Grosvenor,_1st_Marquess_of_Westminster>.

Stephen, Sir Alfred (1802-1894). *Australian Dictionary of Biography*, <http://adb.anu.edu.au/biography/stephen-sir-alfred-1291>.

Stephen, Sir James (1789-1859). *Australian Dictionary of Biography*, <http://adb.anu.edu.au/biography/stephen-sir-james-2694>.

The Fitzgerald Inquiry, *Crime and Corruption Commission, Queensland*, <http://www.ccc.qld.gov.au/about-the-ccc/the-fitzgerald-inquiry>.

The Gatton Murders, 26 December 1898, *Queensland Police Media*, posted October 15, 2013, <https://mypolice.qld.gov.au/museum/2013/10/15/from-the-vault-the-gatton-murders-26-december-1898>.

Tooth, Sir Robert Lucas (1844–1915). *Australian Dictionary of Biography*, <http://adb.anu.edu.au/biography/tooth-sir-robert-lucas-lucas--4732>.

Windeyer, Sir William Charles (1834–1897). *Australian Dictionary of Biography*, <http://adb.anu.edu.au/biography/windeyer-sir-william-charles-1062>.

INDEX

A

A Battery 8, 92, 103, 133, 196, 204, 235
abdomen 28, 31, 34, 42, 43
  see also "mutilated"
Aboriginal tracker 74, 78, 168, 193
abortion 73, 140, 258
accent
  see "Australian accent"
accomplice 9, 33, 62, 199-203, 220, 237
affair 94, 140, 258
Agricultural College
  see "Gatton Agricultural College"
Albany 175, 194-199, 206
Aldgate 28-34, 35-40, 208
alibi 5, 35, 109, 121, 198
All Saints College 75
ambidextrous 222, 223
America 10, 33, 77, 78, 81, 353
anatomical knowledge 28
Anderson, Robert 80
Anderson, William Ross 255
Anglican Diocesan Synod 263
antecedents 41, 75, 207, 216
Archer, Emily 46-49
Archer, George Martin Walter 45-52, 53, 64-67, 260-263
Armitage, William 7, 195, 196

Arrell, William 4, 112-115, 130-167, 177-185, 191-193, 216-220, 235, 275
Ascot Races 66
Attorney-General 204-206, 266
Austin, Thomas ix, 200
Australian accent 36
Australian Club 263

B

Backert, Albert 30
badgered 232
Bailey, Thomas 140, 163
Baines, George 158, 159
Ballantyne, Robert 218
Barber & Co 27
Barber, Constable 80
Barlow, Andrew Henry 191-193
Barney (Aboriginal tracker) 168-171, 188
Barrett, H. 27
Barry, Mary 77
Bathurst 64, 75, 76
Becher, M. A. R. 77
Beck family 109
Belfast Riots Commission 270
Bell, Henry 190
Bengal Merchant (ship) 267
Berner Street 28, 29
Betts, Isabella McInnes 77
Bielby, Agnes 95
Bielby, James 95
Blackstone, William 53, 67
Blair, James William x, 196

Index

blood poisoning 150-157
blood –
- animal 2, 4, 225, 238
- clot 238
- human 2, 4, 172, 225, 228, 238
- smears 43, 44, 141, 142, 238, 239
- smudges 182, 231, 238
- splashes 155, 231, 233, 239
- spots 155, 176, 226-241

bloodstained 4, 30-34, 60-62, 176, 189, 216, 237
bloody (prints) 60, 61
blucher boots 107, 121, 220
blunt instrument 26, 39-44, 142, 143, 222
see also "stick (hardwood)," "umbrella" and "walking stick"
boat 10, 30-33, 91-93, 208
see also "cattle boat"
boiler 246, 247
see also "copper"
Bombay (steamer) 26
Bond, Thomas 31, 42
boot print 121
Boss 36, 73
Botanical Gardens 97
Bowler, Walter 96
Boxing Day night 100, 104-109, 134, 140, 176
brass ring 28-30, 40
bring off that man 180
see also "protected"

Brittain, Charles 27
Brook, Annie 39
Brooking, Arthur 110
Brooks, Henry 36-39
Brown and Walsh's paddock 8, 94-96, 101, 190
Brown, Henrietta Rosa Maria 264
Brown or Browne, Lucy Forest 262
see also "Lady Darley"
Brown, Sylvester John 262
Brown or Browne, Thomas Alexander 262
Browne, Reginald Spencer 130-133, 191, 265
Buck's Row 27
Buckaginga 65
buggery 7, 195, 206
buggy 4, 5, 54, 96, 110-115, 132-138, 172-177, 275
bullet 77, 78, 95, 145-157, 220-224
Bulwer, Edward Earle Gascoyne 270
Bulwer-Lytton, Edward George Earle 270
Bunya Mountains 5, 106, 139, 174, 189-194
Burgess, Richard 5-10, 33-41, 51-63, 75-81, 90-109, 116-121, 139, 140, 168-177, 182-208, 220-226, 237-242, 253-256
Burgess, Richard (Dick) 79-90
Burke, Tobias (Toby) 74-86, 216

Burnett, William 59, 93, 236, 266
Burns, Frank 76, 81, 177, 189, 256, 257
Burton, John 64
Busby, Hugh 257
butcher 10, 29, 33, 78, 114, 182, 183, 226, 241
Byrne, Catherine 130, 131
Byrne, John 92
  see also "Richard Burgess"

C

Cahill, William Geoffrey 203, 266, 267
Callinan, Mary 2, 4, 110-114
Cameron, Thomas 62, 63
Camp, Anthony John 31
Campbell, Alexander 269
Campbell, Constance 269
Campbell, J. A. 206
Campbell, John 75
Campbell, Thomas Robert Curwen 25, 268
Campbell, Thomas Windeyer 268
cannot go strait 3, 189
Carew, Michael 74
Carroll, John 2-18, 108-120, 133, 167, 177-186, 194, 227-236
Carroll, Margaret 110-120, 133
cartridge 131, 192
Carus-Wilson, Claude William 7, 8, 26, 33, 76, 77, 94-100, 195-199, 205, 206
Carus-Wilson, Edward Litton 7-8, 26, 33, 75, 76, 77, 94-101, 175, 192-194-206, 267-271, 274
Carus-Wilson, Margaret 26
Catchpole, Maria 95
Catholic
  see "Roman Catholic"
Catholic priest 140, 259
cattle boat 10, 29-32, 78
Cavanagh, Letitia Frances (Fanny) 54-67, 203, 262
Chadwick, Edwin Andrew (Ted) 104-115
Chancery 268
Chapman, Annie 28, 30, 44
chaste 44
Chaston, William Charles 8-10, 24, 81, 91-98, 102-121, 175, 176, 189, 194-196, 204, 208, 220, 235, 255, 261
Chermside, Herbert Charles 266
Christie, Robert George 59, 96, 179, 180, 185, 191-193, 234, 237, 241, 250, 257, 275
Chubb, Charles Edward 202
Church of England 258, 259, 264
Churchill, Randolph Henry Spencer 270, 271
Churchill, Winston 270, 271
City Bank of Sydney 53-55, 58, 63
Clarke, Arthur George Jnr 223
Clarke, Arthur George Snr 2, 102, 103, 111-114, 134, 176, 182, 183, 192, 194, 205, 223, 236-250, 258

Index

Clarke, Francis William 54, 57, 61, 63
Clarke, John Franklin 223
Clarke's butcher or man 2, 4, 5, 8, 55, 59, 74, 108, 113, 114, 118-120, 130, 167, 177, 181, 186, 192, 194, 227
Clarke's Yard 33
clay pipe 29, 96
  see also "pipe stop"
Clifden, Nellie 32
clot
  see "blood"
Cobb, James Lithgow 62-64
Cochrane-Baillie, Charles Wallace Alexander Napier 73
  see also "Lord Lamington"
Cochrane-Baillie, Victor Alexander Brisbane William 73
coerced 108, 119, 120
Collingham Gardens 34
Collis, Thomas 200
collusion 102
Colquhan (Aboriginal tracker) 166
Commercial Road 29, 79, 80
Commercial Street 27
Commercial Street Police Station 31, 73
complexion –
  - dark 28, 59, 93, 266
  - dark man 57-61, 93, 266
  - sallow 93, 266
concealed 34, 189, 191, 254
Connolly, Mary Ann 27

Connolly, Michael (Mick) 112-115, 130
Connolly, Nathaniel 55
Cook, Annie 112
Cook, Edith May (May) 73, 74, 96, 102, 105, 112, 140, 216, 258
Cook, Walter Albert 112, 130, 170, 174
copper 55, 246, 247
  see also "boiler"
cord (four-lag) 33
  see also "strangulation"
Cornwell, John Phillip 64
Coromandel (steamer) 35
correlation 34, 40, 41, 55, 225, 229, 257, 258
corroborate 27, 33, 45, 61, 78, 117, 224, 226, 238, 266
Cortis, Mrs 63
Cortis, William Richard 62
Covell, Constable 178
cover-up 1, 8, 130, 157, 167, 170, 176, 179, 189, 209, 253
Coworth House 66
Cox (man named) 189, 194, 235
  see also "William Charles Chaston"
Cox, William Sloper 257
culvert 4, 5, 112, 131, 140, 174, 178
Cusack, Martin 259
Cushing, William Heavingham 96, 97
cut –
  - face 54, 58, 146, 155

- throat 27-29, 31, 34, 38
see also "ear to ear" and "left to right"

D

dagger 27
dance 104-114, 134
dark complexion
　see "complexion"
dark man
　see "complexion"
Darley, Captain 272
Darley, Cecil West 269
Darley, Frederick Matthew 41, 42, 50, 65, 66, 262, 263, 267-269, 272
Darley, Henry 268
Darley, Lady 272
　see also "Lucy Forest Brown or Browne"
Darling Point 260, 264
Davies, Frederick George 75
Davies, George 37
Davitt, Michael 91
Dawson, Andrew (Anderson) 254
Day, John 264
Day, John Charles Frederic Sigismund 67, 72, 264, 265, 270, 271, 274
Day, Lady 264
　see also "Edith Westby"
Day, Samuel Henry 264
Day, T. W. 35
Day, Thomas 1-10, 26-34, 35-39, 41-52, 55, 59-67, 73-81, 90, 92-100, 108, 130-134, 140, 157, 167, 175, 176, 180, 182, 186, 200, 209, 216, 225-235, 247, 253, 257-270, 274
Day, William Aloysius 36
Deeming, Frederick Bailey 73
Defence of the Realm 167
Delaney, Edwin (Ted) 49
Delohery, Henry Charles Morisset 257
Derwin, Joseph George (Joe) 54, 60, 63
deserter 9, 175, 204-208, 255
deoxyribonucleic acid (DNA) testing 261
Devitt, William 135, 136, 218
Dickson, Annie 25
Dickson, Frederick William x, 41, 74-76, 93-99, 111-119, 132-158, 179, 180, 195-206, 216-250
Dickson, James 67, 264, 265
Dickson, James Robert 25, 67, 254, 262, 268
Donohue, Michael 115, 116, 120
Double Event 29
Douglas-Douglas, Alexander 265-267, 273
dressmaker 39, 42
Drew, Thomas 115, 116, 120
drover 10, 29, 33, 78
Duff, Lady 262
Duff, Robert William 262, 264
Dungey, Detective 81

Index

Durham, Hubert Roland Pasley 5-7, 21, 22, 79, 193, 194, 197, 198, 201-203
Dutfield's Yard 28
Dutton, Henry Stephen 254
Dying Declaration 55

E

Eames, Caroline Lee 159
ear
   see "right ear"
ear to ear 27, 31, 60,
East End Vigilance Committee 30
Eddowes, Catherine 29, 32
Ellis, James 6, 7, 201, 202
   see also "Thomas Day"
Ely, Ann 25
   see also "Annie Dickson"
Esk 78, 242
Everill, George Everard 37
excommunication 140, 168
exhibit 4, 121, 146, 159, 160, 191
exhumed 190
extradition 194

F

Fallon, Michael 106
Farmer & Co 35, 39, 42, 66, 256, 263, 270
Farmer, William 35, 42, 45, 66, 67, 260, 263-265, 268, 269, 271
Fay, George 198, 199
Feez, Arthur 266
fingernail marks 141-143, 146-148

firecracker 110
firewood 8, 55, 233
fireworks 110-112, 242
fist 40, 146
Fitzgerald Inquiry 275
flirt 190, 191
   see also "put out of the road"
fool 203
footprint 60, 61
Ford, Benjamin 95
Forrest, Edward Barrow 254
Forsyth's farm 106
Fosbery, Edmund Walcott 61, 63, 69, 203
Fox, Francis 95
Foxton, Justin Fox Greenlaw 3, 4, 167, 176, 189, 253, 254, 265, 266, 269
framed 5
Freebairn, William 45
Frewen, Hugh Morten 271
Frewen, John 270
Frewen, John Stanley Angus 270, 271
Frisco 9, 33, 81
Fullerton, John 62, 63
Furner, Edward James (Ned) 54
Furner, Robert 260
   see also "Thomas Day"
Furner, Thomas 235, 257, 258, 260
   see also "Thomas Day"
Furner, Thomas Graham (Thomas) 54, 62, 63, 257

G

Gaffney, John 199
Galbraith, Percy Dumas Fead 137-140, 150-160, 177-180, 184, 193, 221, 265
Galloway, Frederick William 197, 198
gaol 5, 6, 43, 50, 64, 76, 79, 198, 200, 201, 256
Garvin, Thomas x, 99, 103, 113-120, 133, 134, 144-157, 170-185, 191-196, 207, 218-246
Gascoyne-Cecil, Robert Arthur Talbot 261
Gateway 131
   see also "sliprails"
Gatton Agricultural College 96, 110, 114, 130, 202
Gatton track 105
George Yard buildings 27
Geraghty, James 273
get into work 7
   see also "put him on some other job"
Gibney, Desmond 216, 223
Gibney, James (Jim) 216, 223
Gilbert, Charles 132-136, 178, 218
Gillies, James 5, 140, 174, 190, 194
girth
   see "saddle girth"
Glasson, Edwin Hubert (Bertie) 54-67, 93, 225, 257, 262, 263
Glasson, Gustavus Richard 64
Globe Restaurant 92, 98, 103, 104, 200
goat cart 26, 94-97
godson 73, 167
Goodna 94-96
Gordon-Brown, Frederick 31
Goulder, George Edwin 62, 63
Grainger, Mounted Constable 61
Green, Robert 49
Greenmount to Gatton 109, 129
Grenadier Guard 27
Griffith, Samuel Walker 254, 263, 265-268
groom 45, 51, 59
Grosvenor House 79
Grosvenor, Robert 79
gunshot 95, 99, 100, 110, 130, 131, 133

H

Hallas, Beatrice 107-110, 120
Hallas, Frank 107-109, 120
Hallas, Lucy 107
Hallas, Sidney Henry 107, 108, 127, 128
Hallas, Sidney Joseph 106, 107
Halliday, Charles 45-47
Halliday, Isabella 45-48
hammerhead 120, 121
Handbury Street 28
handkerchief 10, 27-29, 33, 62, 141, 144, 199, 228, 229
   see also "silk (pocket) handkerchief"
Hanwin, James 259

Index

Harman, Alexander Ramsay 266
Harris, Henry 64
Harris, William ix, 200
Harrison, Emma 28, 42-52, 53, 66, 141, 173, 262, 263
Hartsinck, Emilie 264
Haslip, George 26
hat –
- felt 2, 29, 104, 112, 115
- hard-felt 28, 104
- slouch 37, 117, 230
- soft-felt 45, 93, 104, 255

Hatfield House 34, 261, 270
Hatton Gardens 79
Hawthorne, Alfred Winter 55
Haye, Constable 6, 201
Hazlett, John Alexander 38
head –
- bashed 141, 155, 159, 217, 219, 224, 225, 239
- turned to the left 31, 42, 43
- turned on the right 28, 44

Head, Thomas 131, 181, 192, 193
Healey, Florence Alfred 53-63
Henry, Hannah 47
Herbert, Joseph Vincent 5, 194-198
Hero (trooper) 188
Hill, Alfred Stephen ix, 7, 8, 26, 75, 94-100, 190, 191, 195, 200, 201, 204-206, 270
Hill, Catherine Maud 33
Hill, Frederick John (Fred) 190, 270
Hillman, Frank 190
Hill-Wray, Charles James 189, 190, 220-228, 239
horse and cart 55
horse-slaughterer 27, 100
Howard Smith and Sons' and Dalgety's wharves 9, 81
Howard Smith and Sons' wharves 77, 93
Howe, Emily Fanny 46
see also "Emily Archer"
Howe, Esmeralda 46
Hughes, Dalrymple 206, 207
hunter 29
hut 36, 204, 270
Hutchinson, George 31
Hutchinson, William 64
Hyde, Frederick Hamilton 78

I

illegitimate 67, 264
Imperil Bank Limited 264
"In Memoriam" notice 74, 96, 216
Innes, Elizabeth 264
Innes, Joseph George Long (George) 45-52, 64, 65, 263, 264, 268
intent 49
see also "motive"
Ireland 31, 59, 80, 91, 92, 168, 256, 262, 267, 268
Irishman 75, 78
Irvine farm 106

Irvine, William 186

J

Jack (trooper) 188
Jackson, James 262
James, Richard 135, 136, 149
Jeater, William Henry 43-45, 48
Jimmy (trooper) 188
job
    see "get into work" and "put him on some other job"
Johnny (trooper) 188
Johnson, Bert 108
Johnson, Edward 98,
Jordan, Joseph (Joe) 110
Jordan, Stephen (Steve) 104, 110, 114, 115
Jordan, Thomas (Tom) 110, 114, 115
jumper 2, 4, 176, 189, 216, 226, 227, 230-248

K

Kelly, Edward (Ned) 168, 171, 188
Kelly, Mary Jane 31, 32, 42
Kent Brewery 259, 260
kidney 30, 31
Kiely, Constable 6, 201
Killarney 6, 97, 98, 103, 201, 202, 220
killing *(animal slaughtering)* 227, 230, 231, 233, 241, 248
Kilpatrick, Robert 201-203, 210, 211
King, Nathaniel Irvine (Nat) 168

King, Robert (Bob) 59, 193, 228-237
King, Thomas Orten Irvine (Tom) 168, 188, 193
King, W. S. (Major) 186
King, W. S. (Reverend) 186
King, Walter Stuart 183-186
Kingsbury, John James 202, 204, 206, 266, 267
kismet 251
knife 27, 28, 40, 146
knot
    see "sailor's knot"

L

Labinsky, Lizzie 139, 168
Laidley 75, 139, 168, 193
Lawler, P. 51
Lawson, Robert Hazlewood 4, 191
Lawton, Charles 49
lead pencil 31, 45, 258
left to right 27, 28
left-handed 223
letter 30-33, 45, 48, 58, 62, 70, 71, 73-75, 78, 82, 83, 87, 95, 216, 258, 270, 277
Lewis 3, 189
    see also "Thomas Day"
Leyburn 77, 78, 169
Lilley, Edwyn Mitford 266
line-up 107, 108, 139, 237
Lipski 29
Litton, Edward 268
liver 30, 208
Lizzie Davis

Index

see "Rose Mylett"
lockup 7, 78, 107, 139, 194, 198, 199, 200, 204, 255
Long Lizzie
see "Elizabeth Stride"
Looby, Michael 64
Lord Lamington 73, 92, 167, 207, 254, 265, 266
see also "Charles Wallace Alexander Napier Cochrane-Baillie"
Lord Salisbury 34, 270
Lowe, Florence (Florrie) 114-120, 236, 237, 248
Lower Tent Hill 73, 109-115, 130, 131, 258
lunatic 31, 45, 261
Lunny, John 74, 78, 216
Lusk, George 30
Lytton Fort 92, 133

M

Macfarlane, Henry Taylor 199, 200
MacKinlay, Mary 25, 268
Madden, George 64
Maitland, Herbert Lethington 39
Malone, Hugh 273
Malone, Patrick 78
see also "Richard Burgess"
Marathon (steamer) 270
Marriott, William Henry 64
Marsh, William 104
Mason 66, 185, 260, 262, 263, 265
Matthews, Henry 261

Mattingly, Thomas John 98, 103, 220
McDonald, Alexander 6, 78, 201
McGregor, Duncan Robert 7, 77, 88, 89, 93, 94
McGrory, Robert 78, 242
McKay, William 255, 257
see also "Thomas Day"
McKenzie, Alice 34, 261, 270
McLaughlin, Austin 5, 194
McNamara, Frank 197
McNeil, Daniel Joseph (Joe) 109
McNeil, Polly 109, 251
McNeil, William 109, 110, 113, 120, 121, 131-137, 177, 186, 216-218
McPherson, Edith 80, 81, 100
McVicar, Agnes 53, 60-65
McWilliams, James 30
meat 55, 134, 182, 231, 233, 243, 248
men's shelter
see "Salvation Army's shelter"
Meo, Paddy 76
see also "Frank Burns"
Meston, Archibald 168-176
mighty magnate 270, 271
Milford, Frederick 42-47
Milk street 79, 80
Miller, John 9, 10, 33, 81, 91-93, 98, 102-104, 108, 110, 115, 120, 121, 168, 177, 189, 200, 208, 220, 237
Miller, Lydia 32
Miller, William 140, 164, 165

323

Miller's Court 31
misfortunate 258
Mitchell, John 49
Mitre Square 29
Moana (steamer) 267
modus operandi 40, 105
Molesworth, Hugh Thomas 269, 270
Monro, James 261
Moore, Richard Albert 79
Moran, Frank 105, 140
Moran's paddock 1, 2, 4, 9, 74, 96, 102-120, 130-133, 140, 166, 170, 186, 191, 216, 244, 258
Morgan, John 64
Morrison, Annie 36-43, 49, 173
Mort, Thomas Sutcliffe 263
motive 49, 65, 236
see also "intent"
Mumford, James 27
Munro, Archibald 197
Munro, Finlay Elgin 259, 260
Murphy, Atoise Jeremiah (Jerry) 104, 105, 109, 131
Murphy, Catherine (Katie) 74,
Murphy, Daniel (Dan) Sen 140, 186
Murphy, Daniel Jnr 166
Murphy, Hnora (Norah) ix, 1, 3, 5, 10, 26, 62, 74, 81, 102, 109-120, 131-162, 167, 189-191, 217-224, 229, 243, 251
Murphy, James 140
Murphy, Joseph (Joe) 131
Murphy, Mary 137, 140, 186

Murphy, Mary (Polly) 109
see also "Polly McNeil"
Murphy, Michael ix, 1, 5, 8, 26, 74, 105, 109-120, 131-162, 167, 219-225, 239, 251, 257
Murphy, Patrick Joseph (Pat) 104, 105, 110-115, 130
Murphy, Theresa Ellen (Ellen) ix, 1, 3, 5, 10, 26, 62, 74, 109-120, 131-162, 167, 189, 217-219, 224, 229, 243, 251
Murray, Albert 115
mutilated 28, 34
see also "abdomen"
Mylett, Rose 33

N

nasal twang
see "Australian accent"
Neil, John 27
New Zealand 9, 26, 30, 80, 207-209, 255, 261
Newcastle 9, 81,
Nichols, Mary Ann 27
nineteen 26, 257
no true bill 206, 267
Noel, Arthur Baptist ix, 59, 102, 103, 113-119, 132-139, 141-153, 158-162, 168-185, 192-196, 204, 207, 219-232, 237-251, 274
Norman (Aboriginal tracker) 74, 78, 169
note
see "suicide note"

Index

O

O'Brien, Charles 76, 78, 92
O'Connor, Stanhope 188
O'Sullivan, J. P. (see below)
O'Sullivan, Patrick (Paddy) 266, 267
order for burial 160-162
Orr, Andrew William 143, 159, 183, 224, 226
Osborne Street 26
Otago goldfields 80
Otter (steamer) 269
our man 7, 202
Oxford Street 36-39
Oxley Creek Bridge 94
Oxley Hotel 95-97
Oxley, Thomas 38

P

Palmer, John 268
Palmer, Mary Maria 268
Palmer, Sophia 268
Parnell Commission 270
Parnell, Charles Stewart 270
Parry-Okeden, Uvedale Edward 196, 203, 204
Parry-Okeden, William Edward 3-9, 12-14, 23, 62, 99, 108, 111, 175, 176, 179, 183, 187, 189-196, 201-209, 212, 226, 254-257, 261, 265, 273, 275
Parsons, Elizabeth 256
Paul, George William 79
Payne, George 73,
Pearly Polly *see* "Mary Ann Connolly"
Pearson, Christina 106
Peerage 34
Pell, Morris Birbeck 263
pencil
    see "lead pencil"
Peregrine (steamer) 9, 81, 92, 199
Perkins, Paddy (Aboriginal tracker) 166
Perseverance 177, 189
Phillip, Arthur 268
Phillips, Annie Dorothy 54-67
Phillips, George Baxter 28
Phillips, Gladys Mary 54, 55, 59, 60
Phillips, John William (Jack) 53-67, 203, 262
Philp, Robert 254
photograph 78, 92, 108, 256, 258, 275
picric acid 104
Pinkenba Wharf 267
pipe stop 96
    see also "clay pipe"
Ponsonby, Henry 33
Pope, John 260
Postman's Ridge 9, 168
post-mortem examination 31, 39, 140, 141, 149-162, 167, 219-222
priest
    see "Catholic priest"
Prince Albert Victor 32, 66, 263
Prince Albert Edward 31, 32, 35, 66, 263

Prince of Wales 32, 66, 263
Princess Mary of Teck 32
Prior, Charles Augustus 57-60, 93
Privy Councillor 262, 265
prostitute 27, 32
protected 1, 3-5, 8, 34, 99, 108, 157, 176, 179, 180, 182, 189, 202, 203, 209, 226, 260, 261, 267
psychopathic killer 200, 207, 209
Ptolomey, Charles 33
Pullitop 41, 65
purse 149
put him on some other job 7
put out of the road 191

Q

quarry 95, 96, 99
Quarry Hill 95
Queen Victoria 30, 32-34, 73, 92, 167, 262, 265, 267,
Queensland Permanent Artillery 92, 103, 133, 175, 196, 202-204, 207, 235, 261, 274
Queensland Police Media 130
Queensland State Archives 1, 3, 157, 173, 200, 274
Quinn, Thomas 64

R

razor 181, 234, 235, 250
Real, Mary 267
Real, Patrick 266, 267
references (from Clarke) 102, 103

related by marriage 64, 263, 271
respectable middle-aged woman 30, 35, 40, 208
revolver 8, 30, 55, 56, 75, 95-100, 130, 131, 192, 233, 250, 256
Richardson, Maud 32, 33
Rienzi 36, 270
right ear 149, 156, 256, 257
right-handed 222
ring 27, 37, 39, 40, 42, 49, 51
   see also "brass ring"
Robbery Under Arms 262
Roche, John 48-51
Rockton (steamer) 98
Rolf Boldrewood 262
Roman Catholic 75, 104, 264, 266,
Rookwood Cemetery 258, 259
Ross, Frederick 59, 68, 91, 92
Ross, Henry 273
rough-looking Irishman 57-59, 93
   see also "Irishman"
Royal family 66, 179, 253, 268
rug 138, 148, 216, 217, 220
rumour 32, 34, 35, 140, 158, 204, 206, 261, 266
Rumpf, Annie 97
Rutledge, Arthur 206, 266, 267
Rutsch, John 77, 78
Ryan, Joseph (Joe) 98
   see also "Richard Burgess"

S

saddle 5, 194, 197, 198
saddle girth 95, 99

Index

Sadleir, John x, 76, 117, 120, 144, 145, 168-170, 172-174, 176-178, 185, 188, 221, 222, 226, 230, 234-236, 246-249
sailor 30, 62
   see also "seaman"
sailor's knot 10, 62
sallow complexion
   see "complexion"
Salvation Army Shelter 91-94
San Francisco 81
Savage, Charles 273
Sawtell, Arthur Caldwell 50, 51
scapegrace 36
Schwartz, Israel 28, 29, 96
Scollay, Thomas 49
Scotland Yard 27, 80, 269
screams 77, 130-133
seaman 10, 33, 35
   see also "sailor"
Selby, Elizabeth 159
semen 143, 152-154, 159, 160, 224, 225
shadowing 6, 7, 63, 203, 253,
   see also "protected"
Shanahan, Denis Collins ix
Shannon (steamer) 207
Sheehy, Elizabeth 45-48
shelter
   see "Salvation Army Shelter"
shot
   see "gunshot"
Siebenhausen, Mary Christina 105, 106

Siebenhausen, William Henry 105, 106
signature (of Jack the Ripper) 29, 33, 199, 229
silk (pocket) handkerchief 28, 199
sine die ix, 200
sins of another 65, 225
Sirius (flagship) 268
slaughterer
   see "horse-slaughterer"
slaughterman 28, 29, 230
slaughterman's knife 28
   see also "knife"
slippers 57, 60
sliprails 2, 4, 74, 105, 108, 110, 112-121, 131, 133, 138, 166, 174, 177, 181, 186, 194, 227, 237, 248, 249
smears
   see "blood"
Smiley, John 106
Smith, Andrew Stevenson 181
Smith, Annie 234
Smith, Emma Elizabeth 26, 35, 40, 228
Smith, H. 28
Smith, Robert (Bob) 131
smudges
   see "blood"
soldier 27, 267
Sparksman, Annie 104, 105
Sparksman, Edward 104, 105
spermatozoa
   see "semen"
Spitalfields 27, 28, 31, 44

splashes
   see "blood"
spots
   see "blood"
Spratling, J. 27
St George's-in-the-East 28
St Helena Island 76, 79, 81, 91, 106, 177, 269
St Mark's Anglican Church 264
St Paul's Church of England 268
stab
   see "wounds"
stable 49, 51, 61
Standish, Frederick Charles 188
Stephen, James 263
Stephen, James Kenneth 263
Stewart-Richardson, Edward Austin 266
stick (hardwood) 155, 219, 224, 239
Stoddart, Susan Jane (Susie) 54-60
Stonestreet, William Thomas 64
stowaway 26
strangulation 33, 44, 146, 147, 224
Stride, Elizabeth 28, 29, 32, 96
Stuart, John 3, 5-7, 19, 20, 98, 178, 189, 196, 200-202, 209, 254
stump 120, 121
suicide note 173, 257, 258
Summerbelle, Annie May 262
swagman 8, 96, 97, 106-108, 110, 120, 192
Swamp Paddock 8, 233

Swanson, Donald Sutherland 27-29
switch 110, 120, 121
   see also "whip"

T

Tabram, Martha 27
teeth –
   • tongue [protruding] between the front teeth 28
   • tongue was clenched between the teeth 44
telegram 3-10, 12-23, 98, 108, 111, 137, 167, 189, 191, 195, 196, 201-203, 206, 253
Thames 10, 29, 33
thigh 31, 143, 147
throat 27-29, 31, 34, 44, 54, 60, 148, 152
Thuerkauf, Louisa 130
ticket-of-leave 267
Tom (pony) 110, 116
tomahawk 54, 56-58, 63
Tomkins, Henry 27, 100
tongue
   see "teeth"
Toole, Henry 255, 256
Toomey, Michael 2-4, 7, 59, 74-76, 93, 107, 108, 113, 117, 119, 121, 124, 125, 131, 133, 157, 167, 176, 179-181, 183, 191, 200, 204, 220, 227, 231-248, 254
Toorak 25, 262, 263
Tooth, Robert Lucas 260

Index

Townsend, Arthur 49
Tracey, James 62, 71, 72
tracks (of two horses) 169-175
    see also "Gatton track"
Trewhella, Benjamin 255
Tunbridge, John Bennett 208, 214, 215
tutor 263
typewriter 275

U

umbrella 40, 41
unfortunate (woman or women) 30, 80, 258
un-guilty conscious 51
Union Club 267
Unmack, Theodore Oscar x, 137, 149, 152, 156, 157, 160, 161, 177, 178, 192
unnatural offence 8, 98, 194, 200-202, 206, 269
Urquhart, Frederic Charles ix, 3, 7, 41, 59, 102-104, 116-123, 130, 133, 140, 156, 157, 162, 167, 170-185, 190-193, 199, 200, 204-209, 213, 223, 232, 251, 254, 261, 265, 269, 273-275

V

vagrancy 5, 79, 198, 200
Vale, Edwin 49
Ville de la Ciotat (steamer) 65
virgo intacta
    see "chaste"
Von Lossberg, William Henry 140-161, 167, 189, 219-225

W

Wagga Wagga 41, 62, 65
walking stick 26, 40, 41, 44
Walsh, Daniel 140, 167, 168, 259, 266
Warner-Shand, Augustus Henry ix, 198, 251
warrant 7, 8, 77, 98, 175, 194-196, 198, 201, 205, 206, 208, 255, 257, 269
Warren-White, John 116-118, 189, 193, 223, 273
Watch belonging to Emma Harrison 42, 49, 51
Watson, Duncan John Reay 266
Weatherstone diggings 80
Webb, Edmund Thomas 64
Weller, George 36, 37
West, Ross 64
Westby, Alfred Ashley (Ashley) 41, 42, 50, 65, 66
Westby, Catherine 264
Westby, Edith 41, 67, 264
Westby, Edmund 67, 264, 265
Westby, Edmund Wright 41, 65
whip 3, 110, 111, 117, 120, 121, 143, 189
    see also "switch"
Whitechapel Vigilance Committee 30
Whitsitt, Margaret Jane 26
    see also "Margaret Carus-Wilson"
Wiggins, Clement Batstone 160-162
Wiggins, John 131

Wiggins, William 131
Wilkinson, William Camac 39, 40
Wilson (man named) 75, 76
Wilson, Annie 112
Wilson, John (Mounted Constable) 6, 78, 79, 201
Wilson, John 36, 39
Wilson, Maude 112
Wilson, Thomas 135, 136, 216-220, 224, 229
Windeyer, William Charles 50, 268
wire 6, 7, 136-140, 157, 158, 176-179, 203, 208, 255, 257, 261
    see also "telegram"
Wolston 95, 97
Wood, Noah 96
Woolcook, John Laskey 266
Wooranalie
    see "Barney"
Woore, John Chadwick 39, 40-44, 173, 257, 258
work
    see "get into work" and "put him on some other job"
wounds –
- blunt instrument 39, 40
- bullet 149, 152, 153, 156, 157, 221, 222, 224
- gunshot 25, 173, 189, 235, 256
- stab 27

Wright, Catherine 264
    see also "Catherine Westby"
Wright, John Arthur 194, 198, 199
Wright, John Waldron 265
Wyer, Joseph 199

Y

Yank 9, 33, 77, 81,
Yankee 33
Yarrawonga (steamer) 194
York 9, 33, 81
young man 28-36, 40, 205, 208
Young-Fullerton, Alexander 194